SPIRITUAL
RHYTHM

SPIRITUAL RHYTHM

BEING WITH JESUS
EVERY SEASON OF YOUR SOUL

MARK BUCHANAN

ZONDERVAN.com/
AUTHORTRACKER
follow your favorite authors

ZONDERVAN

Spiritual Rhythm
Copyright © 2010 by Mark Buchanan

This title is also available as a Zondervan ebook. Visit www.zondervan.com/ebooks.

This title is also available in a Zondervan audio edition. Visit www.zondervan.fm.

Requests for information should be addressed to:

Zondervan, *Grand Rapids, Michigan 49530*

Library of Congress Cataloging-in-Publication Data

Buchanan, Mark (Mark Aldham)
     Spiritual rhythm : being with Jesus every season of your soul / Mark Buchanan.
       p. cm.
     ISBN 978-0-310-29365-1 (hardcover, jacketed)
     1. Spiritual formation. 2. Seasons—Religious aspects—Christianity. I. Title.
BV4509.5.B825   2010
248.4—dc22   2010010797

All Scripture quotations, unless otherwise indicated, are taken from the Holy Bible, *New International Version®, NIV®.* Copyright © 1973, 1978, 1984 by Biblica, Inc.™ Used by permission of Zondervan. All rights reserved worldwide. Scripture quotations marked MSG are taken from *The Message.* Copyright © 1993, 1994, 1995, 1996, 2000, 2001, 2002. Used by permission of NavPress Publishing Group. Scripture quotations marked NASB are taken from the *New American Standard Bible.* Copyright © 1960, 1962, 1963, 1968, 1971, 1972, 1973, 1975, 1977, 1995 by The Lockman Foundation. Used by permission. Scripture quotations marked NKJV are taken from the New King James Version. Copyright © 1982, by Thomas Nelson, Inc. Used by permission. All rights reserved. Scripture quotations marked NLT are taken from the *Holy Bible, New Living Translation,* copyright © 1996, 2004. Used by permission of Tyndale House Publishers, Inc., Wheaton, Illinois. All rights reserved. Scripture quotations marked TNIV are taken from the Holy Bible, *Today's New International Version™. TNIV®.* Copyright © 2001, 2005 by Biblica, Inc.™ Used by permission of Zondervan. All rights reserved worldwide.

The poem "The Sun" by David Whyte is from his collection *The House of Belonging* and is printed with permission from Many Rivers Press, www.davidwhyte.com. © Many Rivers Press, Langley, Washington.

Any Internet addresses (websites, blogs, etc.) and telephone numbers printed in this book are offered as a resource. They are not intended in any way to be or imply an endorsement by Zondervan, nor does Zondervan vouch for the content of these sites and numbers for the life of this book.

Published in association with the literary agency of Ann Spangler and Company, 1420 Pontiac Road S.E., Grand Rapids, MI 49506.

Cover design: Jeff Gifford
Cover photography: Gettyimages
Interior illustration: Shutterstock
Interior design: Beth Shagene

Printed in the United States of America

---

10 11 12 13 14 15 /DCI/ 23 22 21 20 19 18 17 16 15 14 13 12 11 10 9 8 7 6 5 4 3 2 1

To my son,
Adam,
first born,
first man,
apple of my eye,
pride of my heart.
The seasons,
from holding you
to letting you go,
went breathtakingly fast.
May you always walk with Christ,
the man for all seasons.

CONTENTS

WALK HERE, JUMP THERE

The fastest growing sport in Norway is wingsuit jumping. It's the pastime of lunatics, or it's what warrior-knights do in an age without dragons. It requires steel nerves, a cool head, a touch of madness. You must be able to look fast-approaching catastrophe in the face, and whoop.

Here's what you do. Ascend the uppermost point of a fjord, walk to the edge, and jump. The first hundred feet is a free fall, a headlong rush down a granite wall toward a stone floor. The wind pulls your cheeks to your ears. Gravity flips your stomach inside out and pulls it up your throat.

You wear a parachute, but the object of the sport is to put off using it as long as courage and necessity allow. Because — simply — you're wearing a wingsuit, a jumper with webbing beneath the arms and between the legs. It functions like the skin of a flying squirrel. The webbing becomes wings (sort of), and just before your body shatters on the rocks below, you spread-eagle and start to soar (sort of). Your rate of descent is featherlike, around thirty miles an hour, which is about the same as a parachutist. But your rate of forward propulsion is bulletlike — upwards of a hundred miles an hour, which makes you a kamikaze nosediving his target. You're a human cannonball, rushing at dizzying speed toward a very hard landing. Those who have done several wingsuit jumps become daring and agile, trapeze artists who twirl and somersault in thin air. They fly as close to the mountain's flank as possible, trying to graze its side with their outstretched hand, like ordinary people dipping their fingers in a cool lake as they slip along its surface in a canoe. But these aren't ordinary people, and actually touching the mountain at that speed would scrape their hand to bone. When they glide over a ridge of the mountain, their feet sometimes skid across the loose stones before an updraft catapults them freshly over another precipice.

There's a designer who's working on a wingsuit sans parachute; the wings have brakes, so to speak, some device that flares them out at that last critical moment before earth and sky collide, with you caught in the middle. If it works—the suit without a parachute—it will ease you down like an angel catching you. The designer, though, is vague about the details. She doesn't jump herself. But I'm sure she'll have no problem, given the breed of person she's working with, finding a jumper brave or crazy enough to test the prototype.

There's a part of me, brave or crazy, that thinks this will be my next (and perhaps last) vacation.

But maybe I've already been there, done that. I've had seasons in my life when I was flying so high, so fast, that it's hard to imagine wingsuit-jumping notching up the thrill at all. Life was pure exhilaration. Life was the distillate of adrenaline. Life was heart-pounding adventure. I flew on wings like eagles, or at least like squirrels.

I'm exaggerating, but not much. There have been a few brief stretches of my existence when my heart was riotous with joy, and the wind sang in my ears, and I stretched myself wide to catch as much of it as I could, and put off the landing as long as I dared. I twirled and somersaulted midair, and trusted in the next updraft to carry me over the next cliff.

It didn't last.

No season does.

Which is good, because there have been other times, other seasons, when just getting out of bed was an act of holy defiance. Just facing the day was more intimidating than standing down a dozen Goliaths and realizing I'd left my slingshot on the bus seat.

But my life, to date, has been easy compared with most: a lady I know in Canada who, for the past decade, has daily suffered crushing migraines, and no pill or surgery or therapy has brought even a hint of relief, and every morning she wakes (if she slept at all) and endures it one more day; the man I met in Kenya who works all his waking hours at a grueling and menial and demeaning job that barely feeds and clothes him and his family, barely shelters them in their tin-roofed hovel at the bottom of a slum with open sewers and gang riots, and every morning he arises to go through the same thing all over again; the child I visited who ails in the grip of a rare and incurable disease that twists his body in painful contortions and robs him of sight and hearing and speech; the parents who love that child, and are weary and sad with the weight of that love. And every day, spring, summer, winter, fall, brings more of the same.

These, too, are seasons, though some inordinately long.

And then there's everything in between, which most people, for most of their lives, experience—long and uninterrupted seasons of bland ordinariness: work we don't particularly love or hate, health that is neither brilliant nor dismal, circumstances that have their challenges, disappointments, irritations, as well as their surprises, graces, serendipities, but little bitterness or ecstasy.

What I want to know: is Jesus the man for all seasons?

Robert Bolt wrote a play, and a good one, called *A Man for All Seasons*. It was about Sir Thomas More, a principled man of court who defied Henry VIII over his manipulation of the pope to secure an annulment of his marriage to Catherine of Aragorn in order to marry Anne Boleyn. This book has nothing to do with that play, except that I'm shamelessly stealing the idea, if not the title. *A Man for All Seasons*. As fine a description as that might be for Sir Thomas More, it's better suited to Jesus of Nazareth. Here is the man for all seasons: overflowing with joy, intimate with sorrow, hospitable to sinners, nemesis of evil, tempted in all ways, innocent of all wrongdoing, at home in lonely places, the life of the party, one who turns water into wine, just because he can, who multiplies loaves and fishes, just because he cares, but who denies help to his cousin John as he languishes in prison, who, indeed, refuses to help himself when he staggers in a desert or groans from a cross. He goes up on mountains and down in valleys. He preaches to thousands but takes time for any lone beggar, weeping whore, groveling invalid, writhing demoniac, pleading father. He leaves banquets to visit the sick ward. He is silent when talking would help his cause, and talkative when silence seems most prudent. He is rude with bullies and phonies and prigs and, at the same time, tender with losers and seekers and penitents.

He's with us when we soar on wings as eagles, and probably even when we wingsuit jump, and with us, too, when we can't walk for fainting.

And everywhere in between.

In the introduction, which comes next, I'll explain that this book germinated in a dark season. It started not on some Norwegian height but in a deep and lonely valley. A winter, is how I describe it. I am not, now that I've been there, fool enough to romanticize that place and season. I am not masochistic enough to wish its return. But all the same, I met Christ there in ways I hadn't before. I stumbled into the fellowship of sharing in Christ's sufferings, as Paul calls it, and until I'd joined that fellowship I had no idea, really, what he was talking about.

I'm not sure I know now. But what I do know is that Jesus is enough. He has been a good companion all the way through. I have no reason to doubt he will be a good companion for all that lies ahead. I hope there are still many springs and summers and autumns for me. I know other winters will come, and at some point settle in.

Alas and amen. Too bad and so be it.

The Man for All Seasons is here, and there. With him by my side, all is well, and all manner of things are well.

Sometimes reading
... I look out
at everything
growing so wild
and faithfully beneath
the sky
and wonder
why we are the one
terrible
part of creation
privileged
to refuse our flowering

—DAVID WHYTE,
"THE SUN"

***

If some King of the earth have so large an extent of
Dominion, in North and South, as that he hath Winter
and Summer together in his Dominions, so large an
extent East and West, as he hath day and night together
in his Dominions, much more has God.... He brought
light out of darknesse, not out of a lesser light; He can
bring thy Summer out of Winter, though thou have no
Spring; though in the ways of fortune, or understanding, or conscience, thou have been benighted till now,
wintered and frozen, clouded and eclipsed, damped
and benumbed, smothered and stupefied till now, now
God comes to thee, not as in the dawning of the day,
not as in the bud of spring, but as the Sun at noon....
All times are His seasons.

—FROM SERMON BY JOHN DONNE
ST. PAUL'S CATHEDRAL
CHRISTMASTIDE 1624

FOR EVERYTHING, A SEASON

I live in Canada. If you don't, forget your stereotypes: sled dogs and igloos, polar bears and ice palaces, Eskimos in fur-lined parkas and seal-skinned mukluks poised with fish spears over ice holes. Those are rare sightings anywhere in my country, but only myths in the part of Canada I'm from. I'm from Canada's West Coast. Here, even snow in winter is scarce. The grass grows thick and green year round, and flowers start shooting up in early February, or sooner. I write this in January, and already the branches on my willow tree are knuckled with buds, fuzzy and grey, and if the warmth keeps up I expect crocuses by month's end.

I live without four distinct seasons. Winter here is nondescript, and wet. Fall is bland: the few deciduous trees—this is a land of firs and cedars—turn tobacco brown or suet yellow, and blow off in the first strong wind of late October. The only standout seasons are spring and summer—spring a cavalcade of blossoms, summer a tangle of tropical lushness, though without the swelter.

Which is all to say, I did not come by the book you now hold naturally.

This book is about four distinct seasons—not in the natural world but within us. It explores the cycles in our hearts that, like the axial turnings of earth, mark out seasonal rhythms in our lives: flourishing and fruitful, stark and dismal, cool and windy, or everything coming up new. The seasons I'm describing are not the seasons of aging—where youth is spring, early adulthood summer, middle age fall, and old age winter. Interesting as that is, it's not what I've set my hand to here.

This is: our souls, our hearts, have seasons, too. A soul in youth can turn grim and arctic, or a heart in dotage can grow breezy and fragrant. The seasons of the heart are no respecters of age, and seldom of person. I've met children bleak and dour, octogenarians playful and whimsical, middle-aged women enthused about everything, fifty-year-old men bitter about everything. Sometimes this is just the way it is, with no rhyme or reason, nothing to predict or prevent or produce one season or another.

But sometimes we do have a say or a hand in it. And always, we can steward the season we find ourselves in. Just as farmers plow in one season, plant in another, irrigate in another, harvest in another, and let the fields lie fallow in yet another, so there are activities and inactivities that fit our hearts' seasons.

We ignore this to our peril.

I discovered these seasons of the heart late, close to fifty, when I found myself in winter. A friend and colleague, whose presence I depended on more than I knew until it was gone, got sick, and then very sick, and then died. Her name was Carol, and just writing her name opens a door that a cold wind slips through. She was blond, and big, and funny, and could pray heaven close. She forgot details and muddled dates but remembered people, the most quirky and intimate things about them, and she could see deep into them in the way prophets and sages and sometimes grandmothers can.

She had a tumor in her skull, a thing that showed up first as a chronic headache. A mass big as a hardball, nestled just above and right behind her right ear, twined into her brain. Doctors plucked it out, but it grew again, and spread. They went in again, but its roots ran thick and tangled, and all they could do was pare back its wildness a little. We prayed, desperate, confident, declarative, beseeching. We were gallant as knights, then frightened as children. We rode the news, up, down, sideways. We grew, I suppose, but often we diminished, too.

She died. I held myself together, and a few others besides. Carol was not just our friend; she was my copastor, and so our whole church was in crisis. I led well, I think, during her dying and her death. I was in season and out, to know how best to meet him, how best to make the most out of each season and each moment.

After the writer of Ecclesiastes says that for everything there is a season, he remarks about eternity: "There is a time for everything, and a season for every activity under the heavens.... What do workers gain from their toil? I have seen the burden God has laid on the human race. He has made everything beautiful in its time. He has also set eternity in the human heart; yet no one can fathom what God has done from beginning to end."[1]

These two thoughts—for everything there is a season, beautiful in its time, and God has set eternity in our hearts—are joined. Eternity hides beneath the guise of each season's beauty. That beauty is eternity's sleight of hand, the trick it uses to bedazzle and bewilder us, to make our hearts' longing appear and disappear right before our very eyes. You think that you crave the summer of '69, or whatever summer it was you were young and in love. But that summer was only a dress rehearsal for what your heart really wants: heaven.

Heaven whispers in the burden God lays on us. The everlasting flits beneath earth's swiftly fading beauty. God sets eternity in our hearts, and it tells us not to despair of the burden. It warns us not to be overcaptivated by the beauty. For though we want the burden lifted and the beauty prolonged, God has an infinitely better idea: that the Man for All Seasons would walk with us in season and out, and then, when all is done, take us home.

I've divided this book into two halves. The first half—"Spiritual Seasons"—describes the seasons of the heart, beginning with winter, ending with fall. I devote two chapters to each season (to the last season, fall, I devote three). The first chapter on each season simply explores the hallmarks of that season—what it feels like, what's good about it, what its dangers, joys, pitfalls, benefits are. The companion chapter looks at ways to steward the season—what to do and not to do, how to get the most out of it, how to avoid some of its traps. You'll find a certain unevenness from chapter to chapter, though I've taken pains to smooth that as much as I can. Some of that unevenness, beyond my clumsiness as a writer, is owing to the nature of the seasons themselves: just as winter could hardly be more different from summer, say, so each spiritual season differs from the others. There's no way to stuff all four into the same template.

The book's second half—"Spiritual Rhythms"—is a series of reflections on just that: spiritual rhythm, moving with each season's unique flow. Overall in this section, I'm aiming to establish seasonality as an overarching metaphor for understanding our spiritual lives and spiritual development. But you'll see what I mean when you get there.

I end that section with a very long chapter called "In Season and Out," where I look at the spiritual practices that sustain regardless of what season our hearts are in.

You may want to read this book in a straight line, but then again, you may not. It may prove more useful to zigzag through it, going first to the season that most intrigues you, either because you're in it or because you wish you were. You may want to start in the back half, where I deal more directly with issues of spiritual formation.

Whatever you do, my hope is that this isn't just another read. I hope that in these pages you and I become companions. Which leads me to the last thing I want to say by way of introduction.

The worst thing you could do is read this book quickly. It's meant to be savored, not devoured. Any book worth reading is worth reading slowly. It's worth getting into your bones. To skim its pages but not engage its meaning is, frankly, a waste of your time and your money.

So I invite you deeper. If you're going to read this book, plan to get the most out of it. Come prepared to reflect, wrestle, pray, confess, repent, resolve. As you read, pause here and there, ponder this and that, argue with certain points, and talk up other ones. It will make this book worth far more than you paid for it. (And if you didn't pay, lucky you.) It will make the book your companion and mentor, not just a stranger you idled some time with on a flight somewhere.

Every serious reader is coauthor with the writer. This excites me, and humbles me. As the writer, I lay out the ideas like pelts stretched for curing. That takes patience, diligence, some artistry. But as the reader, it's up to you whether you turn those ideas into garments. It's up to you to make something useful, maybe even beautiful, from the raw materials I've handed you.

Even more, every serious reader collaborates with God. Like Adam in Eden, what God makes requires our tending and our naming. That's how earth becomes world and wilderness becomes garden. So with a book. Good books (and even some poor ones) can change us to be more like Christ. That deep change is always a work of God, his subversion and transformation. But we either cooperate with it, or not.

You need to do your part. I've done mine. God's ready to do his. But it's you who'll make the difference. This could be just another book you read. Or it could change your life. Whether it's one or the other is in your hands now.

To help you, I've included along the way—not after every chapter but at points in the book where I think a rest stop would help—a "Time-In" section. This includes questions, points for further reflection or discussion, ideas for prayer, suggested exercises and spiritual disciplines.

Time-in is the reverse of a time-out. Time-out means you cease, for a spell, whatever you're doing. You step back. But time-in means you intensify, for a stretch, whatever you're doing. You plunge in. If, for instance, the section on winter makes you realize that your life is cluttered beyond managing and is desperately in need of a hard pruning, you'll want to do more than just make a mental note of that. You'll want to prayerfully discern what to cut back, and then actually break out the sweet saw and do it. The Time-In sections will assist that. Or if the chapter on summer makes you aware that you're not enjoying God's bounty—you're missing daylight—you'll want to go straight out and eat a bowl of cherries, or nap in a hammock, or swim in your toddler's inflatable pool.

In short, the Time-In sections invite response.

I'm recommending, as part of your Time-In, that you keep a journal. When I keep a journal, I do more than just write thoughts. I write poems. (I've included four in this book, to begin the major sections on each season.) I jot questions. I doodle. (And I'm not an artist by any stretch.) Sometimes I paste a photo or a newspaper clipping.

My journal is bricolage, scrapbook, catchall. Maybe that's of no use or interest to you, but I mention it simply to encourage you to be yourself and to be creative.

Just, please, however you do it, help me coauthor this book. Then one day, if ever we meet, and you're inclined to thank me, it can be mutual. After all, you'll be the one who completed, in the best sense of the word, what I started.

Even better, you'll have joined God in what he was doing. And that is never wasted time, in season or out.

PART I
SPIRITUAL SEASONS

This long dark season
of everything
stripped
to nothing
began so sudden,
overnight,
with the gust of
one phone call,
then never left.
The only miracle here
is waiting
to see
how much night a day
can hold
and still be called
day.

—M. BUCHANAN

CHAPTER 1

WINTER

There is a time for everything,
and a season for every activity under the heavens:
a time to be born and a time to die,
a time to plant and a time to uproot,
a time to kill and a time to heal,
a time to tear down and a time to build,
a time to weep and a time to laugh,
a time to mourn and a time to dance,
a time to scatter stones and a time to gather them,
a time to embrace and a time to refrain,
a time to search and a time to give up,
a time to keep and a time to throw away,
a time to tear and a time to mend,
a time to be silent and a time to speak,
a time to love and a time to hate,
a time for war and a time for peace.[1]

A confession: most my life I've ignored this, that all is seasonal. Maybe I've not even believed it. For *everything* there is a season. For everything? In the natural world, that's obvious: the earth moves in seasonal rhythm:

> Cold, hot
> Work, play
> Light, dark
> Sow, reap
> Fruitfulness, barrenness

Nothing could be more self-evident.

But Ecclesiastes talks about another kind of seasonality, seasons that define not earth's rhythms, its tilting to and away from the sun, but life's seasons, its inevitable tiltings toward light and away from it. Existence is seasonal.

Our hearts know this. Our hearts taste the rapture and leisure of summer, the industry and urgency of fall, the bleakness and loneliness of winter, the busyness and expectancy of spring.

Maybe that, too, is obvious. Only, until lately I had no corresponding spirituality for it. I had ways of adapting my yard and home and habits to the variations of climate and daylight that prevail with each season: I cut my lawn in summer, clean my chimney in fall, stack my wood in spring, wear my boots in winter. But I had no equivalent ways of adapting my spiritual life — my prayer and my worship, my listening and my speaking, my being with God, with others, with self — to the seasonal shifts inside me. Especially, I didn't know what to do with winter. Winter is bleak, and cold, and dark, and fruitless. It is a time of forced inactivity, unwelcome brooding, more night than day. Most things are dead, or appear so. It never seems to end.

I wanted to run from winter with all my might. To disavow its reality. To conduct myself in blatant defiance or outright denial of its existence. I wanted to frolic like it was high summer despite the engulfing darkness and shivering cold inside me.

When my father died in June of 1996, I hardly paused. I came back from his funeral and preached at my church what I'd scheduled to preach. The elders offered me a time of bereavement. I declined it. I didn't alter one thing in my spiritual regimen. I carried on as though a minor interruption, not one of life's hardest and loneliest passages, had just visited me.

In 2001, when three young men in the church died within three months of one another, I did the same. I just carried on. But several months later, I sat in a cabin on a beach and thought I was losing my mind and my faith both, and wasn't sure I wanted to chase either.

That was the start of a slow awareness.

It's foolish to plant corn in January. It's foolish to transplant shrubs in July. Each season has its suitable tasks, its required duties, its necessary constraints.

Concerning earth's cycles, I get that. But it's taken me almost fifty years to grasp this same truth in relation to my own heart. The death of my friend and colleague Carol made it a matter of reckoning. That event, and the events surrounding it, plunged me into winter deep and long, and I couldn't flee it any longer. There was nothing else but to enter it, and dwell in it, and learn from it.

And maybe, just maybe, to grow from it.

But I still don't want to talk about it.

Too raw. Too fresh. Too recent.

Yet in all my conversations with people about these things, it's winter that most intrigues them, and I hazard the guess that it's because it's little understood and often hidden away. Winter shames those in it. It feels like personal failure, something we've caused, or missed, or faltered in. We chide ourselves for being there. We're sure it's our fault. We wonder if we're crazy, lazy, stupid.

And most people around us don't help. They pep-talk us. They serve up warmed-over platitudes. They scold us or offer useless advice. They hold themselves up as examples of how to beat the winter blahs. "I know *exactly* how you feel. I felt that way last month for two or three days. I just cut back my coffee consumption, got an extra hour's sleep each night, got on the treadmill, and I popped right out of it!"

So we tend to close up in our winter houses and smile a lot to divert attention. We nurse our sadness in aloneness, which is kind of how we want it anyhow. It suits the season.

The assumption many of us labor beneath is this: God can't be in winter. God has abandoned me, or I have wandered from him, but this bleakness—this fruitlessness—can't be blessed by him. If I loved God, if God loved me, I wouldn't be here.

It's an assumption I no longer believe.

THE HEART IN WINTER

What I do believe, now, is that our hearts have seasons, and the longest of them, if not in duration then in intensity, is winter. There's no preventing it, though there are ways to steward it. But before we get there, let me attempt a simple description of what the heart in winter is like.

Bankruptcy

Ecclesiastes, again, describes winter.

In this case, it's the winter of life — decrepitude — but it hints at the heart's winter, too. Here's the passage:

> Remember your Creator
> in the days of your youth,
> before the days of trouble come
> and the years approach when you will say,
> "I find no pleasure in them" —
> before the sun and the light
>   and the moon and the stars grow dark,
>   and the clouds return after the rain;
> when the keepers of the house tremble,
>   and the strong men stoop,
> when the grinders cease because they are few,
>   and those looking through the windows grow dim;
> when the doors to the street are closed
>   and the sound of grinding fades;
> when people rise up at the sound of birds,
>   but all their songs grow faint;
> when people are afraid of heights
>   and of dangers in the streets;
> when the almond tree blossoms
>   and the grasshopper drags itself along
>   and desire no longer is stirred.
> Then people go to their eternal home
>   and mourners go about the streets.
>
> Remember him — before the silver cord is severed,
>   and the golden bowl is broken;

before the pitcher is shattered at the spring,
    and the wheel broken at the well,
and the dust returns to the ground it came from,
    and the spirit returns to God who gave it.

"Meaningless! Meaningless!"says the Teacher.
"Everything is meaningless!"[2]

Two details here equally describe both life's winter and the heart's. Verse 1: "I find no pleasure...." Both life's winter and the heart's winter have this in common: pleasure is bankrupt. Things we once craved and relished—our sources of delight—we now avoid and disdain. The food we savored, the friendships we treasured, the activities we cherished—none of it gives us anything other than weariness or sourness. It only deepens our aloneness.

And verse 8: "Meaningless! Meaningless!... Everything is meaningless!" Both life's winter and the heart's winter have this in common: meaning is bankrupt. Things we once found captivating and stimulating—rich with meaning—we now find futile and bewildering. The trips we used to go on, the art we once pondered, the books we loved to read, the subjects we delighted to talk over—winter makes it all dreariness and drudgery. We go from the purpose-driven life to the purpose-starved life. Events and accomplishments are leached of significance. Ambition, accomplishment, aspiration, beauty, courage—none of it means anything in wintertime. I once showed during a Sunday service a video of Baptist missionaries martyred in South America. I was hugely inspired by their example of heroic and sacrificial faith. But a woman came up to me afterward who was in a winter of the heart. All she said was, "That was meaningless."

We savor little or nothing in winter. Pleasure is bankrupt. Meaning is bankrupt.

A Song in the Night

There's another passage of Scripture that, even more than Ecclesiastes 12, describes the wintertime of the heart. It's Psalm 88. As with the passage from Ecclesiastes, this one is lengthy. I'll quote the psalm in full since it renders unflinchingly the experience I'm trying to describe. As you read it, linger over it like a note left to you from a close friend.

> LORD, you are the God who saves me;
>   day and night I cry out to you.
> May my prayer come before you;
>   turn your ear to my cry.
>
> I am overwhelmed with troubles
>   and my life draws near to death.
> I am counted among those who go down to the pit;
>   I am like one without strength.
> I am set apart with the dead,
>   like the slain who lie in the grave,
> whom you remember no more,
>   who are cut off from your care.
>
> You have put me in the lowest pit,
>   in the darkest depths.
> Your wrath lies heavily on me;
>   you have overwhelmed me with all your waves.
> You have taken from me my closest friends
>   and have made me repulsive to them.
> I am confined and cannot escape;
>   my eyes are dim with grief.
>
> I call to you, LORD, every day;
>   I spread out my hands to you.
> Do you show your wonders to the dead?
>   Do their spirits rise up and praise you?
> Is your love declared in the grave,
>   your faithfulness in Destruction?
> Are your wonders known in the place of darkness,
>   or your righteous deeds in the land of oblivion?
>
> But I cry to you for help, LORD;
>   in the morning my prayer comes before you.
> Why, LORD, do you reject me
>   and hide your face from me?

From my youth I have suffered and been close to death;
   I have borne your terrors and am in despair.
Your wrath has swept over me;
   your terrors have destroyed me.
All day long they surround me like a flood;
   they have completely engulfed me.
You have taken from me friend and neighbor—
   darkness is my closest friend.[3]

Scholar Walter Brueggemann calls this psalm "an embarrassment to conventional faith." He even asks, "What is a psalm like this doing in our Bible?"[4] His answer in my words: Psalm 88 gives us language that transposes agony into prayer. Sorrow seeks to render us mute. Psalm 88 gives voice to what is most angry and grief-stricken and frightened inside us. It shapes brokenheartedness into sacrament. It allows us to break our silence even when God refuses to break his.

And it does that, first, by describing what winter in the heart *feels* like. This psalm is no cool, clinical, dispassionate, detached listing of symptoms; it erupts, wild and raw. It's a diary of disappointment, a soliloquy of complaint, a testimony of anguish. It's the howl of a man in the grip of heartache.

The experience this psalm evokes bears a close resemblance to clinical depression. Winter is not exactly that, and not exactly not that. Winter shares a landscape with depression, but I think it has a different doorway: with depression, we enter through a door within ourselves, whereas with winter we enter through a door outside ourselves. What I mean is that depression is triggered mostly by something internal, whereas winter is triggered mostly by circumstances. But maybe the difference is inconsequential. For the record, I have never been clinically depressed. But I've attempted, clumsily I think, to pastor many people in clinical depression. At the least, I've learned a little of depression's tyranny, its whims and wiles and heavy, heavy hand. I don't think it's amiss to read Psalm 88, or my thoughts on it, as equally a description of both winter and depression. But my counsel on stewarding wintertime, in the chapter that follows this one, might not apply equally.

But I'll let you be the judge of that.

Absence of Light

What does Psalm 88 tell us and show us?

To begin, this: winter feels all-consuming and never-ending. It's worth noting the authors of this psalm: the Sons of Korah. These are the same composers who collaborated on many psalms, such as 84 and 87. "Better is one day in your courts than a thousand elsewhere," they effuse in Psalm 84, and celebrate God's intimate protection even of sparrows. Psalm 87 ends, "All my fountains are in you," just before Psalm 88, the bleakest psalm, which ends, "Darkness is my closest friend." The tenor of most of the Sons of Korah's repertoire is upbeat, gladsome, celebrative. They write, mostly, dance tunes, love ballads, patriotic anthems, not blues songs. Psalm 88 is out of character for them. These men have given little sign till now of disappointment with God (though Psalm 85:5 sounds the mood that might have triggered Psalm 88). They are not perpetually gloomy. They are not habitually dyspeptic. They do not chronically murmur. They do not appear to nurse grudges, or keep company with the disgruntled, or rehearse the lament of the victim. These brothers, most of the time, deeply experience God's goodness, and gladly declare it. They know God in the light.

Psalm 88 is a record that, at least once, they lost God in the dark.

Yet to read Psalm 88, it's as though they never found him. It's as though they've never stood in the light of God's favor, never tasted his blessing. It's as though darkness and sadness have marked their existence from the womb and will plague it till the grave. Winter is like that: it has power to eclipse all the good we've stored up, and to plunge us into a nighttime that seems all we've ever known and, worse, all we'll ever know.

Winter seems all-consuming and never-ending.

Absence of God

Winter hides God. It has power to sever my knowledge *about* God from my experience *of* him, and to hold the two apart, so that my theology and my reality become irreconcilable.

The psalmist affirms at many points—starting right at the

beginning—some of the most exquisite and enc
truths about God. He is the God who saves me (v.
is a steady drumbeat of God's attributes: "your w
"your love," "your faithfulness," "your righteousne᠈
This is what this man (the psalm, though composed ᴗʏ a collective,
individualizes the lament, so I will as well) knows *about* God. He
gets an A+ for orthodoxy. There's nothing shaky, vague, or half-
baked in his doctrine.

It's just that his experience and his doctrine bear no resemblance
to each other. What he tastes and sees of God (or doesn't taste and
see) mocks what he confesses and proclaims about God. His everyday
reality taunts his everlasting creed. He talks about God's wonders
and love and faithfulness, but experiences only God's rejection and
anger and indifference. At every turn, he's met with more bad news
—sorrow upon sorrow, trouble upon trouble, loss upon loss. Darkness eclipses light. Sadness consumes joy. Despair overtakes hope. He
experiences a God who simultaneously abandons him and punishes
him, a God of apathy and wrath, a God who hides himself and shows
up only to vent himself.

This is winter. It's when God seems either too far or too near—
aloof in his heavens, or afoot with a stick. Either way, it's as though
there is no refuge.

Winter hides God.

Absence of Friends

Winter is friendless. In it, we experience a terrible, terrifying
aloneness.

> You have taken from me my closest friends
> and have made me repulsive to them;
> I am confined and cannot escape....
> You have taken from me friend and neighbor—
> darkness is my closest friend.[5]

Abandonment. Rejection. Isolation. This is the shape of the soul
in winter. It feels friendless. And it feels this way even, maybe most,

a crowd. At church. In Bible study. At weddings and reunions. Even when many surround us, the heart's winter makes us feel estranged. It makes us feel unloved and unlovable.

Carol was prone to winter—the same Carol whose death threw me into that place. She was unmarried, not by choice. Sometimes her loneliness grew wide and deep and swallowed things whole—her many friendships, her prodigious gifting, her love for God—and darkness became her closest friend. She avoided others, and when she couldn't, she hid inside herself and showed others a mask of herself, a smiling mask that she could barely animate.

I particularly remember a visit she took to Turkey. Something happened there—not an incident but a shifting inside her. She grew fearful, and doubtful. God grew distant. She visited the place where Paul, the apostle, worked and preached and built churches. The buildings those Christians once inhabited, thundering the gospel and storming the gates of hell, were now only ruins, bleached stones scattered in empty fields. The places of heavenly worship had become the haunts of jackals and owls. Mohammed had chased out Jesus and left only rubble to mark the place.

It was a personal apocalypse for her. She nearly lost her faith. And in the pounding heat and wide light of the middle-eastern sun, Carol tumbled down into darkness, and took a year to come out. In that time, she was alone even, especially, when she wasn't alone.

Winter is friendless.

Living Death

Last and worst, winter is death. It is living death. Death haunts us and surrounds those in winter. The psalmist describes in vivid and sometimes lurid terms the pall that death casts over this season of the heart: "my life draws near to death"; "I am counted among those who go down to the pit"; "I am set apart with the dead, like the slain who lie in the grave."

Though he walks through the valley of the shadow of death, he has no assurance that God is with him, that God in any way protects him, that goodness and love are trailing him or the house of the Lord awaits him.

All is dead, or appears so. A tree is so stark and bony in winter, it's almost impossible to believe it will ever bear fruit or give shade again. Winter is when your heart is so closed up you can't imagine it ever opening again, your dreams so buried you can't conceive of them resurrecting.

Winter is death.

When Carol died, this psalm gave voice to my numbness. Even more, it did that for Cheryl, my wife: it was her elegy, the song of her broken heart. It was the bleak inventory of a devastating loss. Carol and Cheryl were closer than sisters. They knew the fellowship of sharing in Christ's suffering, the fellowship of uproarious laughter, the fellowship of voracious God-hunger, the fellowship of movie watching and purse shopping and party planning, the fellowship of carrying each other's secrets and bearing one another's burdens. You don't lose that and keep much else. Cheryl was engulfed, overwhelmed, cut off. "You have taken from me my closest friends." It devastated her. But maybe worse was what replaced the one taken: "Darkness is my closest friend." Her winter, ours, gave us unwanted intimacy with night.

DARKNESS IS YOUR CLOSEST FRIEND

It's how John the Baptist must have felt. He languished in Herod's prison, the cost of meddling in the king's personal life, daring to denounce his brazen immorality. Herod's pride and anger and despotic power converged, and he imprisoned John. But then he froze in indecision. He hated John but also feared him: feared his holiness, his boldness, his wildness. Herod, for all his pagan ways, nursed a deep dread that John might be right, and that the wrath of God would befall him, or that the people would overthrow him, which might be the same thing. And, of course, following in the line of all the Herods, he was paranoid, and superstitious, and egotistical, and insecure, and together that concocted a potent brew of self-doubt.

From prison, John hears of Jesus' comings and goings, his preaching and his miracles. This is the same Jesus whose mother's voice caused John to leap in his own mother's womb. This is the same Jesus whose sandals John felt unworthy to untie, the same Jesus he declared "the Lamb of God who takes away the sins of the world," the same Jesus about whom he remarked, "He must increase, and I must decrease." And this is the same Jesus who declared John to be great in the kingdom of God.

But now, John's not sure. All these bold declarations seem a stretch. If all these things be true, why is he here, rotting and starving? Why does his life hang by a thread held in the hand of a vain and capricious king? If Jesus is the Christ, why is he not coming to the rescue, swooping down in retribution on Rome and all her lackeys? Surely, for the sake of his kingdom, Jesus will act. And if not for the sake his kingdom, then for the sake of John's Elijah-like status as the Messiah's forerunner. And if not for the sake of John's status, then for the sake of Jesus' relationship with him—they're cousins, after all. This is a family matter.

So he waits, and his waiting turns to wondering, and his wondering to worrying, and his worrying to open doubt. He hears about all that Jesus is doing—the astonishing miracles. The people proclaim him as "a great prophet." But something sits askew for John. Something doesn't add up. So he dispatches two of his disciples to ask Jesus a pointed question: "Are you the one who was to come, or should we expect someone else?"

Luke's commentary and Jesus' reply are cold comfort: "At that very time Jesus cured many who had diseases, sicknesses and evil spirits, and gave sight to many who were blind. So he replied to the messengers, 'Go back and report to John what you have seen and heard: The blind receive sight, the lame walk, those who have leprosy are cleansed, the deaf hear, the dead are raised, and the good news is proclaimed to the poor. Blessed is anyone who does not stumble on account of me.'"[6]

Jesus says, in effect, "John, I'm busy. I'm busy being the Messiah—healing, liberating, raising the dead, preaching good news—but if you're asking what this means for you, well, I've got some hard news. I'm not dropping by. Herod will have his way with you. Blessed are you if you don't fall away *on account of me*—if my performing miracles left and right with nary a one for you doesn't drive you into unbelief. Blessed are you if I leave you in the dark and you still trust me."

With that, Jesus sends John's disciples back to him and then turns to the crowd and makes these remarks: "What did you go out into the desert to see? A reed swayed by the wind? If not, what did you go out to see? A man dressed in fine clothes? No, those who wear expensive clothes and indulge in luxury are in palaces. But what did you go out to see? A prophet? Yes, I tell you, and more than a prophet. This is the one about whom it is written: 'I will send my messenger ahead of you, who will prepare your way before you.' I tell you, among those born of women there is no one greater than John; yet the one who is least in the kingdom of God is greater than he."[7]

I don't think Jesus' remarks are unrelated to the message he sent John. Who is the greatest in the kingdom of God? Who *deserves* God's favor? To whom does Jesus, by virtue of their faithfulness or status or kinship with him, *owe* a miracle? Maybe John the Baptist, maybe also the Sons of Korah, as though their closeness with God entitled them to full heavenly benefits here and now, with no deductible.

So John's surprised to find himself in this prison, in this winter, lonely and afraid. Abandoned, while his own cousin saves and blesses and cures every beggar and whore and tax collector he comes across, bestows divine favor on every wayward stranger he meets.

John sits in the dark, waiting, dreading, brooding. He hears the heavy footfall of the dungeon-keeper approaching, hears the clink and thud of the keys in the lock. He knows in his bones what he's come for.

It's not to deliver a pardon. It's not to announce a visitor. It's not to herald a miracle.

Darkness is his closest friend.

TIME-IN 1

YOUR CLOSEST FRIEND

Who's your closest friend?[8]

Your winter, like my wife's, may have descended because you lost—through a move, a death, a fight—your closest friend. Or maybe something else brought on winter, and in it you realized that you have no close friends.

In the preface I allude to Philippians 3:10–11. The full passage is this: "I want to know Christ and the power of his resurrection and the fellowship of sharing in his sufferings, becoming like him in his death, and so, somehow, to attain to the resurrection from the dead." Paul conjoins, here and elsewhere,[9] power and weakness, resurrection and death, glory and suffering. In his mind and experience, the two things are twinned.

I believe every heartache and hardship, and the profound loneliness such things bring, has a back door. They allow us entry into a communion with Christ we don't usually experience in our days of ease and song. Most of us have had our deepest encounters with Christ not on mountaintops but in valley floors.

The word *companion*—a synonym for friend—literally means "one who shares bread with you." In that light, it's telling that Jesus, both to commemorate his death and to anticipate his resurrection, shared bread with his friends.

He companioned with them at a very dark moment.

Here's a simple spiritual exercise. You can do this alone, or with a friend or two. Prepare and receive communion as an act of companionship with Jesus. Drink the cup, eat the bread, with a mindfulness that Jesus shared bread with his friends, including one who would betray him. Soon after, at the darkest hour, Jesus was separated from his Father. He was plunged into the anguish of complete abandonment. "My God, my God," he cried. "Why have you forsaken me?"

For a time, darkness was his closest friend.

Take the bread. Hear his words, "This is my body, broken for you."

Take the cup. Hear him say, "This is my blood, poured out for you, for the forgiveness of sins."

Proclaim the Lord's death until he comes, until that day you see him face to face and sit in the dazzling brightness of his presence.

He entered this darkness for you. There's no darkness in which he hasn't gone. There's no darkness he won't meet you in. There's no darkness that can hide him. There's no darkness he won't, in time, lead you out of.

He's a good companion.

Your closest friend.

***

Perhaps you're in winter now.

I'm sorry.

If I could, I'd stand with you in it, watching, waiting, trusting that my presence and silence were, if not enough, at least something, a kind of light, a kind of lightness.

But now I fear speaking further. Yet at the risk of sounding trite —at the risk of offering cold comfort—I invite you to read on. In the next chapter, I dare to speak of both the gifts and the tasks of wintertime.

CHAPTER 2

WINTER ACTIVITIES

The strangest thing happened this winter: it snowed and snowed, weeks on end. I hadn't seen snow like this since my childhood. Temperatures dipped well beneath freezing. Icicles hung from the eaves of my house; they started no bigger than hairpins, but grew as thick and long as stalactites, as menacing as scimitars. The roof got so snow-laden I feared its collapse, and every day, some times several times a day, I had to shovel the driveway. Mountainous piles accumulated at the edge of my yard. My street narrowed to a single lane, a trench gouged out by plow trucks. Cars navigated down it slowly and cautiously, tires often gnashing and spinning.

This isn't supposed to happen, not where I live. The paper from Victoria, daily, emblazoned startled and startling news about another record broken, and some days it didn't come at all—the paper, that is—because of those record-breaking conditions.

Christmas Eve the sky opened like an ancient sorrow and let loose a blizzard that didn't let up till early morning. The snow was so deep and heavy that my makeshift carport, constructed from metal poles and heavy tarps and lashed down with an elaborate spiderweb of rope, collapsed. I discovered it Christmas morning when I let the dog out. The mangled structure trapped my car beneath it. It took me two hours to dig the car out, banged up like someone had pounded one side with a truncheon. The damage was almost artistic, the top of the car's door rim fluted the way my mother used to pinch the edge of a pie crust. The car's side mirror had snapped clean off at the neck but still hung on, skewed and drooping, dangling by its adjustment cables.

All this surprised me with an insight I already had, except I hadn't paid close enough attention to it: winter imposes work. There are certain kinds of labor, and certain kinds of play, only possible or required in winter.

During those days when the snow kept accumulating, when the sky was a blur of white and the ground a sea of it, I had to shovel for the sake of sheer survival. My driveway is short and steep: it climbs a height of five feet over a run of thirty-five feet, a pitch of 7:1, which makes it equivalent to a gabled roof, a billy goat's bluff, a sudden escarpment. The thinnest veneer of ice makes ascent a carnival of antics—spinning wheels, fishtails, abrupt rocketing. Anything more means we're homebound. I had to stay on top of the work to keep up with it at all. Whenever three or four inches accumulated, I bundled up again, braved the blizzard (usually with my trusty dog lolloping through the deepening banks with a kind of drunken abandon), and hunkered down to the task. I developed a rhythm akin to rowing: push, scoop, lift, fling. After clearing the ground, I filled a plastic bucket with coarse salt and scattered it like an ancient farmer sewing barley seeds, broadcasting it side to side as I took long strides up and down the driveway. Grains of salt pocked the crusts of ice until they became filigree that I then scraped off with my shovel blade tipped upside down.

My muscles, not used to this exact combination of demands, ached for the first few days. Truth is, at first I resented the labor. Each time I cleared the driveway it took close to an hour. It consumed time I might have spent doing other things. I went to the task muttering, returned from it relieved, and also a tad sore at those who sat by the fire while I toiled in the storm. They were lucky to have me. They were lucky I didn't perish in the wilds. Maybe, in their self-absorption, they wouldn't even have noticed my absence till morning. Then, alarmed and duly smitten, they'd send out a search party that, hours later, would discover my carcass, rigid with death and ice, ashen with cold, buried beneath a layer of snow so thick I barely left a bump on its surface.

But soon I got to enjoy it. The work, I mean. I relished when the snow reached the magic depth that warranted another round of push, scoop, lift, fling. My body adapted admirably to its new role. I'd come back in the house steaming like a horse. The labor, its vigor and purpose, shook me from the lethargy induced by idleness. I felt that God, for a spell, had granted me an urgent and necessary work, one with measurable results. I even bought winter boots, manly clodhoppers with knobby treads, zippers and laces and flaps, and steel toes, just in case. I had, briefly, joined the ranks of farmers and carpenters and lightbulb makers, people whose efforts we rarely stop to appreciate but which, should they cease, we'd suffer for want of.

For the record, I don't always feel this way about my day job.

Now, mid-January, my world has resumed the winter I'm accustomed to—drab, cool, wet, grey. All that remains of the mountainous snow piles are ridges of dirty slush. Bundling up means putting a windbreaker over my sweater. Winter footwear means I lace up my runners rather than slip on my loafers, and I've resumed wearing only slippers for my little jaunts to the curb, to take the garbage out or let the dog do his business.

It's all rather depressing.

I'd forgotten winter calls forth deep and almost dormant reserves of manliness, or at least fortitude (to which no gender lays special claim). There's work in winter only winter knows. (And play in winter that only winter knows, but more of that later.) It's hard work, and good, and needed, and restoring, in its own way.

WINTER'S WORK

Prayer

The Sons of Korah discover a good work in winter.

I'm back where we started in the last chapter, in Psalm 88, that dispatch from the heart of darkness, that song in the key of desolation. I'm back with those psalmists in the throes of their wintertime, in the grip of their wild harrowing sorrow. They, too, find that there's work in winter that only winter knows.

It's prayer.

The psalmist prays like never before. He prays day and night. He cries out, he calls out, he spreads his hands to heaven. Winter tries to bury him, and he keeps digging his way out.

Prayer is the ongoing work of winter. But this can go either way. Wintertime can poison the life of prayer as much as awaken it. It can deaden it, or revive it. Usually, it forces a fluctuation between the two. Cheryl, my wife, illustrates this as much as anyone I know. My wife and Carol, my colleague, did many things together — shopped, watched movies, attended conferences, planned renovations to my house. Mostly, though, they prayed. Theirs was a sisterhood anchored in intercession. So it was natural, as Carol fell ill, for them to pray together for God to do something big, decisive, impressive — to step in and save the day. To heal her. They prayed many other prayers besides that — prayers for family, for friends, for the church, for courage no matter what. But always, they prayed for healing.

The healing never came. There were hopeful turns of events that seemed to bode well — the day, for instance, Carol's eyesight, damaged from the first surgery, recovered enough that she could drive again. And prayer oftentimes did give them the courage they asked for. They found the redemptive, defiant, subversive power of laughter in the face of adversity, and so made jokes of Carol's baldness, puffiness, her black eye-patch that made her look like a rotund and hairless pirate. Neither the praying nor the laughing staved off the dying. The disease's retreat was only ever a regrouping, and the next visit to the oncologist always brought troubling, sometimes devastating, news.

A day came when Cheryl had to pray alone. Carol was too bloated, addled, groggy to join her, and besides, she was moved to a hospice in another town. So Cheryl began a journey that was mostly solitary, and almost wordless: the groaning Paul describes in Romans 8, where words fail. This is prayer matched to the rhythm and pitch of the entire broken, frustrated creation, that song of lament and protest in a minor key, mournful and defiant as the song slaves sing picking cotton or prisoners sing breaking stones.

During this time, Cheryl was part of a prayer team at church. She headed it, in fact. Every Sunday, people came to her for prayer. Many asked her to pray for strength and faith to cope with Carol's illness. Some came with illnesses of their own, or on behalf of loved ones struggling with cancer, lupus, renal failure, multiple sclerosis, congestive heart condition, chronic depression, bipolar disorder, and many other strange or common ailments that mess with us. Cheryl prayed, dutifully. But later she would confess how hard it was to pray believing. Her words in her own ears sounded rote, trite, mechanical, and often she fought down an inner voice that mocked her, that told her this was an exercise in futility, putting band-aids on mortal wounds, singing lullabies to breaking hearts, crossing her fingers as the sky falls.

That's where Psalm 88 helps. In this man's wintertime, he prays, too, though his capacity to believe is strained almost to extinction. He prays anyhow, and in this way: according to what he knows of God, not what he sees of God. Or put it this way: his praying is anchored in God's revelation of himself in Scripture, not in his first-hand experience of God in daily life. He doesn't pray because he can taste and see that the Lord is good. He prays in spite of that, contrary to the evidence at hand. What he tastes is bitterness; what he sees is darkness. Circumstances erode his faith rather than buttress it.

So he pushes himself beyond circumstances. He resists the temptation to equate circumstances with God. He prays not because God's been good to him but because God's Word says God's good, and he's betting the whole farm on its being so.

That's biblical faith. Everything short of this is a hedged bet. Everything short of this is a faith based on what I can, at least dimly, see. And to the extent I can see it, it's not yet pure faith.

Winter grows pure faith. It grows almost nothing, but it grows biblical faith like no other season can. It combines the unique conditions that nurture the certainty of things hoped for and the assurance of things unseen. It is the season above all seasons when we walk by faith and not by sight. There is no better ground for growing an abiding faith that weathers the worst life can throw at you. In later chapters, we'll talk about the seasons we love, especially summer. As delightful, as fertile, as the summertime of the heart is, it is almost useless for growing faith. It may produce a bounty of joy, vast crops of thanksgiving. But not faith, that fierce, hardy Scotch broom of a

lose heart. Though outwardly we are wasting away, yet inwardly we are being renewed day by day. For our light and momentary troubles are achieving for us an eternal glory that far outweighs them all. So we fix our eyes not on what is seen, but on what is unseen, since what is seen is temporary, but what is unseen is eternal."[3]

The maiming became the sculpting. The paring back gave way to a vigorous flourishing.

I'm wondering what this means for you. If you are in winter, there may be, hidden in its bleakness, a rare opportunity. You may be able to lose some weight: the weight of unneeded responsibility, the burden of useless activity. It may be the season to say an unapologetic no to the things to which, recently or long ago, you said a hardy or an unenthusiastic yes. I'm not advocating irresponsibility. But I am advocating simplicity. I'm saying that this may be the one shot you have at becoming less so that, in time, Christ's fruit in you might become greater.

Waiting

Another good work of winter is waiting. Winter forces us to wait. And waiting forces faith to grow.

In winter we pray, call out, cry out, spread our hands. God seems indifferent, or absent, or opposed to us. He doesn't show up. He leaves things unchanged, or lets them change for the worse. Still we pray, day and night. It's met with silence. With hardship. Those who wait on the Lord *will* renew their strength, we remind ourselves. But in the meantime, in the waiting, our strength languishes.

The psalmist in Psalm 88 unintentionally gives us a hint about what to do with that. He points to something that only those whose faith is grounded in resurrection hope can grasp. It's this: he says his closest friend is darkness. This is meant to be a statement of hopelessness. But how could it be for people of the resurrection? No moment in history was darker than the day after Good Friday. No day ever seemed so devoid of light or comfort, so desperately lonely.

The day after that day, it's still dark. Two disciples, grieving and bewildered, walk toward Emmaus. Darkness is their closest companion.

They're joined by a third, a stranger. His presence, at first, is an annoying intrusion into the splendid isolation of their gloom and misery. But he talks, and talks, and slowly the two disciples' hearts warm.

And then, just as night comes, so does day: the stranger, he reveals, is no stranger at all. It's Jesus, who's been with them all along, in the darkness, in the grief, in the bewilderment, walking with them in the fellowship of sharing in their suffering.

It's odd. Why didn't Jesus announce himself or disclose his identity the moment he joined them? He does that only in his departure. This is often the shape of winter—the Christ who meets us and walks with us all along doesn't reveal his identity until we arrive at an end.

But why? Why not tip his hand sooner, when it would mean so much to us, when even a glimpse into the eternal would relieve completely our doubt and sadness and pain? Why not turn the lights on straightaway? Why wait?

My guess is that the waiting builds faith's backbone. The waiting is necessary to cultivate a faith to die for and live for, a faith that will literally change the world. Waiting is necessary for faith in the same way a chrysalis is necessary for a caterpillar, to change it from a grub that crawls the earth to a butterfly that dances the air. Many of Jesus' disciples, then as now, would die for their faith. That kind of faith isn't grown in a week. And, mostly, it's not grown in warmth and sunshine. Miracles can take it only so far, and after that can actually stunt it. Its hardiest growth, where the roots get deep and tough, happens in darkness.

In winter.

That would be true of Cheryl. Carol has been gone a while now. There was no miracle that intercepted her dying, and only one miracle that came out of it that I know: her brother, long estranged from God, put his faith in Christ just before he died of cancer almost a year to the day after Carol died. It was Carol's courage in the face of her own death, and Cheryl's friendship with him in his own sickness, that turned him round.

Cheryl's faith today is leaner and tougher and less prone to doubts and setbacks. It's more a faith that is certain of things hoped for, assured of things unseen. It's more based on who God is, not her circumstance of the moment.

It is a gift only winter could devise.

Which brings us to the strange bounty of winter.

WINTER'S GIFTS

A New You

Winter calls us to some good work — praying, pruning, waiting. Improbably, it also gives us a few good gifts.

Like the opportunity to reimagine our lives. Indeed, it almost demands that. By reimagining our lives, I don't mean indulging the fantasy of escape, conjuring the mirage of a tropic isle in the thick of an arctic storm. I don't mean the reverie of an "Ah, if only . . ." What I mean is that we see our lives in their truest light: see them for what they truly are, and know what really matters, and what doesn't.

My son's friend Thomas, at this writing, is gravely ill. He is only eighteen. Last year he was at the crown of his young years. He had graduated early from high school, with a scholarship to go to the University of Victoria. He finished the school year by cleaning up at the awards ceremony — athlete of the year, top academic, all-round student. He was valedictorian for his graduating class. He was musical, funny, good looking, popular. He was pursuing a career in law.

Then Thomas started to lose his balance. Walked into walls. Fumbled things. Slurred words. His parents grew alarmed, ordered tests. Those found a large growth in his brain. Malignant, they said. That was a year ago. Since then, Thomas has had several operations, radiation, and hundreds, maybe thousands, of people praying for him, and no clear diagnosis.

But one clear prognosis: if this thing, whatever it is, doesn't stop, he'll die.

Thomas's family are good people, kind and generous. They've never lived lives of coveting or complaint. But Thomas's illness had pared their existence down to a fierce simplicity. Before, their dreams were like most of ours. They were simple and modest enough: to live comfortably if not lavishly, to retire early, to travel a bit, maybe take up a new sport. A good dream. But now they'd throw all of that away just to have Thomas well again. This wintertime has forced them to reimagine their lives.

And what has come of that is beautiful.

My son left for university two weeks ago. The night before he left, we had a barbecue for him and his old classmates and their families. Craig was there, with his parents and sisters. Paul came, with his mom. Sean and his parents were away but sent a gift.

Thomas was conspicuously absent.

So after dinner, the three boys, now men, went to his house. They came back with Paul, Thomas's dad. And with Thomas. He was in a wheelchair, in a van the family recently acquired to lift and hold Thomas, chair and all, with the flick of a switch. All of us piled into the cul-de-sac for a visit; Thomas perched in his chair inside the open van.

Thomas is whittled and bloated. His once sinuous arms, nimble at catching any flying thing, potent at tossing it back, hung limp. His once muscular legs, fast and agile, draped over the chair like newsprint. His eyes shuttled sideways. His face was puffy from medication.

But his wit was undiminished. He got us all laughing at his wisecracks, his puns, his kind but sharp ribbing. Standing there, with Thomas and his dad, it was obvious their life has enlarged as much as reduced. It has a simple beauty and clarity about it. There is not one ounce of striving here. There is no pretension. There is no idle chatter. There is no gossip, or boasting, or foolish speculation. There is just hope, and thankfulness, and pain, and an enviable ability to cherish and inhabit the moment.

Before they drove away, my son kissed Thomas on the forehead. "I love you, man," he said. "I'll see you at Thanksgiving." Then he looked away, but I could see he was close to tears. I could see that through my own tears.

Except for winter, none of us would be here. None of us could have imagined it.[4]

A New Heaven and Earth

Maybe the greatest gift of winter, a gift that winter alone gives, is that it makes us heavenly minded. It breaks our addiction to this-worldliness and nurtures in us an anticipation of things unseen. We begin to long for, not death, but what takes death's sting away, and makes earth's many trials seem light and momentary.

We are not made for this world.

Only those who deeply suffer learn how to fully anticipate. For the writer of Psalm 88, he knew God, but not the God revealed in Jesus Christ, whose greatest defeat and darkest hour turned out to be his greatest victory and finest hour. The Christ whose triumph means that, even when we draw near the grave, we can say, "Death, where is thy sting?"

Harry Robinson is a preacher of legendary status in the city of Vancouver. For years, he was pastor at St. John's Shaughnessy, a vintage Anglican church in one of the most upscale areas of that city. He once performed a funeral for a nominal Christian who had attained great stature among his peers. He was a man of social clout, business savvy, financial success, cultural refinement, political sway. Eulogizer after eulogizer said so. A long parade of his admirers stood and sang his praises, citing his numerous earthly accomplishments that earned him these accolades.

The last man to pay tribute forgot his notes on the pulpit.

Harry Robinson followed him. Harry is a big man, tall, well built, with hands as large as wings. For a long time, he stood in silence behind the pulpit, his head sloped down toward one shoulder. Then in a deep gravelly voice he spoke. "All these things," he said. He picked up the notes that had been left behind, held them up, looked at the congregation. "All these things," he said again. Then, in his massive right hand, he curled in his fingers and crushed the paper into a tiny ball. "All these things," he said, "mean nothing"— and at that, he let the ball of paper fall to the floor—"if you do not know, and are not known by, the Lord Jesus Christ."[5]

It takes more than unceasing summertime to teach a man that.

WINTER'S PLAY

Loving Black Diamonds

There's one last thing, and it allows us to end on an upbeat note. Just as there's work in winter only winter knows, so too there's play in winter that only winter knows.

I started skiing when I was twelve. It was a way to break the endless dreariness of the winters where I lived.

My first time skiing was a near disaster. It was at Mount Tabor, a modest ski hill that stood right alongside the Yellowhead Highway, the lone straight strip of asphalt that carried you north from our already northerly town, and eventually threaded you through the Rockies in all their terrifying grandeur. But Mount Tabor was a long way west of the Rockies, and maybe technically not a mountain at all but just a hill, though I forget at what height one becomes the other. It was served, those days, by a T-bar—a large upside-down *T* attached to a cable that pulls two skiers at a time up a hill. It started off mildly enough, skating you over a nearly flat stretch, but then shot you up the flank of the mountain at a precipitous angle and an alarming speed. (At least, my memory has it thus.) The T-bar track crossed, two or three times, the cat-trail that the grooming machines used to traverse their way up the mountain, and here you had to make a quick body adjustment—from leaning steeply forward as you went up the incline to standing straight up as you crossed the trail, and then back to leaning forward as you started the incline again.

No one explained this to me.

So first time out, never before on skis, I failed to stand up straight when we hit the cat-trail. I fell off in a tangle of limbs and poles and skis.

There was no way out but down. That meant creeping along the cat-trail until it opened on what, it turned out, was the farthest run. Now, indeed, there was no out but down. And it was almost straight down (making allowances, again, for my preadolescent memory). The run was called, I found out later, O My Gawd, which was roughly what I exclaimed when I saw it.

If you're not a skier (or that awful parody and desecration of a skier, a boarder), let me give a brief explanation. A ski hill is divided and categorized by terrain—steepness, flatness, width, hazards, the like. The widest, smoothest, shallowest runs are designated with a green circle. Your hundred-year-old rheumatic grandmother could manage it. The next level—a few wild pitches, a hillock or two, a narrower berth—these are designated by blue squares. Your waddly, goutish middle-aged uncle could get down alive.

Then come two categories of black-diamond runs—single diamond and double diamond. There are double-diamond runs so steep you can stand at the top of the run with your ski tips hanging over the edge and, looking down between them, see the bottom of the mountain. There are double-diamond runs where, coming to a ridge, you have to inch near to make sure you're not on the lip of a hundred-foot cliff. Every year, skiers die miserably on double diamonds—tumbling headlong over bluffs, shattering at the bottom, or sailing spread-eagle into Douglas firs, just like Wile E. Coyote, but not so funny, or racing hard against an avalanche sweeping down on them, and losing. You need to be as fit as the new James Bond and half again as crazy to attempt one, and even still there are no guarantees.

Single black diamonds aren't as dangerous. Not quite.

O My Gawd was a single black diamond.

It took me close to an hour to negotiate my descent. It was a slapstick of pratfalls, body sprawls, flailing arms, wild careening swoops. I can still see myself as I must have looked to anyone watching—a small boy overdressed against the cold, with a parka that made him look swaddled in pillows, hollering as he came, an object of terror and humor, a spectacle of mayhem and folly, a vaudeville act of bungling and antics.

Anyhow, I survived it, in case you are wondering.

And went up again. This time, I managed to stay on the T-bar right to the top, and chose, until day's end, easier runs—green circles, blue squares. I steered clear of black diamonds. For the time being.

But some virus got into me that day. And every winter weekend after that, there I was—at Tabor or, later, Purden Ski Village, which had a chair lift *and* a T-bar, and a quarter of the mountain covered in black diamonds. By the end of that season, I was skiing those runs regularly, if not elegantly.

Eventually, black diamonds were almost all I skied, those and the notorious double black diamonds. At close to fifty, it's still almost all I ski.

That longish, somewhat self-promoting story is all to say that

---

TIME-IN 3

YIPPEE YI YEAH!

I have a friend who moved, several years ago now, from the almost tropical paradise of Vancouver to the far north of Canada. He moved for work. The intent, for a long time, was to get back down to the coast. The winters up there are brutal. They take up most the year, starting in late August or mid-September, ending in late May or early June, with usually at least one summer blizzard just to let everyone know who's boss.

His intent was to move back, until his intent was to stay. Somewhere, things shifted. Now he wouldn't move back for love or money. He wants to finish his days in that cold lonely place, and have them bury him, when it's warm enough to break ground, in a wide open space so that snow will blanket his bones most months of the winter, and in late summer the northern lights will dance the night sky above him, dazzling as a rush of seraphim wings.

He learned to play. That's what shifted. He learned that he lived in an Arctic paradise, a vast playground of snowshoes and skidoos, skis and skates, a wonderland of ice fishing and snow camps and hockey games that ranged over whole lakes. Snow-men populated the town like a colony of happy, chubby albino trolls. At lunch, he'd lace up his skates and knock a puck around with his friends. His children came home from school every day and, before dinner, swooped down a nearby hill on toboggans, inner tubes, all manner of plasticky torpedo things. He'd gather

---

such play is possible only in winter. (I know about glacier skiing in summer, and have done it several times, but it simply isn't the same thing; skiing a few hundred yards on an ice sheet that you spent an hour clambering up in order to spend a minute schussing down — what was the point, again?) Until I was twelve, growing pudgy and indolent in my semihibernation from late November to late April, I'd found little to make winter anything but a trial and a curse. I

with friends at least once a week, make a bonfire in one or the other's yard, and roast things in it, and not just hot dogs but tendons of elk, sausages made from wild venison, whole pigs.

I asked him if he'd ever again want to live in a more agreeable climate.

He really thinks he's in one.

What might be your game in winter?

Carol got sick just as we started planning for her to take a sabbatical. Her illness interrupted that. But in a way, it provided it. "Why don't you," I told her, after her first surgery when she was feeling well enough to do most things but lacked energy to return to work, "why don't you treat this time as a sabbatical? Why don't you do those things you planned for your sabbatical — the novel reading, the getaways, the quiet days?"

So she did.

Winter might be handing you a gift like that. There may be something you can do now, here, that's hard or impossible to do anytime else. Maybe you've always wanted to read the entire oeuvre of Tolstoy or Dickens. Maybe you've wanted to learn bonsai. Maybe you've always wanted to visit Toledo. Maybe you'd just like to sleep one hour more a day.

There's no time like winter. Sure it's cold outside. But those skates work only when it's freezing.

spent my winters loafing about the house, drowsy and grumpy, eating too much.

Skiing snapped me out of that. It took me where eagles dare. It took me up up up so I could go down down down.

For years after, winter became my most longed for season. That sudden turn in the weather in late fall, when you wake one morning and the air is sharp with cold and the lawn hoary with frost—that always thrilled me, and still does, though age and duty have muted the joy. The first snowfall was sheer festivity, a gift as pure and elating as a windfall of money. I worked hard all summer at menial jobs, and saved most of what I made, so I could buy some new piece of ski equipment—newfangled boots with buckles and pistons and velcro straps, or the latest innovations in retractable bindings, or goggles that had little self-regulating vents at the brow to keep the lens from fogging up. I was a sucker for all of it. I would buy these things in late August and touch them daily, like heirlooms or talismans, until first use, usually in early December.

Because I fell in love with a sport you can engage only in winter, winter became not a season I endured but the season I anticipated most, and hated most to end.

Spiritually, that has a certain resonance. Winters of the heart are rarely playful, and there's nothing about them that makes us wish their return. But there can be a kind of sideways pleasure in it all the same. As a tree in dormancy exists only for its own sake, so a heart in winter does much the same. The burden of responsibility loosens and lightens in that season. In mine, I felt a release of sorts to do things I longed to do but seldom took the time for—sleep in past eight, read long novels, watch mindless movies, play Scrabble. I indulged myself in small diversions without so much as a twinge of puritan guilt. Again, nothing here that caused me to miss winter once it went, or that made my winter of the heart equivalent to the winters of my youth. But there was enough that even here, joy found a way.

SNOW CHILD

There's a lovely Russian folktale called "The Snow Child." It's the story of an old couple in a small Siberian village. Their love for each other is strong and deep, but they live beneath a shadow of sadness: they are childless. They watch the children of the village play in summer and winter, all year, and the sight delights them but also deepens their sadness. It reminds them that, except for each other, they're all alone. One winter evening, after they watch the children make snowmen in the village commons, they bundle up and trundle out and, together, make a snow child—a girl with bright dark eyes made from stone, wild tousled hair made from brambles, a flowing dress of pure ice.

She comes alive. She is a sprite of untamed energy. She dances, and sings, and laughs. The home brims with her voice and her mirth. The one oddity is that she never sleeps in the house. She only ever sleeps outside, in the wintry cold. Her parents worry for her, but she simply explains, "I am a snow child, and I need to go where the cold winds blow."

Her presence awakens youthfulness and vigor in the old man and old woman. Their sadness flies away.

But spring changes things. As the earth warms, as birds appear, and then flowers and blossoms, the snow child stops singing, stops laughing, stops dancing. She grows listless and morose. The old man and old woman grow alarmed and seek remedy. None's to be had. Then one bright morning, as spring tilts into summer, she's gone.

It is the saddest summer of their lives. Every day, with diminishing energy, they wake hopeful and anxious, wondering if she'll return. Every night, with growing sorrow, they bed down despondent and bewildered, wondering where she went.

All summer. Not once do they enjoy the sunshine, the flowers, the play and laughter of the village children. Darkness is their only friend.

The leaves turn color and fall. The air gets cold. And one day a snowflake spins down from a bleak sky.

And there she is, the snow child, her happy, sprightly, dancing self. Back for winter. The old couple are more elated than even the first time she came to them. This winter is brighter than the last. It becomes a long season of celebration that they never want to end. But it does. Spring comes, then summer. And as before, so again, she leaves. She is a child of the snow, and she goes where the cold winds blow. But as before, so again, when the cold winds blow, she returns.

The couple learn to wait. They learn to enjoy her presence and stay productive in her absence.

But what changes, and completely, is their orientation. Winter is no longer the season to endure, no longer the season you wish to come late and depart early. It is not the season any more they would foreshorten but the one, if they could, they'd prolong. Winter is the only season they're fully alive.

And it's not that it is less brutal and dark. It's simply because then, of all times, their beloved abides with them.

Jesus, the Man for All Seasons, abides with us always. But because he is a man of sorrows and familiar with suffering, he comes closest in winter. It's then, of all seasons, he moves into the house.

In the next chapter we move to another season. If these past two chapters seem a little too close to the bone, that may be all you need to know: spring is coming, summer's close behind.

But maybe it's coming too soon. Maybe my descriptions of winter, and my meager advice about stewarding it, have stirred more than settled you, disturbed more than consoled. If that's so, I'd invite you to stay a while. I've written a special piece in the Time-In 4 section that will help you abide here a little longer.

TIME-IN 4

STAY WITH ME

"Don't you care if we drown?"

Jesus' disciples asked him that in a moment of terror, when the storm-battered boat they were in was keeling to the gunnels, and Jesus just slept through it. The storm didn't wake him, but his disciples did, angry, frightened, desperate.

"Don't you care if we drown?"

Most of us have asked Jesus that, one time or another. He sometimes seems utterly oblivious to our plight, indifferent to the peril right before us, threatening to destroy us.

But then Jesus has a question—two, in fact—for his disciples. "Why are you so afraid? Do you still have no faith?"

This seems rankly unfair to me—accusing men who have left everything to follow of lacking faith—but let's leave that aside for now. What I'm wondering is if the disciples, one or two of them anyhow, remembered this moment in the garden of Gethsemane, when Jesus faced *his* biggest storm. When he felt he was going to capsize. He asked his disciples, three times, to wake up, to stay with him.

"Do you not care if I drown?" he might have asked.

"Why are you so afraid?" they might have retorted. "Do you still have no faith?"

I referred earlier to the "fellowship of sharing in Christ's sufferings." I think that fellowship is a mutual waiting with Jesus. It's a mutual standing with each other in the dark, when we are afraid and it's as if we have no faith. But maybe Jesus wants us to stay with him as much as we want Jesus to stay with us. It's a radical idea, maybe heretical, but there are hints here and there in Scripture that Jesus invites us to abide with him not just for our sakes but for his as well.

I'm not suggesting the risen Christ is ever afraid, wavering in his resolve. But when Christ dwelt on the earth, he certainly had such moments, and he sought both the consolation of his Father and the companionship of his friends to ease his dread and his sorrow. The biblical portrait of Jesus mostly depicts his earthly incarnation, not his heavenly exaltation. We know far more about Jesus' humanity than his divinity. We see him more in his humility than in his glory. I don't think the Bible tells and shows us all that except that God intends to draws us alongside Jesus not just in his divinity but just as much in his humanity.

"Will no one stay awake with me?" Jesus asked. Sometimes, I think, he still asks it.

Is it possible that in this winter of yours, when you desperately need Jesus to stay with you, he's just as happy for you to stay with him?

If you can, right now, spend time with Jesus. Tell him all the ways you need him to be near you. But dare to ask him if there's some way he needs you, or at least longs for you, to be near him, too.

And when you're ready, I invite you for a walk in spring.

Life protests
death and starts
a riot underground
uncontained and so
it breaks out
everywhere
(every hairline crack of pavement a
breeding ground for insurrection)
spreading
far and wide
up and down
until the whole
wide earth
brims full
and wild
and hidden in it manifold
flowers
fade and knot
into
fruit
    nut
    seed
drawing life into
themselves
to give it
back
a thousandfold.

—M. BUCHANAN

CHAPTER 3

SPRING

I spent my early years in a northern Canadian mill town whose reputation, such as it is, I'll protect by not naming. It's the place they make ice in winter and mud in summer, and where they breed mosquitoes so large and hungry, and loud as war jets, that they seem a species of prehistoric bird.

The winters were memorable only for their endlessness. They were long, dark, despotic seasons. The ground hardened up like marble. Sometimes boulders split from sheer cold. In January or February, a cup of coffee poured out on the air would freeze solid before it hit the ground. Every car's engine was fitted with a block heater, a device that kept the oil from thickening beyond motion. If you failed to plug it in overnight, you could no more turn that motor over than raise the dead. And touch your tongue to metal—the piping that suspended the schoolyard swing set, or the aluminium fence post in the neighbor's chain link fence (I tried both)—and it fused instantly. The only way out was to tear your tongue away and suffer a week's healing, or press your mouth closer until the heat of your breath loosened the ice's death grip, and even then your tongue felt abraded all day, like you'd been licking splinters. That iciness worked its way into fingers and toes, even swaddled in thermal wear, like fire works its way into wood or water into cloth. I frostbit my fingers so many times that I lost feeling in their tips for several years, and even today they tingle slightly, and a mildly cold day can turn them numb and white in minutes.

The doors and windows on our house grew, around the inside edges, a rind of frost that daily we'd have to chip off with hammer and chisel. Some days it got so cold they closed the schools—blissful news, but muted by the fact that we had to stay housebound lest we perish in the outdoors. We'd get cabin fever, go stir crazy, sitting in that house, getting fat from our indolence, the furnaces wheezing to keep up. Whenever the brutal cold would break, and the temperature soar to a balmy minus five or so, we'd spill out of our homes like victors after a great war, giddy in triumph, delirious with relief, glad to be alive.

A few years ago, on a flight to Toronto, I watched the movie *March of the Penguins*. I found it gripping and moving. But I also found it, with its footage of thousands of featherless birds crowding together to keep from freezing to death as an Antarctic storm pummeled them half to death, and the temperatures, with wind chill, dipped down to minus eighty, disturbingly reminiscent. My fingers ached with the memory.

Spring seemed never to come. Many a May, I, trembling with hope and dread, watched for the first hard bud to pinprick the branch of the birch tree outside our front window. I'd scour the field for any sign of life, even if only the hieroglyphs of birdclaw in snow. I'd time the number of minutes of daylight we gained over the day before, and the week before that, and every moment of sunshine was an auspice of joy.

And then one day, usually in late May, sometimes even early June, it would appear, suddenly and all at once: spring. The trees frothed with leaf and blossom. The ground softened to mud, then thickened with an embroidery of flowers. Birds whirled and swooped and sang, and colts and calves tottered or gamboled in farmyards. The back of winter finally broke, and warmth and color came rushing in.

And hope. Always, hope.

Spring is a good season. In the previous two chapters, I talked winter. In the winter of the heart, I said, we experience a wide gap between what we know of God and what we taste and see of God. Our theology says one thing—God is loving, faithful, righteous, bestowing wonders. But our experience says another—that he's aloof, angry, capricious, dealing bruises. And we feel deeply alone;

even when we're with others, we're estranged from them. Sadness is a room we can't find the door out of.

And, worst of all, we feel the encroachment of death. Everything looks dead. We feel dead. Sometimes we wish we were dead.

But Christ, the Man for All Seasons, meets us even here, in the depth of our wintertime. He waits with us. He prunes us. He breaks our self-dependency and deepens our God-dependency. He brings us into a fresh encounter with the God who raises the dead.

And always, the Man for All Seasons leads us out of winter.

And what he leads us out into is spring. (Or usually so. The logic of spiritual things is that sometimes we skip a season or two, go straight from winter into fall or summer into winter, and the like.)

THE HEART IN SPRING

Isaiah, I think, best captures the experience of the springtime of the heart. This is Isaiah 35:

> The desert and the parched land will be glad;
>   the wilderness will rejoice and blossom.
> Like the crocus, it will burst into bloom;
>   it will rejoice greatly and shout for joy.
> The glory of Lebanon will be given to it,
>   the splendor of Carmel and Sharon;
> they will see the glory of the LORD,
>   the splendor of our God.
> Strenthen the feeble hands,
>   steady the knees that give way;
> say to those with fearful hearts,
>   "Be strong, do not fear;
> your God will come,
>   he will come with vengeance;
> with divine retribution
>   he will come to save you."
>
> Then will the eyes of the blind be opened
>   and the ears of the deaf unstopped.

Then will the lame leap like a deer,
  and the mute tongue shout for joy.
Water will gush forth in the wilderness
  and streams in the desert.
The burning sand will become a pool,
  the thirsty ground bubbling springs.
In the haunts where jackals once lay,
  grass and reeds and papyrus will grow.

And a highway will be there;
  it will be called the Way of Holiness.
The unclean will not journey on it;
  it will be for those who walk in that Way;
  wicked fools will not go about on it.
No lion will be there,
  nor will any ferocious beast get up on it;
  they will not be found there.
But only the redeemed will walk there,
  and the ransomed of the LORD will return.
They will enter Zion with singing;
  everlasting joy will crown their heads.
Gladness and joy will overtake them,
  and sorrow and sighing will flee away.

This passage, obviously, doesn't speak of spring. But it does describe a transformation of desert into garden. It's a surprising springlike flourishing in the waste places, an exultation of flower and beast and human. The deserts of the Near East and the long winters of the Canadian north are not so unalike. They share this in common: nothing much lives or grows in them. They're dead zones. Each is a sprawling fastness of barrenness.

Until that day God chooses otherwise. Until that day, all at once and everywhere, life and life to the full returns.

And with it, hope.

***

This past year, my family and I spent several Sunday evenings watching the remarkable BBC documentary series *Planet Earth*. David

Attenborough's measured and dignified voice narrates this sweeping story of forest and ocean, desert and tundra, whales and winged things, polar bears and tree frogs — the infinite intricate strangeness and beauty of this resilient yet fragile planet we inhabit. My favorite parts were the time-lapse sequences: a forest that moves from the bony starkness of winter to the pastel softness of spring to the verdant lushness of summer to the wild mosaic of autumn, all in a minute or less. There were many of them: cacti blooming in the austere landscape of Arizona, mountain meadows blushing with wildflowers before turning sere in the Yukon.

But the time-lapse sequence I liked most was the Kalahari Desert.

It starts in hot and dusty bareness. The few animals out in it are barely surviving. They're gaunt from hunger, half mad with thirst. A herd of elephants makes a desperate journey to find water. Their massive footfalls send thick plumes of dust hundreds of feet sky high, trailing them for miles. The weak ones lay down and die. The rest walk, day after day, past the skeletons of trees and animals.

And then one day, a trickle of water, flowing from seasonal rains in the highlands of Angola, threads down to the desert floor. In time lapse, we watch a miracle unfold: the thread of water becomes a stream, and then a river; the river carves a bed, then spills it, sprawling over parched earth. Grass springs up beneath its kiss, then trees, seemingly dead, burst with bloom. Great reeds flourish. It becomes a lake, a vast glinting wetland surrounding an archipelago of lush ground.

Everywhere and all at once, death turns to life.

> Water will gush forth in the wilderness
> and streams in the desert.
> The burning sand will become a pool,
> the thirsty ground bubbling springs.
> In the haunts where jackals once lay,
> grass and reeds and papyrus will grow.[1]

The cameras take us back to what's happening in the Kalahari. It's become an aqua playground. Amphibious things teem along reedy shores. Baboons wade through lagoons like fastidious old women in their Sunday best trying to stone-step a creek. Spindly-legged birds with scissorlike beaks wait still and watchful in the shallows, then, lightening quick, plunge their heads in the water and come up with fish (where did *they* come from?) bejeweling their mouths.

But best of all are those elephants. They play in that water like otters. They dive and torpedo, splash and dance. They gallop along the bottom, and thrust their huge heads up, trumpeting water through their trunks in a fanfare of joy. The long desperate march through desolation could not be farther behind them, even though —implausibly—the place they now frolic, only weeks ago, was that very wasteland.

I can't think of a more vivid picture of hope flooding where hope had died.

Isn't that spring?

The beauty of Isaiah 35 is that it captures both a reality and a hope. Isaiah prophesies an actual desert place springing forth in Edenic abundance. It's a reality: this, indeed, will happen, just as the Kalahari will bloom. But Isaiah also uses the desert-into-garden image to portray a hope fulfilled, a spiritual longing coming to fruition. In essence, he tells us what it *feels* like when God is on the move. God changes everything and utterly, and with breathtaking swiftness. The impossible becomes the inevitable. Desert turns to garden. Where death reigned, life triumphs.

I wonder if C. S. Lewis was thinking of Isaiah 35, and transposing the desert imagery into winter imagery, when he wrote *The Lion, the Witch, and the Wardrobe*. If you've read the book (or seen the movie), you know that when the Pevensie children first arrive in Narnia, they learn that a curse is on the land. The curse has very real manifestation: it's always winter, never Christmas. Winter is the perennial season. The whole land is in its icy grip. All toil beneath its bleak prospects. Winter never ends, and no festival makes it bearable, no robin singing or crocus blooming promises its subversion.

But then the children begin to hear mysterious, thrilling, earth-shaking news: Aslan is on the move. The Great King is back. He's already at work, and what he's planned will change everything.

The sign and symbol of that promise is that winter's despotic reign ends. The snows melt. The ice breaks. The cold lifts. The trees blossom. And out of the bleakness, spring:

> Every moment the patches of green grew bigger and the patches of snow grew smaller. Every moment more and more of the trees shook off their robes of snow. Soon, wherever you looked, instead of white shapes you saw the dark green of firs or the black prickly branches of bare oaks and beeches and elms. Then the mist turned from white to gold and presently cleared away altogether. Shafts of delicious sunlight struck down to the forest floor and overhead you could see blue sky between the tree tops.
>
> Soon there were more wonderful things happening.... The ground [was] covered in all directions with little yellow flowers—celandines. The noise of water grew louder....
>
> Then came a sound even more delicious than the sound of the water. Close beside the path they were following a bird suddenly chirped from the branch of a tree. It was answered by the chuckle of another bird a little further off. And then, as if it had been a signal, there was chattering and chirruping in every direction, and then a moment of full song, and within five minutes the whole wood was ringing with birds' music.[2]

Everywhere and at all once, spring. And with it, hope.

TASTING SPRING

What does springtime of the heart feel like?

It pulses with joy. The opening verses of Isaiah 35 are a refrain of celebration: "glad," "joy," "rejoice greatly," "shout for joy." Spring is a raucous fanfare of jubilation. And it's the creation itself that rejoices—the once parched land, the once barren wilderness, begins the parade. Trees and rivers and mountains and billy goats and ducklings—yes, and elephants—frolic. Creation itself delights in the newness that breaks forth from the deadness.

When God moves, creation responds. This is a biblical theme, and especially in Isaiah. It's Isaiah who envisions, as the people of God respond in obedience to the commands of God, that creation strikes up the band—whole mountains sing, whole forests dance. And the Psalms, too, are suffused with the theme—Psalm 29, for instance, where cedars and oak trees bend and shatter beneath the voice of God.

But the theme moves from metaphor to reality in the New Testament. The winds and the waves obey Christ's voice. The creation itself mourns when Christ is crucified—midday becomes night, the earth shakes in anguish. And earth, too, exults at Christ's presence. If we are silent, the rocks themselves will sing. Given Christ's track record, it's possible he didn't mean that as a mere figure of speech.

But implied in the joy of creation is joy among God's people. Isaiah 35 hints at Romans 8: "I consider that our present sufferings are not worth comparing with the glory that will be revealed in us. The creation waits in eager expectation for the children of God to be revealed. For the creation was subjected to frustration, not by its own choice, but by the will of the one who subjected it, in hope that the creation itself will be liberated from its bondage to decay and brought into the freedom and glory of the children of God."[3]

TIME-IN 5

GREEN THUMB

Every spring I *need* to plant at least one thing—a wisteria, a plum tree, an azalea, an English rose, a wandering Jew (well, there are so many to choose from, I usually need to plant more than one). The need is fed by the miracle, year after year, of what the ground does with its foundling: nurtures it into a great gangling thing, many limbed as a Hindu goddess, or shaggy as bison, or bejeweled with flowers. I think if I live to be 103, the magic act of seed and soil will never cease to astonish me.

It's also true spiritually: every spring I *need* to plant at least one thing, usually many. I try a new preaching style. I revise or revive or renovate a ministry. I roll out some newfangled, never-heard-of-before thing—an outreach to Elvis impersonators, or a worship service with dancing bears, and suchlike. When the

Here, the creation follows our lead, not the other way around. It waits for our cue. The people of God experience liberation from bondage *first*, and then the whole creation takes up the chorus, joins the dance. Isaiah himself says as much in his famous passage where "the mountains and hills ... burst into song before you, and all the trees of the field ... clap their hands." But what happens first? Watch:

> As the rain and the snow
>   come down from heaven,
> and do not return to it
>   without watering the earth
> and making it bud and flourish,
>   so that it yields seed for the sower and bread for the eater,
> so is my word that goes out from my mouth:
>   It will not return to me empty,
> but will accomplish what I desire
>   and achieve the purpose for which I sent it.
> You will go out in joy
>   and be led forth in peace;

ground is right, and the air is right, what God does with our small efforts is breathtaking.

If you're in spring, why not do both: plant something in the ground, and plant something in the world? Let each betoken the other.

Here's something you might try: gather a group of friends, and clean a local park or street. You may even want to talk to city hall and ask if there's any creation care they'd like done. I know of a church in New Brunswick that started doing this. They got a list of nearly a hundred small tasks the city wished done, and they did them all. They've gone out into their community to serve it so often, gone out with joy and been led forth in peace, that now their community's starting to come to them.

Spring has a way of growing small things big.

the mountains and hills
   will burst into song before you,
and all the trees of the field
   will clap their hands.[4]

God speaks first. Then you — *you* — "will go out with joy and be led forth in peace." Then the creation joins the song.

Here's one way I've seen that happen. A number of times in our church, the congregation's gone through a tangible renewal (an experience I'll describe in personal terms in the next section). Always, a reawakening to God's voice sparks this. We hear with clarity and respond with swiftness to God's Word and presence. These seasons are always marked by repentance, but they are also characterized by joy and peace. We have a fresh hunger for prayer, preaching, worship, service, evangelism, friendship. We work hard and celebrate often. Our joy is obvious and infectious, our peace deep and inviting.

When these seasons are upon us, creation booms. We tend gardens, walk the woods, play in the parks. We pick up litter we didn't leave. We notice birds, trees, clouds, frogs. The natural overflow of our reignited love for God and humanity is our awakened love for creation, our enlarged capacity to see it, enjoy it, and care for it.

When we go out in joy and are led forth in peace, trees clap, mountains sing.

And the opposite is true. I can tell at a glance when a church, my own included, is joyless and without peace. The grounds and buildings tell the story before anyone else does. Neglect. Withering. Rankness. Debris. Trees dying, weeds run amok. When there's no song from the hills or applause from the trees, it's a given that there's not much singing and clapping, joy and peace, anywhere close by.

SPRINGTIME RENEWAL

God's springtime begins with renewal within you.

The renewal comes out of dryness and wilderness. *Dryness. Wilderness.* Hear those as bywords for crisis. Spring springs forth from death. It unaccountably, inexplicably, unexpectedly shows up in the least likely places and most unpromising circumstances.

Maybe the death of someone you love. Maybe the loss of a job, or a torturous stretch of poor health, or a long and twisting road of emotional upheaval, or a deep valley of depression. Maybe a season of conflict in your home or workplace or neighborhood or church. Whatever, the crisis makes your heart bitter soil or frozen ground, too hard or too parched or too leached to nourish any seed to life, maybe even to receive any seed at all.

And then one day it breaks, suddenly and everywhere at once. And the only way you can explain that is God did it. God acted. God intervened. Aslan is on the move.

And when God moves, everything's different. Isaiah gives us three vivid touchstones—emotional renewal, physical renewal, and moral renewal. Any of these alone is good indication that spring is upon you. Together, it's certain. In fact, one form of renewal implies and invites the others. Just as earth's sudden flourishing implies that almost anything will grow, and invites you to plant a garden, so an emotional renewal implies and invites physical and moral renewals. Restored joy often prompts renewed physical activity, which often leads to fresh resolve to live well. And the sequence can work in any order. We'll look at that in detail in the next chapter. But for now, let's understand each of these renewals.

Emotional Renewal

Emotions that winter (or desert) have bruised to withering, spring heals and restores to vigor. Look again:

> Strengthen the feeble hands,
>   steady the knees that give way;
> say to those with fearful hearts,
>   "Be strong, do not fear;
> your God will come,
>   he will come with vengeance;
> with divine retribution
>   he will come to save you."[5]

Times of crisis often enfeeble and terrify us. We hide in clefts and jump at shadows. We cower in upper rooms. Our confidence in God, in ourselves, in our church, in others, whittles down to nearly nothing. We just want to go away, but we're not sure where. Anywhere but here. Better, we want to fall asleep like bears do, all winter, and wake up hungry and feisty and curious again.

Sometimes those around us try to cheer us with platitudes. These are galling. We do not need people, in winter, telling us to buck up or snap out of it. We do need people (more of that in a later chapter), but we mostly need their silence or their laughter, their willingness to stay with us in the darkness or their ability, sometimes, to distract us from it. But their lectures and bromides are typically worse than useless.

But when springtime arrives, words of cheer are the only ones that make sense. Hearty exhortation is the order of the day. Such speech, to use a popular phrase, *resonates*. It matches our mood, and heightens it. Triteness sounds profound in springtime. Be strong. Cheer up. Do not be afraid. Get out in the garden. Strengthen those feeble hands and shaky knees.

Buck up, indeed.

Yes, we say. Exactly what I was thinking.

Isaiah gives and commends such pep talk: "Say to those with fearful hearts, 'Be strong.'" What sounds shallow and hollow in winter booms deep and rich in spring.

But the pep talk turns quickly sour. God, he says, comes with vengeance and retribution. He's gonna get the bad guys. There'll be blood on the tracks when this is over.

Grim, but if you've ever had an enemy, this, indeed, has the ring of good news. Isaiah was writing to a people who had an enemy, several in fact. They endured much from bad guys. The chapter preceding this one announces judgment on the nations who have opposed God and, by implication, God's people. And Isaiah lived and prophesied in the days when looming over Israel was the ever-present threat of a brutal and bloodthirsty regime, the Assyrian powerhouse. Those are the people Jonah wanted nothing to do with, and for good reason. They carried out retribution with ruthless efficiency. They conducted military campaigns with a scorched-earth policy, leaving rubble and smoke in their wake, and vast fields of the dead. For

Israel, there had to be a certain satisfaction in knowing that what goes around comes around. God has marked a target on their enemy, and it's them, not you, who will soon be cowering.

That's good news to my ears.

Only, I'm not supposed to admit that.

But here's what I can admit, and long for: vindication. Underneath Israel's thirst for vengeance was a hunger for vindication. Vindication is when the wrong done to us is set right, fully, finally, and publicly. The insults we endured are rebuffed. The wounds we took are healed. The gossip that assassinated our character, ruined our reputation, blighted our influence, sidelined our participation—it's proved empty and false. The hurt done to us boomerangs on those who caused it.

That's vindication.

And when it happens, something inside us that crawled into a hole and curled up to die is suddenly given a new start and a fresh resolve. We stand tall again, and stop shaking.

When I first became a pastor, I stumbled across a prayer of St. Augustine's: "Lord, deliver me from the lust to vindicate myself." At the time, I hardly knew what it meant. Now, a couple of decades into this work, I pray it almost daily, with great feeling. And my wife does, too, often with greater feeling.

Not that I have many enemies. I've a few, and at least half of them well-earned. But still, it's just a few. What I have lots of, though, are critics. There are people—more than a handful, I'd say—who find fault with me. Things I say, or don't say, deeds I do, or don't do, attitudes they detect in me or detect the absence of. Sometimes, I'm scorned or scolded for personality deficiencies, which—admittedly—I abound in. I am not warm and cuddly like pastor so-and-so. I am too bloody-minded, or—conversely—an incurable soft touch. I don't preach a clear vision. I do preach a clear vision, but not a compelling one. I do preach a compelling vision, but compelling us toward the wrong ends. I talk too much about money from the pulpit. I don't talk about it enough.

When winter is upon me, all this makes my hands feeble and my knees weak.

But spring brings vindication. The vision proved right after all. More money came in, with just the right amount of talking about it and not talking about it, and with it we hired a pastor three times as warm and cuddly as pastor so-and-so. My bloody-mindedness routed a coup, and my soft touch won all the culprits back.

At least, that's what it *feels* like. It feels like I'm winning again, after such a long dismal season of losing.

All this raises the question, What if there's no "enemy" that drove me into winter? My own wintertime, following Carol's death, had an enemy, for sure, but the battle wasn't against flesh and blood—or it was, but only obliquely, at a slant. It was a battle against death and its cruel devices, the twisting and breeding of cells, the vandalism of a body turned in on itself. So it was a battle against death in the lowercase: resisting death's plundering, inch by inch, by throwing at it whatever surgeries and therapies, diets and regimens, we could muster. But it was just as much a battle against Death in the uppercase: standing down, like that lone man who stopped, for mere seconds, the convoy of tanks in Tiananmen Square in 1989, the bureaucratic violence of a ruthless faceless principality as it lumbers ever closer. The body count of nature is genocidal. It's rigged to win, by hook or by crook.

Spring is vindication against that cosmic rigging. The church (in the northern hemisphere, where most of its story unfolded until the past few hundred years) has always connected the happy coincidence of Christ's resurrection with the advent of spring. Both spring and resurrection are a kind of insurrection against death's domain. Both are vivid object lessons of death being swallowed up by victory: put a dead thing in the ground—a seed, a bulb, a body—and just wait. Each spring reminds us that death doesn't have the last word.

Paul calls death the last enemy. With quiet confidence, he announces its defeat at the hands of Jesus. "Death," he asks, rhetorically, tauntingly, "where is your sting? Where is your victory?" The enemy casts a shadow, big and dark and menacing. But there's no substance behind it. It has a stinger, but it's lost its venom. It has a bark, but no bite. We'll all suffer death in the lowercase. But by Christ's good graces, no one need suffer death in the uppercase.

Death at that scale has been undone. Death still has battalions on the ground, pitching battle, making havoc, quibbling and collaborating among themselves. But the empire backing them has collapsed.

The paintings of Jesus during the Middle Ages and into the Renaissance largely depict him in his death throes: staggering beneath the weight of the cross, hanging limp and bloody and cruciform, held pale and lifeless in the arms of his mourners. There's a morbidity to it that has more to do with certain fashions in art at the time than with any fascination with the atonement. During this period, few painters depicted the resurrection. But the few who did brought an exhilarating vigor to the task. My favorite work in this motif is by Piero della Francesca. The painting is simply called *Resurrection*. A muscular Jesus, draped in a red cloth, stands triumphant, one foot raised up on a marble pediment, his left hand resting on his bent knee with an athlete's ease and poise. Four Romans soldiers swoon or sleep at his feet. Jesus is wounded—hands, feet, side—but they're clearly the wounds of a war he's won, and they're not slowing him down any. His expression is candid, serene, assured. It's as though he's saying, "Told you so." He holds in his right hand a flag emblazoned with the cross.

In the backdrop, a row of barren trees stands on one side of Christ, but a forest of flourishing ones stands on the other.

It's spring.

Spring is vindication. It's a season of emotional renewal. The barren tree grows fruitful.

Death, where is your sting?

A clear sign of this emotional renewal—in part causing it, in part announcing it—is springtime's physical renewal.

Physical Renewal

Isaiah lists a series of miraculous restorations that happen once God is on the move: the blind see, the deaf hear, the lame leap, the mute speak.

These are signs of the Messiah. Isaiah 35 is the very text Jesus alludes to when John the Baptist is rotting in Herod's prison and he sends his followers to ask Jesus if he really is the one they were to expect. Jesus sends word back to John that, as we saw a couple of chapters back, must be cold comfort. All the same, don't miss the substance of Jesus' message: on his watch, physical restoration, just like Isaiah foretold, is taking place. "The blind receive sight, the lame walk, those who have leprosy are cured, the deaf hear, the dead are raised, and the good news is preached to the poor."[6]

The Man for All Seasons knows winter. He is a man of sorrows, familiar with suffering. He is close to the brokenhearted. He is maybe closer to John in his darkness than he ever was to John in his limelight. We can know the fellowship of sharing in Christ's sufferings because, first and foremost, he's entered the fellowship of sharing in ours.

Jesus reserves his deepest intimacy for winter. But he displays his greatest handiwork in spring. He brings living water into thirsty lands, emotional strength to faltering hearts, physical wellness to the sick and the lame.

And just as the entire creation responds to God's presence, so too this "liberation from bondage to decay" among the Sons of God is felt creationwide. Not only are the lame cavorting about like deer, the deaf listening to Bach or Bachman-Turner Overdrive, the blind gawking at all the pretty flowers, but everything wakes up with eyes to see.

Sometimes we experience this in the most literal way: God heals us of a lingering illness or a debilitating condition—not doctors, or medicine, or therapy, but God, direct and unmediated. I've seen that, though not as often as I'd like or my Bible leads me to believe I should. But I've seen it.

One story will suffice. Helena came to me dying. She was pared down to less than a hundred pounds. Her skin was grey as ash and taut as wax. She had a rare incurable blood disease, and her doctor gave her less than a month before the long sleep in the pine box. She came to plan her funeral—songs she wanted sung, texts she wanted read, the story told of how God rescued her from a life of drink.

We planned that.

Then I had an unction, as the old time preachers called it. It was to pray for Helena's healing. I asked her if I could, and she didn't think it would hurt.

That was nearly ten years ago. She got well straightaway. She got fat and sassy in no time. The next year, I performed her marriage to Jim—she nearly seventy, he already in his eighties. A favorite photo in my office (besides those of my wife and children) is of Helena and Jim on their wedding day, both smiling like imps, her cheeks plump, a halo of wildflowers in her hair like a forest nymph. She became a workhorse around the church, and three years ago decided to move, compliant husband in tow, back to her homestead in Saskatchewan, where she could repair her old house (she was a carpenter by trade), nurse Jim in his dotage, and save all her relatives from the coming wrath. She phones me approximately every three months, hails me like a barmaid, and sounds hearty enough to outlast another dozen or more prairie winters.[7]

I love that story. I wish I had more of them.

What I've seen hundreds of times, though, is physical restoration that overflows from emotional renewal. Vindication brings a second wind. Our feeble bodies grow robust. In winter, you want to sleep half the day. You lack energy for simple tasks. You're not hearing well, seeing well. You slur and mumble words. But when spring arrives, you leap from your bed. You accomplish a whole day's work by nine in the morning, and feel you're just getting started. You run and don't grow weary.

When I plunged into winter, one sign of that was I could hardly wake up, and I ached most of the time. People had to repeat things to me because I wasn't listening as carefully as I should. I often had to repeat things to others because I wasn't speaking as clearly as I might. I failed to notice much. I dragged myself around. I was half deaf, almost blind, borderline lame.

But when spring started again—the rivulet on the desert floor that became a flood, the bird chirping in the tree that became the woods ringing with birdsong—the old energy and focus and clarity returned.

I've also witnessed the physical beauty and vitality that bloom on those in whom God is doing a deep work. I have seen this so many times—a brightness in the eyes, a glow in the skin, a sheen in the hair, a bounce in the step, a squareness in the shoulders, a lilt in the voice—that I use it as a touchstone for gauging people's walk with God. I can, generally, at a glance know when someone is close to God or far from him—or, better put, whether they are *experiencing* God's closeness or distance. Their bodies tell me. Their eyes say so.

Even those who do not get physically better in any medically significant way—the cancer victim who doesn't experience remission, the MS sufferer whose eyesight continues to fail, the Parkinson's struggler whose limbs just shake and stiffen, unremitting—even they experience a form of physical renewal in springtime. Springtime brings the consolation of hope. It gives the assurance that death has lost its sting. There is beauty in this hope and this assurance. There is beauty in the woman whose chemo-induced baldness, unswaddled, shines like a pearl, in the man whose palsy makes him shimmy like a Spanish dancer. There is beauty in their defiance and their acceptance. There is beauty in their standing in the hope that death can't steal or destroy.

Carol got that beauty.

The drugs she was on puffed her up like dough and made her as tipsy and groggy as a drunk. She would blurt out strange utterances like she had Tourette's syndrome. Her cascades of blond hair molted and regrew in bristly tufts poking up here and there on the waxy sheen of her scalp. Her right eye, damaged by surgeries, drooped permanently. She was unrecognizable from her former self. When we escorted people who'd last seen her well into her hospice room, it was with the caveat that her appearance was "shockingly altered." It was one more indignity death heaped upon its stockpile of them.

But at the end the beauty returned. She was just as bruised and bloated and bald as ever. But a light had turned on inside, and all the ruination in the world couldn't hide it. It got through the cracks and rubble.

The last time I saw her alive was in her hospice room. Cheryl and I had been called to come quickly. She was dying, we were told, within hours. We rushed to her side, along with a few others. She was comatose, her breathing heavy and ragged. We spoke to her, prayed over her.

And then we sang. We sang, a capella, clumsily, all her favorite songs. We sang for ourselves as much as anything. We sang in the hope that words and melodies she loved and once sang with gusto, arms lifted in extravagant love, would sift down to her inmost self and speak.

And then she woke. Not sit-bolt-upright-and-hail-us-loudly waking. But her lips began to move, and words formed on them, and sounds came from them. She was singing with us. We sang and sang, and she sang and sang with us. And in all my knowing her, I never saw her more beautiful.

She died two days later. She's home now, her lowly body transformed to look like Jesus' glorious body. That night, I got a little glimpse of what that might look like.

Spring is a time of physical renewal. But there's one more renewal spring brews. It's a restoring of moral bearings and a deep surge of energy to live in the light. The best part of spring is that our hearts are scrubbed clean.

Moral Renewal

And spring is a time of moral renewal. If it is about vindication and restoration, it is also, maybe more so, about sanctification:

> And a highway will be there;
>   it will be called the Way of Holiness.
> The unclean will not journey on it;
>   it will be for those who walk in that Way;
> wicked fools will not go about on it.
> No lion will be there,
>   nor will any ferocious beast get up on it;
>   they will not be found there.
> But only the redeemed will walk there.[8]

In spring, God gives our hearts and lives a thorough cleaning, top to bottom. Areas in our lives where we've compromised, become tainted, allowed a bitter root to grow or some poisonous attitude to creep in or some dirty secret to harbor or some noxious habit to take hold or some foolishness to befuddle us — God comes in and scours it all spotless.

I love this about springtime most of all. I love the way God renews my spirit. The way the things inside me that have become dark and dank and musty are flooded with light, washed and rinsed and disinfected. Back in the late nineties I went through one of the most spectacular springtimes of my life. I experienced all that I've talked about—emotional renewal that felt like vindication, a second wind that felt like physical restoration. But what was best was the moral cleansing. It wasn't that I was wallowing in sin. More wallowing in self-pity. I had lost the joy of my salvation, and I had a scab of cynicism on my wound.

And then, suddenly and all at once, it broke, and God began to renew a right spirit within me. Cynicism gave way to hope and boldness. Self-pity was replaced with sound-mindedness. The joy of my salvation came back in a rush, and I thirsted and hungered after righteousness.

Since I've told you I spent a while in winter recently, you might be worried about my fitness to be a pastor or a Christian author, dispensing moral and spiritual guidance. I didn't in that season slip

---

TIME-IN 6

I'M WALKING ON SUNSHINE

Think about one of your personal spiritual springtimes, and then ponder these questions:

1. Do the three renewals I describe in this chapter—physical, emotional, moral—fit with your experience of springtime? Or would you describe it differently?

2. Can you trace the event or events that triggered your last spring? To what extent did your efforts delay or hasten its coming?

3. How did it end? What season followed? To what extent did you precipitate its end or prolong its duration?

4. How did you use your last springtime? Next time, what will you do the same? Differently?

into a morass of sin and rebellion. But I was weary and had to fight a spirit of jadedness. My heart crusted with pessimism. Wrong attitudes accumulated. For me, the accumulation was mostly self-pity. I could, in a single evening, nurse a woe-is-me feeling from a twitch to a spasm to convulsions. But I was getting sick of it. I wanted the whole cellar cleaned out.

As spring stirred again, it happened. With strengthened hands and feet, ears to hear and eyes to see again, God as my vindicator and restorer, holy things took root once more where selfish things had overspread.

Unclean things and devouring beasts stopped walking the road with me.

***

Vindication. Restoration. Sanctification. Emotional renewal, physical renewal, moral renewal: these herald spring. They're what spring produces in rich profusion. They are gifts and they are invitations. The opportunity spring provides — to grow things in abundance — can be missed or seized. The next chapter is about seizing spring's opportunity. But before that, Isaiah has two more images that describe a springtime of the heart.

HIGHWAYS
AND HOMECOMINGS

Isaiah concludes with two images that sum everything up — a highway and a homecoming. The first seems to sit out of kilter with the passage as a whole: "And a highway will be there." After all the garden imagery, this is jolting. It's as if, smack-dab in the paradise of the Kalahari in full bloom, an expressway is built.

But of course, that image is misplaced. A highway in Isaiah's time meant something substantially different from what we mean by it — overpasses and underpasses, cloverleafs and multiple lanes, guard rails and exit ramps. Yet our highways and his highway share this in common: they make hard places easy. Terrain that once was difficult, dangerous, and grueling to cross becomes smooth and straight and safe. Spring is when what has been tortuous, arduous, perilous becomes otherwise. The yoke seems easy, the burden light.

The hardest time, generally, to get from one place to another is winter. Navigating through the bleakness or wildness of a winter landscape is harrowing. That's true literally and figuratively. Where I grew up, a February blizzard imperiled just getting to the mailbox. I can think of many winter car trips I've taken—one through the southern mountains of British Columbia under three feet of snow comes vividly to mind—that were muscle-clenching, white-knuckle affairs from start to finish. I can think of many flights I've had canceled or delayed by the treachery of snow and ice. Likewise, when I was in my wintertime of the heart, just doing ordinary, routine things—getting from one end of day to the other—was exhausting, precarious, sometimes unmanageable. The idea of writing one more sermon (someone described preaching as delivering a baby on Sunday and finding out Monday that you're pregnant again) was as daunting as crossing the Khyber Pass in January. Every counseling session set me on edge like I was venturing down a jungle trail in Vietnam in, say, 1967. Meetings were exercises in joyless endurance.

But spring made a highway. I could hardly wait to dismount the pulpit so that I could start gearing up to mount it again a week later. Counseling sessions intrigued me, how I might become to someone a fellow traveler and together we might discover God in the midst of their pain or sorrow or confusion. Meetings were war councils, where we plotted strategy to push the kingdom deeper into enemy territory, or they were parties, where we loudly celebrated God's many good surprises.

The desert had become a highway.

One of the most obvious and practical ways I see this at work in people's lives is when their devotion to God shifts from burden to delight, from struggle to glide. They read God's Word with hunger and the thrill of discovery. They pray with a sense of intimate closeness to God. They experience the joy of the Spirit shivering down their bones, as if what they just thought or said or did tickled God's indwelling presence in his rib cage, and his laughter shook them, too. They seek and enjoy the company of other believers. They share with wisdom and winsomeness their faith with unbelievers.

It's as if the narrow way Jesus describes becomes, for a season, broad, smooth, flat, straight. It's like the goat path of obedience becomes an autobahn. A road that used to be hard and lonely and long is now quick and easy, and almost always traveled in company.

Twice I've been to the Massai Mara in Kenya, the sprawling wilderness park crowded with wildebeest and zebra, abounding with cheetah and gazelle, trampled by elephant and grazed by giraffe, and much else besides. The first time I went by plane, a brief skip and jump from Nairobi. The second time, I went by car. That was its own kind of safari: a seven-hour trip over roads that, at their best, were narrow and potholed, at their worst were virtually nonexistent. We inched along dusty, rutted shoulders, drove through scrub brush and trenches, corkscrewed down mountain switchbacks with rusty semis riding our tail. Twice we got stuck and had to have another vehicle winch us out. We arrived parched and grimy and bone bent. We just wanted to shower and sleep. I enjoyed the animals both trips, but the second time my enjoyment was shadowed by the thought that soon we'd have to drive back the same route.

Not long after I got back to Canada after that second trip, I drove to a community north of where I live. The highway is two lanes the entire way, with little traffic. It's well maintained. Well lit. It has a concrete divider running its whole length to separate the opposing lanes of traffic. The road runs almost impossibly straight and flat from here to there: huge mounds of granite have been carved out to make it so. You can drive, legally, 75 mph for most of it. I arrived at my destination in less than two hours, fresh and strong, ready to do what I came for.

I'd covered the exact same distance from Nairobi to the Massai Mara.

Oh, the difference a highway can make.

TIME-IN 7

I'M ON THE HIGHWAY TO HEAVEN

I grew up in the era when AC/DC's song "Highway to Hell" was the national anthem for angry young men, and a few women. It was a brazen declaration, a proud rallying cry to choose the netherworld. Confession: I went to an AC/DC concert in the late seventies. The crowd was a mob: drunk, high, brawling, ranting. The floor writhed with teenage angst and revolt. Everywhere, arms were held aloft with the two-fingered salute to Satan.

Highway to hell indeed.

Not long after that, I met Jesus. I chose, as he describes it, the narrow way that leads to life. I got off the highway to hell — broad, fun, fast — and squeezed through the small gate that leads to life. I started the journey on Jesus' winding, climbing path. It tapered down in places to a single-file trail. It cut the edges of steep cliffs. It twisted down into dense ravines, and traversed scorching deserts. It wasn't fast, and often not fun.[9]

But it's become so, mostly.

Following Christ isn't easy. It requires tenacity and endurance. But there come seasons, springs, when "a highway is there," free of fools and beasts, thronged with fellow travelers. What took so long, took such effort, entailed such danger, involved such loneliness, becomes a breeze.

I think of a friend who entered the narrow way carrying a bulging gunnysack of anger. He was the proverbial time bomb. He had almost to tie himself down and gag himself to keep from causing all kinds of damage when his anger roused, which was often. But then he went through a very deep, very real renewal, and a highway got built. He would be in situations that once triggered explosions, and he not only didn't react that way, he had no desire to. It took a while for his wife and children to believe it was real.

It was.

It is.

An exercise: map your Christian journey so far. Literally. Draw a map that shows when and where you took the narrow way, and all the places it's taken you since, all the things you've learned along the way. And especially note this: where the road narrowed so that it was just you and Jesus, and maybe it felt like just you. And note where the path became a highway. Identify the highways this way: what used to be a struggle is now a snap. What used to take forever, now comes quickly. What used to be lonely, now abounds in friends.

Spend time thanking God for the highways.

Look at the map again. What paths do you hope become highways soon? Is there anything you can do to aid construction? Ask God to show you, and to help you.

***

And spring is a homecoming. After long exile, return. After deep loneliness, reunion. The sorrow and sighing that marked our exile and our winter flee away.

Raucous, joyous singing take their place.

And best of all, the joy is everlasting. It seems it will never end. It seems, in fact, it never ended, never left. That spring has always been here.

It's good to be home.

Antwone Fisher is a movie named after the man whose story it tells. Antwone was a profoundly troubled youth, raised and abused in foster homes, who sought refuge in the navy. But his past kept catching up with him. His anger was hair-triggered, and he would brawl with almost no provocation. Inside, he was empty and tormented.

At the urging of a psychiatrist, Antwone goes on a journey to seek his mother. He eventually finds her. But the reunion is brief, painful, and awkward. She is bewildered and terrified by his presence. She never speaks a word to him. He leaves sadder than if he'd never found her.

Antwone returns to his aunt's house. He found his aunt in his search for his mother. While he's been gone visiting his mother, his aunt has assembled every living relative Antwone has: uncles, aunts, cousins, nephews, nieces, brothers, sisters, grandparents. Roomfuls of people. And everywhere, tables laden with food.

Antwone walks into the house. He walks from room to room. His family, every last one of them, welcomes him home.

I think of many of the men and women I've watched come into our church. Many arrive alone, afraid, broken, sad. Many have never known their families; they've been raised in foster homes. Some wish they'd never known their families; they've been harmed deeply by neglect or abuse by the people who were meant to love them deepest.

I think of the day we baptize many of these people, usually in the river that runs close to our church. I think of them coming out of the water, leaping, yelling, weeping. We gather at the shore with them, hundreds strong. We pray for them. And then I ask them to look up. Look around. Make eye contact.

"Here's your family," I say. And to those who surround them, "Here's your newest brother, your newest sister."

Then I look the new brother or sister in the eyes. "You're home," I say. "You're really home."

It always feels like spring then.

CHAPTER 4

SPRING ACTIVITIES

Spring here is pungent. The air is heady with smells. Some are hypnotic —the fragrance of certain flowers, lilacs, koreanspice, forsythia, and the like. Some are a tonic—the smell of turned earth or cut grass. And others are unpleasant and overpowering—the reek of manure on wet fields, the stench of rotting things churned up by the blades of plow and hoe, the smell of daisies.

I variously breathe in, holding inside myself these perfumes as long as I can, or plug my nose and mouth, holding these smells outside myself as long as I can.

I walk my dog down a trail near my home. The trail, long ago, was the bed of a railway track, and so it's wide and flat and mostly straight, no sharp turns. A creek runs down one side of it. Most of the year that creek meanders, shallow and clear, and you can easily ford it with a bit of agile hopscotching on rocks. But in spring it swells to wild waters, deep and churning and silty, and you can cross it only by walking atop fallen trees that straddle it here and there, but that's unnerving: fall in, and it will carry you fast away until you entangle downstream in some wild nest of bramble, and they'll pull you out only much later, bluish white and bloated.

I walk this trail all year, but spring is best. The thin scrim of forest either side of the trail shimmers with newness. The creek, in its swollenness, gives me a visceral thrill. My dog finds it fascinating; it's a potpourri of aromas he finds irresistible, and he roots and rummages along its spongy banks. I'm always calling him back from the brink, fearing for his life lest he lose footing and tumble in, but this adds an element of high suspense to our walks.

But it's the smells, equally alluring and repelling, that make the whole thing so memorable. Some spicy bloom I can't identify wafts by. Some sappy fragrance tingles in my nose. The pleasant mustiness of moldering leaves pulses like a bass note everywhere. The pungency of raw earth teeming with seed and root and fiber and millions and millions of creepy-crawly things burrowing through it pervades the whole. And then, mingled throughout, other smells catch me in the throat — piles of swiftly rotting debris, farm fields close by being readied in the organic way for planting, the rank wetness of my own dog, his paws and belly slathered in composted muck.

All of it, fragrance and stench alike, are part of spring's magic. They are spring's raw apparatus to ring our bell, shake us loose, call us out. What sleeps in winter wakes in spring, loud and urgent, and you either get out and smell the roses, and everything else besides, or you move to Antarctica.

All's to say, the first activity of spring is to wake up. It's to get up. It's to plunge in, all senses wide. Dead things recycle as nutrients in spring. Dormant things shiver to life. That is as good a template as any for us: the accumulation of all winter's losses and sorrows breaking down into something useful and life-giving, the hidden stillness of all sleeping things leaping up, tumbling forth.

Susan, for example. Susan's the pastoral assistant at our church. She juggles the details of four pastors' comings and goings, and many things besides. We would be walking into walls without her. She is ruthlessly efficient. I call her "boss" and don't mess with her. But she's not ruthless. If anything, she's the opposite; she has a heart so big and soft that sometimes I have to talk her out of helping people in crisis that, I fear, will only pull her in neck deep. But I'm not always sure I give the right advice.

The thing is, Susan comes by her heart honestly, which is to say she has suffered to get it. Just a few years ago, Susan was a drunk. She worked in a management position and her job was to keep the employees up to high standards of production quotas and quality, or fire them. She was just plain ruthless. Her employees feared her. Some hated her. She took no pleasure in that, but it was nothing that a couple dozen beers or a twenty-sixer of gin couldn't solve. She was life trying to take root inside us? James, Jesus' brother, puts it this way: "Humbly accept the word planted in you, which can save you."

Jesus speaks this parable to "the crowds," a favorite audience of his. No one can make head or tail out of it. It's too cryptic. Is he giving agricultural pointers, or spiritual guidance? If the former, everyone knew all that already. If the latter, what's it all add up to? What's this have to do with me?

The disciples, who have been tagging along with Jesus for a while, are as stumped as everyone else. Maybe more. For one, he'd hand-picked them from trades other than farming. And most of them came from the kind of work where you don't sit around all day pondering the inner workings of the universe or the mysteries of providence. They had fish to catch, taxes to collect, Romans to assassinate. There was little idle time on their hands to toy with riddles.

But here's the difference: the disciples have a hunch that this is important and harass Jesus into explaining things. Whereas everyone else just goes home, scratching their heads, shrugging their shoulders, forgetting about it.

Ears to hear doesn't mean, always, a mind to grasp. It means you listen. You lean in. You wait, you pester, you dig. You hang on to God and wrestle him all night if you must, and refuse to let go until he blesses you.

So the plowing of springtime is the discipline of deeper attentiveness.

Pastoral work allows me to see this often. At any given time, I'd guess, about a third of a congregation (at least the congregations I've been part of) is in some season of spring. They're in renewal. The world tastes fresh to them. They can spot God at work at every turn.

One mark of this renewal is a desire for prayer and Word. They're hungry to meet with God in spirit and in truth. That hunger is typically just a by-product of the waking up. But what starts spontaneously must be sustained deliberately, else it quickly shrivels. That's where plowing's needed. This season is best for establishing spiritual practices—holy habits, as I call them in one of my other books. It's the time for *resolve*, a clear and firm decisiveness around what matters. From now on, you will live this way, not that. From now on, you will go in this direction, not that. And with this resolve, you then reorder your life—how you give, pray, read, serve, think—to both reflect and nurture your resolve.

If you're in springtime or just coming into spring, by all means enjoy it. But don't squander it. Look closely at your life, decide where you need to join God in this season of renewal. Then take plow blade to hard earth, open it wide, and harrow it soft.

William now comes to mind. William and Grace started coming to church not long after I arrived as the new pastor. In his words recently, "We've come to New Life for twelve years. We've been part of it for six."

The first six years, when they merely came to church, William had a nasty secret and a dirty habit. William was in the clutches of a pornography addiction. It had gone from a diversion he indulged now and then, out of boredom, to a full-scale obsession he rearranged his life to feed. It started as something he could bid come to suit his pleasure; it became a tyrant that commanded his total allegiance. When the problem came to light, its hooks were deep. He was embarrassed, remorseful, full of self-reproach.

None of that proved enough.

So William had an affair with his next door neighbor.

The next several months were a wild ride. William slept on the couch. He quit all his junk cold-turkey, and some days, like a heroin addict in withdrawal, shook with craving for one last fix to ease him through. He met daily with other men who, like him, were limping toward the light. In time, he established a men's group where, every Monday night, a mob of men descended on his house and gathered in his basement. They chastened one another with blunt talk, primed each other with raucous laughter, bolstered each other with hungry prayers. Grace hid upstairs, glad it was happening, though not particularly caring to know exactly what was happening. As long as William kept walking in the light, she was for it. Slowly, their marriage, the trust and intimacy that William had shattered, revived. And then it grew. And then, preposterously, it became magnificent.

Then they went to Africa. I was leading a large team from our church to Kenya to work among a dozen churches there. One of the and didn't much seek it anyhow: it was rickety and itself heaped with bric-a-brac. I would think every month or so about cleaning and renovating the whole thing, but grow so weary with just the thought of it I'd walk away defeated without even an attempt.

Then my wife and one of our daughters went for a ten-day trip to California, and I decided I'd renovate the workshop as a surprise, and a kind of cockeyed gift. What I conceived as a renovation became, in the doing of it, a top-to-bottom remaking. I hauled out old cupboards and shelves, shaggy with cobwebs, diced them up with my (new!) Stihl chain saw, and tossed it all in a bonfire I had blazing in the back yard. Thick plumes of white smoke billowed into the cool spring air, and my dog ran around trying to snap flakes of cooling embers in his jaws as they sparked up and then floated down. Watching that, I was so happy I felt like fiddling like Nero as Rome burned. But I had work to do. As it burned, I built. Tools lay every which way in my carport. Sawdust accumulated at my feet. Camp gear and paint equipment and bicycles and boxes of unsold books lay piled in corners in several rooms.

The shirring of saw blade.

The clap of airgun.

The slap of level on beam.

The muttering of an amateur carpenter.

And the pride—raw and undisguised—when my wife came home and I escorted her down to show off my shiny new thing: bicycles hung in alternating pattern from the ceiling, a work bench you could eat off of, little stacking trays holding nuts and bolts and screws and nails and door stoppers and brass hinges and rubber washers and, even, an extra wax ring for putting underneath a toilet, should the need arise. There's a peg board bristling with tools like a bricolage, and drawers brimming with more tools, and cupboards with spare things that one day I might need, and a whole wall of shelving lined with Rubbermaid bins containing all the stuff we hardly use but sometimes do.

It's so beautiful that for the first week after it was done, I'd wander downstairs in my housecoat and slippers after everyone was in bed and all the lights were out, turn on the new florescent work light hanging over the bench, and just take it all in.

All the rubble and dirt and grime was more than rubble and dirt and grime: it had become a symbol of some deeper disorder and accumulation in my life. But now the old was gone. The new had come.

A clean start.

Again, I think of William and Grace. They used their springtime not just to scour out all the mildewed things in William's closet but also everything everywhere in their personal world. They had grown an attachment to stuff and status that they hauled out to the curb, dumped there unceremoniously, and never looked back. They had neglected relationships that had to be repaired, and had acquired one or two that needed jettisoning. Grace, "the victim," had a few things hidden in her own dark corners that she needed to rummage out and dispose of.

And now they can stand in the light of it, the old gone, the new come, and savor the sheer orderliness and brightness of the whole thing.

Here's one simple way to engage that. It's borrowed from an ancient prayer practice called the examen. The examen is a form of personal inventory. At day's end, spend time in prayerful reflection on your day: your comings and goings, routines and disruptions, work and play, discoveries and disappointments. Think about who you met, or missed. Think about your moments of aloneness. In all, ask two questions: when was I most alive, most present, most filled and fulfilled today? And when was I most taxed, stressed, distracted, depleted today? A simpler, and more spiritually focused, version of those questions: when did I feel closest to God, and when farthest?

A pattern will emerge over the course of several examens. (It will be helpful to keep a journal.) From the pattern will emerge a portrait. The portrait will be of you. It will reveal to you your own heart, its passions and quirks and aversions. Where it leaps, where it sinks, where it feels safe or imperiled, where it just beats in steady contented rhythm. All that will guide you. Few of us get to shape our lives to suit ourselves, not entirely at least, and I'm not suggesting that anyhow. I am suggesting that most of our lives are cluttered and need to be pared back and reorganized. I use the examen to sort myself out in that way. I use it to reorder the gathering and dispersing of my time and energy. I use it, in short, to spring-clean.

Here's how that works. Because the examen helps me understand my spiritual and emotional rhythms, it helps me live with greater focus and effectiveness. I can see the clutter to remove it. I distinguish the habitual from the purposeful, mere busyness from real productiveness. I separate actions that are fruitful from those that are fruitless, ways of thinking that are self-generating from those that are self-defeating, relationships that are life-giving from those that are life-sucking. And then I rearrange or rebuild the "workshop" so that I operate out of strength and joy. It doesn't mean I avoid hard things or difficult people. It means I'm more likely to deal with such things and such people from a place of wisdom, grace, clarity, and peace.

TIME-IN 8

YOUR OWN REALITY SHOW

Budget constraints and innovation created the first reality TV shows that emerged at the dawn of the new millennium. Greed and cheap imitation made them, within the decade, a glut on the airwaves. Now we have one for every imaginable scenario—the bored couple wanting to rev up their marriage, the tawdry dresser whose friends want her looking like a starlet, the fat man whose family wants him consigned to dieter's hell, the poor family who wants a mansion, the millionaire who wants to buy it.

I heard an interview not long ago with a female jockey who stars in a reality TV show called—ready?—*Jockeys*. Part of the story line focuses on the stormy relationship she has with another jockey. The interviewer asked her if having the intimate details of their private lives openly divulged and minutely examined was awkward. "No," she said. "It's good. It's forced us to have those really deep conversations that otherwise we avoid."

Well, okay. I must be missing something. When did it become easier to reveal our inmost thoughts and feelings when voyeurs and eavesdroppers thronged the bedroom?

But let's have some fun. Imagine you have your own reality show, except the only ones watching are you and God. But it's *your* show. You're the star. It works kind of like *Jockeys* and its ilk: the camera eye follows you everywhere. It's there when you wake up, there when you bed down. It watches you eat, work, daydream. Some invisible director encourages you to think out loud. What were you *really* thinking when you were talking with that man? How are you *really* feeling about your friend not inviting you to her party?

But, mostly, this: where did you experience God today? And where did you miss him?

Novelist Walker Percy once lamented that we can learn everything there is to know about Uranus in five minutes, though it's 1.6 billion miles from the earth. But we live with ourselves our entire lives and, at best, maybe know 10 percent of what there is to know about ourselves.

Get to know yourself. Not in a narcissistic way. But know what makes you shine, or fade. Know what makes your heart glad, or heavy. Especially, know where you most often experience God. When you find that place, go there more often.

***

If you're in springtime, enjoy.

Wake up.

Strengthen your feeble hands and steady your shaking knees.

Smell the roses, and everything else besides.

But there is a field or two, or maybe three, God wants you to plow. And there are seeds he wants you to sow, and seedlings he'd have you plant. Maybe he is calling you into a new ministry, or a deeper engagement in one. Maybe this is the moment to get serious about a relationship that you've only dallied with up till now. It may be the moment to make that bold career move, or to launch into that ambitious project you've dreamed about, or to take the trip you always think you'll get around to next year.

And there are corners of your life he wants you to clean. Things that you've had long enough, to no good purpose, and you'll only be better off without them.

So go ahead—plow, plant, clean.

What's to lose, except the moment itself, and a few things you didn't need anyhow?

Thin girls
reedy and brown
dance in firelight
sleep in shade
wake drowsy
and hungry and throw
back their heads
to fill their mouths with
laughter.
At night the air
holds its warmth
like skin
and breathes out
slowly
awake and watchful
waiting for
light. In my dreams
I'm always here
never aging and that
sadness that now haunts
my days
not even
rumor.

—M. BUCHANAN

CHAPTER 5

SUMMER

"Love Will Keep Us Together." That was the hit song the summer of 1975, by Captain and Tennille. I openly scorned it and secretly loved it. I wasn't in love, not then, but the song made it easy to imagine love-smittenness, its bliss and agony, its power to make you foolhardy or brave.

I don't remember it raining once that summer. Every day dawned in a rapture of sunshine. The air was a spice of sea breeze and coconut oil. And, oh, this: I was living in Vancouver, a city dazzling even in gloom, and I was fifteen: thin, with hair, with a body so pliant I could bend it in two. I spent most days traipsing the beaches of the city or running harum-scarum through the trails of Stanley Park. I had wellsprings of seemingly bottomless energy.

One day, my brother and I walked all the way from downtown Vancouver to the University of British Columbia. It was about ten miles, and a hot day, and partway I wondered if we'd overstepped ourselves. But when we got there, I forgot all that. I was seduced straightaway by the place, its combination of stately gothic brick buildings, draped in ivy, and the foreboding hugeness of sixties-style institutional architecture, streaked with gull stool. The grounds were shaded with maples and oaks, and summer students tossed a Frisbee on the commons. Someone had backed their Camero close to the field, popped the trunk, which was one massive cavity for a sub-woofer that physically throbbed, and cranked up the tunes: ZZ Top first, with their wild hillbilly rock that, I don't care how pious you are, it's impossible not to toe-tap to, the mighty Zep and their legendary, even then, "Stairway to Heaven," with Robert Plant hitting

111

and sustaining a high A that seemed supernatural. Then Captain and Tennille, letting love keep them together. And though I remember making a snide remark to my brother about the song, in my heart of hearts it was the song that sealed it: I was coming here.

I'd never before had any thoughts of further education. My one aim academically was to finish high school and get a real job, and never read another book, never write another essay. But something about that day, that place, that song, wove a romance around the idea of UBC, and so seven years later, astonished, drunk with elation, I walked onto that campus again, this time a student. And my life thereafter, including the book you're now holding, can plausibly be blamed on the summer of '75.

Love will keep us together.

I believed it.

If I'm not careful, my nostalgia for the summer of '75 spoils all the rest. It was my perfect summer. It was my endless summer (only it ended). It was my died-and-gone-to-heaven summer.

Which in some ways is what summer is: a foretaste of heaven. It's a rehearsal of paradise, a preview of the promised land.

THE HEART IN SUMMER

The book of Revelation describes the kingdom of God in its fullness, and it's a good place to begin understanding what the heart in summer feels like: "On each side of the river stood the tree of life, bearing twelve crops of fruit, yielding its fruit every month. And the leaves of the tree are for the healing of the nations."[1] Endless summer.

The sign of summer's endlessness is an amazing tree — singular, one tree, according to the grammatical logic — that stands on *both* sides of the river and bears "twelve crops of fruit, yielding its fruit every month." In God's kingdom, the progression of months remains intact — one through twelve — but the cycle of seasons ends. Each month simply flows into another month of fruit-bearing sunshine and warmth.

Jesus explicitly equates the kingdom of God with summertime.

"He told them this parable: 'Look at the fig tree and all the trees. When they sprout leaves, you can see for yourselves and know that summer is near. Even so, when you see these things happening, you know that the kingdom of God is near.'"[2]

When you see leaves, you know summer is nigh. When you see "these things," you know the kingdom is near.

We'll circle back later, in the next chapter, to what Jesus means by "these things."

But reflect for a moment on the connection he makes between summer and the kingdom. What do we associate with summer? Fruit, warmth, light, rest, play, wonder, festival, joy, reunion, holidays. All, Jesus implies, are kingdom experiences. The kingdom of heaven, Jesus told us in story upon story, is a banquet, a homecoming, a joyful reunion, a festival. The writer of Hebrews says the kingdom is a true Sabbath, a sustained and restoring rest, a full and final reprieve from life's misery and drudgery and loss.

In the heart's summertime, we experience all this—vitality, connectedness, rest. It abounds in play and fruitfulness, warmth and shade. There's ample daylight, and we find sheer delight in God and in what he's made. It's the diametric opposite of winter. In winter, God is like an enemy, friends become strangers, and death and darkness sidle up close. But summer flips that: God and others draw intimately near, light and life surround us, and night and mourning flee away. Darkness seems a tacky rumor, death a feeble opponent.

So summertime's a taste of the kingdom. It's savoring a morsel of heaven, sweet and brief, where God, fully present, shines his light day and night. Fresh fruit's in season twelve months of the year. Reunion and retreat alternate.

How do you know you're in summer? Simply, things *flow*. Your life is marked by effortlessness. Fruit comes easily. Joy rises naturally. Light shines everywhere. You have energy to spare. Most seasons of our hearts demand something from us, some sacrifice, some labor, some deep wrenching adjustment. But summer just wants to give and give. Its only demand is that we surrender to it, bask in it. Spiritual insight hangs plump from low branches. It's easy to nourish ourselves, warm ourselves, refresh ourselves. In our hearts' summertimes, God seems giddy with beneficence, prodigal with welcome. Every other day he's serving up the fattened calf and throwing a Mexican fiesta for no good reason except, maybe, it's Tuesday.

There's not much here not to like. It's as good an apprenticeship for heaven as I know.

***

I write this in summertime. The river near us runs clear and warm, and grown men, their woolly white bellies shamelessly flaunted, play in its currents like otters. Every few miles down the highway another roadside stand overflows, cornucopia-like, with peaches sweet as sugarcane, watermelon with rinds thick and green like tortoise shells, huge ears of corn with parchment leaves and silk-tasseled heads, twelve for two dollars, mounds of apples whose stems still have a leaf or two attached.

Day comes early and bids you rise. Night comes softly and bids you linger. Birds fill the sky in the mornings, dancing, singing. Bullfrogs and cicadas take up the refrain at dusk. There is a flower in my garden that, at sundown, releases a perfume so hypnotic it tricks me into thinking I'm young again, and I want to dance, do handstands, woo my wife with fool's talk.

Throughout my neighborhood, starting early afternoons, men in shorts and straw hats fire up barbecues and grill savory things — herb-tossed vegetables, marinated beef, sauce-basted chicken, prawns fresh from local waters — so that the aroma weakens me in mind and body, and I understand how Esau gave up his birthright.

I never get tired of summer. I want it here forever. I do, though, try to stay up late, if for no other reason than to watch falling stars race down the sky like sparklers, and to clap my hands at a God so playful and resourceful.

FIRST SUMMER

Most people experience a summertime of the heart right after conversion.

Zechariah 8 is a vivid description of a city—Zion—when God comes near. Here are a few verses, from Eugene Peterson's *The Message*: "God's message: 'I've come back to Zion, I've moved back to Jerusalem.... Old men and old women will come back to Jerusalem, sit on benches on the streets and spin tales, move around safely with their canes—a good city to grow old in. And boys and girls will fill the public parks, laughing and playing—a good city to grow up in.... People and their leaders will come from all over to see what's going on. The leaders will confer with one another, "Shouldn't we try to get in on this? Get in on God's blessings? Pray to God ...? What's keeping us? Let's go!"'"[3]

Most people come to Christ exactly the way Zechariah describes it. They witness a vibrant church or household of Christians, or meet just one man or woman fully alive. They see life as it is meant to be, with God at the center. They confer with someone, maybe just themselves, and say, "Why miss out on this? Let's go!" And, getting up and going, they typically go straightaway into summertime. Everything is right. Everything is bright. Everything works. The old is gone; the new has come.

A few weeks after I came to Christ at age twenty-one, I went on a fishing trip with a group of guys from the church. I had never before been among men who, when they gathered, didn't speak in lewd, demeaning ways about women or turn the air blue with cussing, who didn't guzzle beer until they got bleary-eyed and slurry-mouthed. I didn't think men like that existed. And now I'd spent a whole weekend in the company of six or eight such men, who began and ended each day with prayer and Scripture reading, who spoke lovingly of their wives, who honored one another and served one another, who told and laughed at jokes that were clean. I came back and, trying to describe it to Cheryl, broke down and wept with utter joy.

In that season, I heard God crystal clear. I could almost *see* him.

Every conversation I had—with fellow believers, with nonbelievers—was holy. Every Scripture was a revelation. God was, as the child's prayer has it, in my seeing, in my hearing, in my speaking, and in my understanding. He was tangibly growing fruit in my life. The world seemed light and bright and full of color, and warm all the time.

Summer.

Maybe you know exactly what I'm talking about. Typically the first big disappointment in our Christian lives is when that initial summertime turns cool and grey. A dampness of complacency creeps into our bones. Icy winds of doubt chill us. Spiritual abundance becomes barrenness.

And we are dismayed.

But we learn that other springs and summers are coming, and each becomes a foretaste of that endless summer, the kingdom of God in its fullness.

I think our hearts' summertimes get both sweeter and more melancholy with the passing years (much as our earthly summers do). That's been my experience. I've been following Christ nearly thirty years. My first summer of the heart was spectacular. But my current summer is better. And the best, I know, is yet to come.

The years have seasoned me. I have a capacity for enjoyment I lacked in younger days. I've learned the art of slowing and savoring, and I've gained a width and depth of perspective. Problems are less problematic. Simple pleasures are more pleasurable. I laugh and cry with less inhibition. My wife looks dazzling to me. My children—just the lilt or pitch of their voices—delight me. My friends seem pure gift.

Yet a sadness tints, sepia-like, the edges of it all. Heaven's growing nearness seems at once to quicken my pace and to weigh it down. Summer's light remains full, but grows heavy with shadow. I find each summer of the heart deepens my joy and, strangely, my sense of loss.

For this reason, I've learned that I have to guard my heart in summer, more than any other season, against the wiles of nostalgia.

BATTLING NOSTALGIA

Nostalgia is an inescapable part of summer, part of its lure and magic, its strange tint of melancholy. Every summer since 1975 has, for me, had this tint. Its joy, bright otherwise, shades darkly at the edges. Its melody, mostly happy throughout, shifts at the bridge into a minor key.

I'm occupationally obliged to be an enemy of nostalgia. It's not good for church growth. I have to deal with it weekly, sometimes daily: the stalwart charter member who laments the passing of those golden days when "we didn't have to pay people to do [fill in the blank: custodial work, grounds maintenance, Sunday school supervision, office help]." It's a long list. I deal with the transfer or defector from another church who remembers, constantly, the way it was done back then and there, and holds that up as a model of superiority and a standard of excellence even if, just months ago, they were telling me how bad it was back then and there. I even deal with the fourteen-year-old who bemoans a change in the youth group or complains that "we never do those old songs anymore," then by way of example cites a song that, from my perspective, is still warm from the printer.

So I've had to set my face like flint against all that. It's onward, upward. It's charting a bold course into the future. It's taking hill country, and leaving pastureland to the sissies. And so on.

But I also have to deal with myself, with my own nostalgia, my own tendencies to scavenge among the bones. I lost things I can't recover: my hair, my elasticity, my knees that could ski moguls all day and still carry my body upright the next, unimpeded. A dog who romped and bounded, and always found me companionable. And those are the specifics, the things I can name and picture. Mostly, I've lost something I can't name, can't see, never held in my hand. A mood, a tone, a note. A quality underneath things that was easily missed at the time, and dearly missed ever since.

The summer of '75 was, at the time, just another summer, more or less. I had, in June, left that awful place I describe in my chapter on winter and moved to Vancouver, which was as exotic for me as moving to Morocco or Rio de Janeiro, or Narnia. So I was primed for magic. But all the same, I was too young to know that I'd one day be old. I was too happy to know that life has long stretches, unavoidable, of sorrow. Simply, I didn't know what I had until I didn't have it. I didn't even have the dog yet, let alone know the deep sadness of losing the dog.

And, what's more, death in any significant way had not yet come remotely close. My brother had a friend die in middle school—he was large and clumsy and fell down a steep bank and broke his neck—and my brother was asked to be a pallbearer, which seemed to me a dark honor. And my crazy violent grandfather whom I'd never met—whom, indeed, my mother, his own daughter, hadn't seen, spoken to, or heard from since the forties, when he hightailed it out of her life and left my grandmother to raise four children—was found dead in a rooming house in Victoria, smelly and gaunt and penniless. These things were more rumors to me than realities, and more titillating than devastating.

So I had the hubris of youth, that sense of invincibility and immortality. I was Icharus, and believed I could fly near the sun and not melt my wings. I was Achilles, and thought I could fight all wars and never expose my heel. I was Tithonus, and had forgotten to ask for eternal youth along with eternal life, but at this stage of the game that seemed no great oversight.

Now I'm nearly half a hundred years, and the hubris, for the most part, is gone; it's unsustainable in the face of reality. It's hard to be proud and paunchy both, to be cocky and cockeyed at the same time, to swagger with a limp. It's hard to think life goes on and on when the weight of evidence is overwhelmingly otherwise.

And it's hard to fully enjoy summer when your body bears the scars and stiffenings of many winters, its diminishments and accretions. It's hard, in fact, not to be a tad nostalgic for other summers, perfect summers. It's hard not to pine for the summer of '75.

Now, I've come a long way to say a simple thing: I think nostalgia is really misplaced anticipation.

I will speak more fully about this later on, in my chapter on heaven, but now I want only to sketch the idea. The idea is that nostalgia is expectancy in reverse. It's our instinct for heaven rummaging in the storage closet, hoping that our heart's true desire is in there somewhere, hidden amid a clutter of keepsakes and accumulated debris.

It's not that we fall prey to this only in summer. I just think we're more susceptible then. Because summer evokes heaven so potently, we're most prone to misinterpret it then. I'm thinking of a biblical passage we looked at early in this book, from Ecclesiastes 3. "I have seen the burden God has laid on the human race. He has made everything beautiful in its time. He has also set eternity in the human heart; yet no one can fathom what God has done from beginning to end."[4]

Earth's beauty—its summertime vivacity—is a gift that can become a burden. If we don't fathom that summer's beauty is a rumor of heaven, we'll make a fetish of the rumor and miss what it's pointing to. We'll try to cling to summer's beauty, and resent its fading.

We'll become nostalgic.

We all know the past was never as clean and bright as we remember it. Nostalgia paints history gold, just as unforgiveness paints it black. Actually, nostalgia, besides being misplaced expectancy, is also second cousin to unforgiveness. Both unforgiveness and nostalgia share the trait of an unreconciled past. Nostalgia is a vain attempt to reconcile the past through wistfulness, whereas unforgiveness is a doomed attempt to reconcile it through vengeance. The past is actually only ever reconciled through four things: thankfulness, forgiveness, acceptance, and repentance. Most of us have a season or two when we try to reconcile the past in these other ways, through wistfulness or vengeance. But all we find (if we're noticing) is it makes the past accumulate, not resolve. It makes history's hand on us heavy, not light, confining, not liberating. The past ends up claiming us in ways God never intended it to; rather than imparting clear identity that shapes destiny, it twists identity and thwarts destiny. Nostalgia and unforgiveness both do this.

In fact, one easily becomes the other. He who waxes nostalgic will usually, in time, turn bitter about how the past won't return to him; she who nurses unforgiveness will usually, in time, pine for some pristine beginning, some imagined prehistory before all the trouble began.

Consider my nostalgia for the summer of '75. That year, for many on the earth, was dreadful—runaway inflation, the threat of food and fuel shortages, the ever-growing specter of nuclear war and silent spring. My father had a miserable summer that year, dragooned as he was to move to a city he loathed, triple-mortgaging to buy a house four times the price and no more the quality of the one we'd sold. So my version of that year was idiosyncratic, a measure of my self-absorption. To use another Greek myth, I was Narcissus, and the summer of '75 was a still pond that reflected my image and pulled me deeper into self-love.

But ever since, I've had inklings that it wasn't as good as I remember it, and that what was really going on for me was not the enshrining of memory but the waking of hope. Summer, I'm saying, never really evokes a "back there" experience. It jolts an "up there" one. It calls us not back to a garden we once enjoyed and then lost but to a city we've yet to visit and barely imagined. And where summer keeps changing, but never ends.

Spiritual nostalgia bears some semblance to this. The church of our first summertime, whether we're still in it or long ago moved on, seems holier and truer than wherever we are now. We remember fellowship groups, potluck dinners, Bible studies, worship services, three-point sermons as having a purity and beauty that everything since falls short of. And we tend to remember the former glory most vividly in subsequent summertimes.

There's a scene in the book of Ezra that describes it as well as anything I know. It's during the rebuilding of Jerusalem's temple—surely, a spiritual summertime for Israel. When the foundation for the new temple is laid, a worship service marks the occasion: "When the builders laid the foundation of the temple of the LORD, the priests in their vestments and with trumpets, and the Levites (the sons of Asaph) with cymbals, took their places to praise the LORD, as prescribed by David king of Israel. With praise and thanksgiving they sang to the LORD: 'He is good; his love to Israel endures forever.' And all the people gave a great shout of praise to the LORD, because the foundation of the house of the LORD was laid."[5]

It says all the people shouted their praise, and likely that's true. But not everyone rejoiced: "But many of the older priests and Levites and family heads, who had seen the former temple, wept aloud when they saw the foundation of this temple being laid, while many others shouted for joy. No one could distinguish the sound of the shouts of joy from the sound of weeping, because the people made so much noise. And the sound was heard far away" (vv. 12–13).

Nostalgia got the better of many—not all, but many—of the older ones. They "remembered when."

If any of them, old and young alike, knew what they really wanted—that they were "looking forward to the city with foundations, whose architect and builder is God"[6]—then this current temple would have been nowhere near what they hoped and so much better than they remembered. Anticipation would have replaced nostalgia.

Instead, some looked back, and their gladness turned to mourning.

But more of that later, when we come to the chapter on heaven.

Right now, let's ask, What's a summer for? The next chapter attempts an answer.

TIME-IN 9

LOOK BOTH WAYS
BEFORE YOU CROSS?

This counsel was drilled into most of us from an early age: "Look both ways before you cross the street." It's wise, deep, versatile. It's served me well for a whole lifetime. I failed to heed it just once, at age six. I'd just learned to ride a bike, and coming to my first intersection, I sailed straight through. I never looked either way.

I nearly became a hood ornament. The driver of a big bulky car caught me in its sweet spot. The impact folded my bike like newsprint and sent me tumbling across the car's entire length, landing me in a heap at the tailgate. I ended up in hospital, bruises everywhere, a mild concussion. The pudding, the coloring book, and the day off school made it almost worth the while.

Still, I learned in my bones the sagacity of that counsel. "Look both ways before you cross the road." I've never since done otherwise.

But does the counsel apply elsewhere? Is it also a metaphor for life? Should I, should you, always look both ways—to the past, to the future—before crossing the street, before stepping into a new place?

Yes.

And no.

Memory is a gift. It makes maps of human terrain—our emotional and intellectual and spiritual and social worlds. It tells us where we are, and where we need to go to get someplace else. Philosopher George Santayana famously said, "Those who forget the past are doomed to repeat it." Much of the Holy Spirit's work is to remind us of Jesus and his ways.

But memory is also a trap. It makes fetishes of some things, taboos of others. It woos or terrifies us too easily, dictating our future with an authority it's rarely earned. I know scads of people whose hurts from the past foreclose the risks they need to take to get to the other side. I know many people whose idealizing of the past has turned them bitter in the present and wary of the future.

They're stuck. That is not memory's best work. It is memory gone rancid, memory turned maggoty.

Take a moment to be still before God. Ask him to search you and know your heart. Ask him to show you any area where you're stuck—where, for fear of the dangers on the road, you refuse to cross it, or where, missing something you once had, you long to go back. Ask him to help you identify the memory (or memories) that controls that. Then interrogate that memory. Is it really telling you the truth? Does it wield a power greater than it should? Is it the *last* word?

I had a habit of aloofness that was hurting people I love. I dug down to the memories that drove this—the experience of growing up in a town where stepping into another's personal space meant a fight. It was never a gesture of friendship or intimacy. So I learned to keep my distance, avoid eye contact, give short answers.

It was keeping me from crossing the street. But once I hauled into the witness stand those memories and cross-examined them, they proved contradictory, full of lies, trafficking in rumors.

So I rejected their testimony.

And now I hug a lot, and look people in the eye, and give long answers.

That's a lot of room created from kicking one bad memory out.

CHAPTER 6

SUMMER ACTIVITIES

What do we do in summer?

First, most: enjoy.

Warm up and rest up. Frolic with childlike abandon. Play with our children. Wrestle with the dog. Visit people we haven't seen all year, or longer. Take holidays—holy days, times of Sabbath renewal, touching earth and breathing heaven. Repose: rest until our pose of anxious weariness gives way to one of limber readiness, until our two speeds of rushing and crashing become a seamless rhythm of receiving and giving.

Grow strawberries.

Eat watermelon.

Lie in the sun.

Sleep in the shade.

Read in a hammock.

Swim naked.

Do all this in the most earthy and ordinary ways. Summer is a time for enjoying God and others, without reserve and without apology. It's a time for rediscovering the sheer pleasure of simply being alive: waking early or sleeping late, wading lakeshores or tenting in rain forests, talking late under starlight or staring silently, for hours, at clouds. Likewise, the summer of the heart is marked by leisure and pleasure, a kind of holy hedonism. We strive for nothing and yet have everything. We relish abundance without needing to hoard it or feel guilty about it. We heed the counsel that Scripture gives to rich people: don't trust in your wealth, which is so uncertain, but trust in God, "who richly provides us with everything for our enjoyment."[1]

In the summer of the heart, we get that: abundance isn't for trusting in; it's for enjoying.

But there are a few opportunities, even necessities, of summertime.

THE RHYTHMS OF KINGDOM LIVING

The people of God are already, the Bible says, citizens of heaven. That's our true identity. Our heavenly citizenship doesn't get transferred upon death, like a widow's pension, but is established the moment we turn to follow Jesus. Part of our apprenticeship in Jesus, then, is learning to live the kingdom life even now, especially now, that we're not home. If summer is equated with the fullness of the kingdom, we should pay close attention to the activities — and inactivities — of summertime. That, indeed, is a major clue to what it means to do God's will on earth as it is done in heaven.

Let's look at three rhythms of kingdom living, modeled on summer living: it is not hurried, it is not worried, and it abounds in fruit.

Kingdom Living Is Not Hurried

Kingdom living is not hurried. It luxuriates in the sheer abundance of God's watchcare. In summertime you begin to live in the way A. W. Tozer describes: "Those who are in Christ share with [God] all the riches of limitless time and endless years. God never hurries. There are no deadlines against which He must work. Only to know this is to quiet our spirits and relax our nerves. For those outside of Christ, time is a devouring beast; before the sons of the New Creation, time crouches and purrs and licks their hands."[2]

In *The Rest of God*, my book on the gift of Sabbath, I note that it is often in stillness that we discover, anew, God's bigness and goodness. "Be still and know that I am God." In our busyness, we often miss God: the whirlwind of our doing becomes a smoke screen for evasion. Endless busyness is earwax against God's voice and a blindfold to God's presence. God grows mute in the din of our shouting, remote in the blur of our rushing. But stillness reawakens our wonder and attention, and allows us to become freshly present with God, keenly attuned to his speaking.

We see this played out in the story of the two sisters, Martha and Mary. Martha's failing is not her commitment to hard work—that's commendable, and good news for those of us who like eating and clean houses. Her failing is that her drivenness has struck her deaf and blind, so that she can neither see nor hear Jesus when he's sitting right in front of her. Sabbath rest is a way of rendering ourselves still, but not still in the way of slumber: still in the way of a fox when he crouches to catch the rabbit, or still in the way of the birdwatcher when she espies some rare breed of cockatoo perched nearby. Sabbath, in this way, provides an intersection with eternity. It is an earthly practice toward a heavenly reality. It trains us in the rhythms of kingdom life. Hebrews 4 says that heaven is the true Sabbath, so all our intervening Sabbaths are preparation for and anticipation of that.

But here's an irony: winter, for all its enforced silence and stillness and waiting, is seldom restful. It is often toilsome, or tedious, or both. Summer, by contrast, is typically active and restful altogether. We feel deeply alive and deeply relaxed. It is the season par excellence for repose—to take our pose again, this time in a posture of ease and gratitude. The Bible tells us not to be anxious about anything. Not to be anxious. That's a spiritual discipline needed most in seasons of darkness but rarely cultivated there: it's only tested and proven there. Peace—shalom, the presence of God so vivid and real that anxiety doesn't stand a chance around it—is summer's birthright but winter's lifeblood. So in the summer of the heart, when God seems most visible and available, learn the rhythm, the action and inaction, that avails you most of his presence. "Remember your Creator in the days of your youth, before the days of trouble come."[3]

Recently, I took a week of summer holidays with my wife and our youngest daughter. Our oldest daughter joined us for the last couple of days. Our son, alas, had to work (though I took him surfing in Tofino the following week, to make it up to him).

We went to Whistler, a playground for children and grown-ups alike, and on a grand scale: a mountain over a mile high where, even in July, skiers schuss the glacier and, lower down, cyclists on bicycles with more springs and pistons than a cotton gin swoop down switchbacks. There are lakes by the dozen, and icy rivers teeming with fish, and golf courses sprawling every which way. Paved trails for walking or cycling spiderweb it all together. There's a township at the mountain's base modeled on a Swiss alpine village, with brick streets and awninged shops and restaurants with ample patio seating. The children's play areas are made from river driftwood, artfully fitted together like some marshwiggle's teepee and darkly lacquered. We brought our bikes, and fishing rods, and walking shoes, and several good books, and a few good movies. Every day, we chose a new activity. We tramped up craggy snowy mountains, walked along wild swift rivers, swam and kayaked and fly-fished in lakes. We slept on grassy banks. We read and read and read. We picnicked on beaches. We returned to our condominium, showered up, and made a late dinner, and then read some more, or watched an old movie, or played a game, or went to bed early so that we could wake early, or not.

I hadn't been that active in a year. Yet I hadn't been that rested in a year. When I returned to work, the first few days everyone commented on how relaxed I looked.

This was the best part: I wasn't striving for a deeper relationship with my wife, or with my daughters, or with God. I was just taking time to enjoy those relationships, and they got deeper in spite of that. Or, maybe, because of that.

The summer of the heart is like this. It's a time for activity; why not start something new, attempt something hitherto avoided because you didn't have the time, the spunk, the pluck? But there's little striving in such activity, strenuous as it is. You're not in a rush, not trying to prove anything, win anything, finish anything. It's just that the day is long, and you're alive, and feel younger than you look. O happy day.

One simple application: I renovate my spiritual practices most often during my heart's summertimes. I experiment with prayer techniques, for example, or try new ways to read the Scriptures. Most Mondays throughout the year, I hide away for a few hours in the afternoon to pray, read, reflect, journal. It's a restorative practice. I don't tamper with it—where I go, how I spend the time—when my heart is beleaguered. Then, I need the tried and the true. I need a secret garden, one sure safe place in a world of dubious advice and treacherous ground. But when my heart's in summer, I play with this practice. I go to different places. I try new ways of meeting God. I tinker with the tried and the true, and sometimes make wholesale changes. Some work, some don't. In summer, it doesn't matter much. There's nothing to lose. It's no more wasteful than trying a different flavor of ice cream—mango cherry coconut, say—and finding you don't like it quite as much as vanilla. But then again, it just might be the world's best kept secret.

Kingdom Living Is Not Worried

Kingdom life, like summer living, is not worried. You bask in the sheer abundance of God's goodness.

Winter is when we walk by faith, not sight. God is good, all the time, but winter is when that truth is a conviction we nurture, not an experience we savor. In winter, the goodness of God is our creed, true always, seen or unseen, recited regardless of present feelings. In summer, it's our testimony, true because it's obvious, and deeply felt. Summer is when we walk in the light—we can see, at every step, that God is good, and near, and *for* me. And it's not that you take any of that for granted; you just don't turn your nose up at it.

You bask in it.

As a pastor, I love to help people to enjoy, without apology or guilt, a summer of the heart. For some reason, most of us, even those of us (like me) with pagan roots, carry a residue of Protestant angst that makes us feel guilty if we feel good. This is odd, given that we follow a savior who is borderline obsessed that his joy fill us to overflowing. Odd, given we worship a king whose first miracle— *archē ho sēmeion*, in the Greek, which could be rendered "greatest miracle"—was to turn water into wine, for no greater reason than that the party might go on. Odd, given that we take our ethical cues largely from the apostle who wrote, "Finally, my brothers and sisters, rejoice in the Lord!... Rejoice in the Lord always. I will say it again: Rejoice!"[4]

Joy is our birthright. Joy is a sign of the Messiah's presence, the wine at his banqueting table. Joy is the savor and aroma of heaven itself. Jesus didn't let his disciples fast during his time with him any more than he would encourage fasting at a friend's wedding. It would be bad manners, Jesus said, not to mention poor timing. It would be strange, and laughable, and regrettable, like dressing for Antarctica to visit the Bahamas.

I have a photo on my mantle of Cheryl and me on the night I turned forty, almost a decade ago. We are standing on a beach in Mexico, as the setting sun melts gold into sky and sea. We are thin and smiling and relaxed. Cheryl is gorgeous in an evening gown she sewed just for this moment, to surprise me with. She has a string of pearls she borrowed from her mother around her slender neck. I don't look bad myself. In a moment, I remember, we'll go in to the restaurant and eat a seafood dinner to celebrate my birthday and, two days belatedly, our fifteenth anniversary.

It was an amazing season in our lives: my first book was due out in six months, and we were just starting a building program in our church to accommodate the rapid growth. Our children were young enough that they still loved being with us (as opposed to now: loving us, but preferring to be with friends). They were sad we were away in Mexico but thrilled they could spend a week with Grandma and Grandpa. (Several years later, when we visited Mexico again, they were happy we were away but miffed that Grandma and Grandpa were brought in to take care of them.)

It was a summertime of the heart for us. Many times since then, I've looked at that photo and rejoiced that in that season we simply basked in God's goodness, without guilt or apology. We took the season for what it was, a brief preview of the kingdom in all its fullness. It didn't last, not in that distillate form we tasted then, but it betokened that time when the kingdom of our God will be the kingdoms of the earth, and for that alone it's a memory worth keeping alive.

As I spoke about in the last chapter, I try not to idolize memories, try not to make them sirens of nostalgia. But I do derive residual joy from them, savoring them like the faint lingering fragrance of a garden I once walked in.

Kingdom Living Abounds in Fruit

Kingdom life, like summer living, abounds in fruit. It relishes the sheer abundance of God's provision.

God has a knack for doing "exceedingly, abundantly more than we ask or imagine." For wide swaths of our existence, we take that on faith. But in the summers of our hearts, we acknowledge it as fact. The evidence is everywhere. In earth's summer, most gardens and fruit trees produce more food than the average householder knows what to do with. (Where I live, late summer is a potlatch of neighbors trying to give one another zucchinis and apples, plums and cabbages.) Likewise in summers of the heart, God provides more than most of us have capacity to hold. When I'm in summertime, God gives me insight into the Bible faster and thicker than I can write it down or share with others. I live in a perpetual state of discovery. I'm Indiana Jones on the scent of the Spirit. And virtually everything seems another clue. Every book I read, movie I watch, conversation I have, situation I encounter—with minimum effort, each brims with meaning, illumines some idea, connects with some truth or another. What I can dredge only in trace amounts in winter tumbles down in vast abundance in summer. Which leads to a caution. In summer, it's easy to become a spiritual consumer—picky, wasteful, taking it all for granted.

Maybe the best way to understand this is to compare it with our tendency to ordinary consumerism. Consumerism's worst symptom is that nothing's enough. It imposes no outer limit or inward restraint on our appetites. The result of this is we crave many things and enjoy none. That's what an unchecked appetite does: increases hunger but diminishes satisfaction, so that we're always wanting and never happy. We're addicted to pleasure but never pleased.

Perhaps the greatest irony of consumerism is that, for all its treasure-hounding, the one thing it's robbed us of is the capacity to treasure. Everything is disposable in a consumerist culture. In an article I wrote years ago for *Christianity Today*, I called it the "cult of the next thing," an almost religious devotion to chase what I lack rather than enjoy what I have.

So this is where a clarification is crucial: kingdom living (which summer gives us a taste of) could not be more different. It delights in the abundance that's already here rather than looking for more. It takes pleasure in bounty. It treasures treasure. In other words, the kingdom is not when we need more but when we rejoice in the sheer muchness, the ampleness, of what we already have. One sign of this is you share that abundance and, even, give it away. The boy who offered the little food he had to Jesus had personal abundance— five loaves and two fishes. It was more th[ ] he cared about was himself. But in sharing his ab[ ]esus, who shared it with everyone, scarcity turned t[ ]all. Which is another irony of consumerism: it te[ ]d, to keep abundance to ourselves, and so fosters [ ]rcity. Only abundance shared lets us discover more [ ] imagined.

I've learned a lot these past few year[ ]friends, the Cowichan people. One of their traditions, for year[ ]nned by the Canadian government, was the potlatch—roughly translated "the great deeds." The government banned the potlatch because they deemed it wasteful. That's because the potlatch is not about hoarding wealth—a great Canadian tradition—but about giving wealth away. In the potlatch, a tribal chief would flaunt his wealth by bestowing it on another. This struck Canadian lawmakers as counterintuitive, which it certainly is, and opposed to all that is right and good and decent, which it certainly is not. Because in the potlatch tradition, what goes around comes around, and the result is wealth for all, not the few.

What grieves me is that early missionaries didn't see the potlatch for what it was: a sign of the kingdom, a token of the one who "though he was rich, yet for your sakes he became poor, so that you through his poverty might become rich."[5] The potlatch was perhaps the most ready-made container for explaining the gospel and the kingdom of God, in all its counterintuitiveness, to native people. Abundance, like love and honor and peace, is increased by giving it away. Instead of seeing that, the Canadian government saw the potlatch as a threat, an upheaval, to our economic system, and got rid of it right fast.

Hoarding wealth, so much the way of the world, is the opposite of enjoying it. Thus, the world is the inverse of the kingdom, where wealth is only wealth when enjoyed, and that only when shared.

The kingdom rhythm of summertime is when we stop living in the mode of craving and complaining and instead live in the mode of giving and thanksgiving. It's how it must have been in Eden before the serpent began to preach the doctrines of consumerism and scarcity. It's how Adam and Eve, naked and without shame, must have spent their days, relishing each moment, the cool shimmer of morning, the drowsy heat of midday, the golden light and purple shadows of late afternoon, the riot of song and fragrance that broke out each

---

TIME-IN 10

POTLATCH

"The great deeds." That's, roughly, how to translate *potlatch*, a Hul'qumi'num (*Hull*-cum-*me*-num) word. For Coast Salish people, the potlatch marked a great deed, a great happening—a victory, a wedding, a funeral, a birth. The potlatch was the party you threw, the banquet you held, the festival you hosted, to announce that something much bigger than yourselves had taken place. Something's happened, maybe by your own doing, maybe not, that defines those who are part of it in new ways. You are now a chief, or a husband, or a victor, or a father.

Only a potlatch can adequately mark the occasion.

At the heart of the potlatch was sheer bounty. It was pre-eminently about giving and receiving. It was sharing wealth in the most literal and extravagant way. Everything was up for grabs. No possession was so valuable it couldn't be vouchsafed to another. One's riches were measured by one's generosity. The more you gave, the wealthier you were.

As I said in this chapter, the Canadian government condemned it and outlawed it. A culture that measured wealth on the scale of possessions could not grasp wealth measured on the scale of donations. Away with the heathen nonsense!

night. They must have gone from tree to tree, sampling the vast array of fruit, overwhelmed by the abundance, the variety, the goodness of it all. Relishing every flavor, every texture, every everything for its own sake, not wanting it to be otherwise, not wishing for it to end or, for that matter, to stay. The joy of having a thing, they knew by holy instinct, was completed only by sharing the thing.[6] All was pure gift, undeserved but gladly received, to be neither hoarded nor squandered, only shared, only enjoyed. The one response to all this: "Thank you!"

Of course, that heathen nonsense was closer to the heart of God than our materialism. It's not unlike the exchange of wealth described in Acts 2 and 4, where a Spirit-emboldened people can't give away their wealth to each other fast enough.

Why not host a potlatch? Invite friends over—or make it a churchwide thing—with the sole purpose of giving things away to one another—treasured things, beautiful things, useful things, rare things. I'm not talking about the "one man's junk is another man's treasure" principle. I mean sharing your wealth. I mean gathering things that are hard to part with, and parting with them.

Of course, the brilliance of potlatch is everyone goes away newly provisioned. You gave a blanket and gained a teepee. You relinquished a copper plate and acquired a silver bowl. For five strips of dried venison you received three smoked sockeye. You hauled in a twenty-pound squash, and hauled out a twenty-two-pound turkey.

Likewise, this. The irony is that, giving all that wealth away, you end up wealthier.

THE WARNINGS
AND WORK OF SUMMER

I've already hinted at some things we should attend to and some things we should beware of in summer. But let me speak more directly.

Beware Dehydration

In the summer of the heart, live in the rhythms of the kingdom. But beware dehydration. The danger of summer is drought—plants and animals and people just not getting enough water. I put potted flowers and hanging baskets around my house every summer. And on a hot day, I can water these thoroughly in the morning and by afternoon the plants are wilting. Living things parch quickly in heat. And though in summer it's good to play and rest, we do something in this season that we do more than any other: we soak things down.

You and I hold the glory of God in clay jars. We hold it, but thinly. We dry out quickly. We need a continuous inpouring of the Spirit and a deep saturation in the Word. Jesus, in the parable of the seed and sower, says that one of the greatest threats to fruitfulness is not a lack of warmth and light but too much: "When the sun came up," he said, "the plants were scorched."[7] Summertime, both in the natural sense and in the spiritual sense, is a good time for some intentional inactivity—the resting and playing we've talked about. But the one thing you cannot neglect is water—a life of prayer and the Word. In the closing part of this book, I'll speak about those practices that we must attend to in season and out, those spiritual disciplines needed regardless of whatever season we are in. The Word and prayer are such practices. There is never a time, never a season, when we can neglect these without the neglect hurting us.

I just finished memorizing Psalm 19, sometimes called a tribute to "God's two books," the created world and the revealed Word. Psalm 19 begins by exclaiming the wonders of creation: it's a showcase for God's glory and a bullhorn for God's voice. The psalm then shifts. It becomes a paean to the beauty and power of Scripture.

Israel and the church, throughout the ages, have cherished this psalm because it reminds us that God speaks to us both through what he's made — rivers, mountains, stars, bullfrogs — and through what he's revealed — his statutes, laws, ordinances, commands, to name a few things listed in Psalm 19.

But a part of this psalm has puzzled me until just now. The pivot between the psalm's two halves, the hymn to creation and the paean to revelation, is this:

> In the heavens he has pitched a tent for the sun,
>
> which is like a bridegroom coming forth from his pavilion,
>   like a champion rejoicing to run his course.
>
> It rises at one end of the heavens
>   and makes its circuit to the other;
>   *nothing is hidden from its heat.*[8]

The psalmist uses summer imagery here — a wedding, a sporting event. The imagery is richly evocative and deeply inviting, until the very last line. We can almost hear the laughter, feel in our guts the butterflies of anticipation, see the dazzling brightness of banners fluttering in sunlight. We taste the exuberance of festivity.

But it's so hot.

That sun is brutal, relentless, inescapable.

Abruptly, after the psalmist presents these summer images, he starts his ode to the Word: "The law of the LORD is perfect, reviving the soul. The statutes of the LORD are trustworthy, making wise the simple," and so on for another five verses.

Here's what I make of it: happy times are both a gift and a curse. Festivals, weddings, sporting events, holidays, getaways, all the rest — all are lovely. Endless summers. The sun shines all the time.

But nothing is hidden from its heat.

The only remedy for drought is water. And the only remedy for spiritual dryness is the water of the Word. That is "perfect," "trust-worthy," "right," "radiant," "pure," "sure," "more precious than gold," "sweeter than honey," "reviving the soul."[9]

In summer, drink often. Related to the caution I gave earlier about spiritual consumerism, summer's abundance can seduce us into spiritual complacency. We can become so accustomed to the bounty of God that we grow indifferent about seeking his gifts and stewarding them. The lake brims and is so refreshing we fail to notice that the river that feeds it has dwindled to a trickle. I met a man recently who said he rarely reads the Bible anymore. He feels that God has given him a lifetime of insight into his Word, and now the task is simply to live it. There's a part of me that rejoices at this; surely, this "go and do likewise" attitude is a great good. But there's an equal or greater part of me that cringes. When will the reservoir run dry? I need a "constant washing with the Word," a continual inflow of it, just to prime myself to do what it says.

So drink. Soak.

And then there's the next thing.

Gather Firstfruits

Summer is a time to gather firstfruits. "A wise youth harvests *in the summer*, but one who sleeps during harvest is a disgrace."[10]

In the next chapter, I'll talk about the primary season of harvest, autumn. But there are crops in summer, too. Those crops are called firstfruits: the first apples the tree yields, the first corn or wheat the field produces. And if you know anything about firstfruits biblically, you know that they belong to God. Repeatedly, the Old Testament instructs the people to bring the best of their firstfruits to God.[11] In the New Testament, it gets even more interesting: Jesus is referred to as God's firstfruit *to us*,[12] and we are to give ourselves as a firstfruit to God.[13]

This is all getting complicated. Let me simplify it: summer produces an early crop called firstfruits. In a spiritual, new-covenant sense, this is both what God gives you — his best — and what you give God — your best. So when you are in a summertime of the heart, don't sleep through the moment. Don't be a disgraceful son or daughter. Be wise, and harvest God's best for you, and your best for God.

I have been both a son of disgrace and a son of wisdom in my two score and ten years. And, of course, given my day job, I see both kinds of sons and daughters. I think of two Daniels I have known, both of whom died young, but one whose wisdom turned to folly, and the other whose folly turned to wisdom. Daniel means "God is my judge," and in the end that's where it stands. The final verdict on any life God alone renders. Our judgments are only ever partial, flawed, penultimate at best. But to the extent I know the details of the two Daniels' lives, I dare to say one was a wise son, the other not.

The unwise Daniel was a young man from Ghana who came to Canada to help his aunt with her two small children. He was the son of a pastor, and he was wise when he first showed up, one who gathered summer crops. He was eager to seek God's best for himself, and to offer his best to God. He was musical and often helped with our church's worship, playing his *jimbe* with skill and sensitivity and a joy that must have thrilled the angels. He became friends with many of our young people, who loved his sweetness and kindness. Many of the young ladies noticed Daniel, too—he was handsome as a prince, and the very soul of chivalry. He fell in love with Canada and wanted to stay here, get an education, stake out a career in engineering, establish a home and a family. So he went to Vancouver to pursue his dreams.

It was his summertime.

In Vancouver, Daniel discovered a shortcut to all he sought: selling street drugs. It was easy, and big money, and bestowed a kind of status and respect that he'd not experienced before. But he was inept at it, clumsy and nervous. His suppliers had told him to keep his vials of crack cocaine in a balloon and, if ever the police were bearing down on him, to swallow it, and retrieve it later, when it had worked its way through his body. This happened—the police came after him, and he swallowed his balloon. The police detained him anyhow and put him in a holding cell. And there a terrible thing happened: the balloon burst, and the drug, all of it, spilled its poison inside him, and he died in agony.

His grieving father, Abraham, the pastor, came from Ghana to perform the funeral. There were, before Abraham spoke, a few eulogies from people who hardly knew Daniel. These were lullabies of treacly sentiment, hardly the honest talk needed at such a moment.

But father Abraham was made of sterner stuff, and he cut through all the nonsense to speak a clear word of truth. He openly grieved the choices his son had made. He openly hoped that God in his mercy would forgive him. And he openly warned all present, and especially the youth, not to be a fool like his own Daniel had been. To seek the Lord while he may be found.

The other Daniel sold drugs, too, and with a lot more savvy than the first Daniel. He sold drugs, and did drugs, and much else besides. But in his thirties, he literally got sick and tired of all that, mostly sick, and one day Daniel walked into church midway through a ser-

---

TIME-IN 11

A BUSHEL HERE, A BUSHEL THERE

Take a look at how you spend an average week.

Who gets the best of you? I'm not asking who gets the most of you—the most time, the most attention. Your family and work likely get that. But who gets the best of you?

The beauty of giving your best to God is that it's an unmatched exchange—God gets more out of it than you put in. But giving God your best opens you wider to receiving his best.

Here are a few simple questions to measure that:

- Do I enjoy my time with God? Do I wish for more of it? Or does it often feel like a duty?
- Is God's Word shaping me—my attitudes, my actions, my thoughts? Are these prompted by and submitted to Scripture? Or am I mostly influenced by other things—television, moods, circumstances, the morale and morality of my workplace?
- When I feel overwhelmed by stresses and demands, are the time, energy, and resources I give to God the first things or the last things I let go? Does kingdom work seem like an option to me? Or do I seek *first* God's kingdom and righteousness, and trust God for my needs?
- What is one area where I will begin to give God my best?

vice. The Holy Spirit accosted him almost physically (and this in a Baptist church), and that day he walked away from who he was and what he did, straight into the kingdom of God. In the next few years, he rode out the storm of that decision. But he never looked back. He came into a summertime of the heart. His life was made new in every aspect. During his second year at Bible college, where he was preparing for the pastorate, he woke one morning, walked out of his bedroom, and fell over dead.

I preached his funeral. God, I said, had brought to us a wreck when Daniel first showed up. By God's grace, we sent back to him a saint. And if I had to sum up how that happened, why that was so, I could do no better than to say that Daniel had become a wise son, gathering his firstfruits. He had given his best to God, and he had received God's best for him. He hadn't slept through the summer.

I'm not assuming that you, like either of the two Daniels, have ever trafficked drugs; fortunately, that's not a prerequisite for gathering firstfruits. This is: recognizing the urgency of the moment. Awakening to the fact that diligence in the short run will provide abundance for the long run. Effort now, *but only now*, will pay extraordinary dividends. Give God your best, and reap God's best for you.

Don't Mistake Leafiness for Fruitfulness

The first year I lived on Vancouver Island, I built a grape arbor and bought two tiny grape plants from a local vintner, whom I reckoned must know a good grape plant when she saw one. I asked her for plants that produced the sweetest, most delectable grapes, good for eating or juicing. She sold me a breed she said were like candy when eaten, nectar when drunk. I tenderly planted and lovingly tended those sprigs until they grew into sinewy rough-barked trees that twined their thick trunks through the lattice of my arbor. Every year since, they've brought forth dense clusters of grapes. Every year since, I've waited in eager anticipation to drench my mouth in their sticky juice.

And every year since, I'm disappointed. I wait until they look ready—a bursting plumpness, a dark purple hue. I pluck one and pop it in my mouth. And I wince like I'm sucking lemons. It's hard as stone and bitter as gall.

After several summers of this, I asked another green thumb what I was doing wrong. He told me I wasn't cutting back the leaves to let the sun shine on the grapes.[14]

The problem is, I like all those leaves. They throw a cooling shade. They look great. And they seem to furnish irrefutable proof that I have a green thumb in my own right. But what I've nurtured, with my green thumb, is a mass of big leaves at the cost of a good crop. I can either have much shade and little fruit, or I can have much fruit and little shade.

I just can't have both.

Jesus cursed a fig tree that was thick with leaf but absent fruit. In the end, the abundance of leafiness means nothing. It's by our fruit that we're known.

Apply it this way: we can get spiritually busy during summer in ways that make us feel productive—look at all the leaves! But make sure there's something else growing beneath the busyness. And if you must, sacrifice some of the leaves for greater fruit.

Many people get so busy during their holidays, they need a holiday to recover. They water-ski, paraglide, camp, fish, visit all the long lost cousins and aunts and uncles and people they haven't seen since high school. But the busyness is not always fruitful. My family once returned from such a holiday so worn out, in moods so foul and bleak, that any benefit the time might have bestowed was destroyed in our sheer nastiness to one another.

All those leaves, and not one piece of fruit to show for it.

In similar fashion, the summer of the heart can lure us into saying yes to so much that activity overtakes productivity. Most spiritually oversubscribed people I know got that way in high summer. They had so much energy, so much vibrancy, it created its own magnetic field. They were asked to teach this, be part of that, help over here, render an opinion over there. Everything sounded great, nothing seemed too much, and they didn't want to miss a thing. No opportunity was a bridge too far. Indeed, opportunity became, in their minds, the same thing as call: that which they *might* do became that which they *must* do. For a time, it worked. But the sheer accumulation of all of it got tangled and unwieldy.

Lots of leaves, little fruit.

Winter, we've seen, is the season for pruning. It's then we set our hands to the task of ruthlessly excising what we want only proliferated in summer. But if you have any say in the matter, and you at least have some, better to restrain some of the wild growth and sucker shoots before they start. A gardener, with a flick of the wrist or a pinch of the fingers, can nip in the bud or pluck the head of something that, if it's left to grow too long, can be removed only with chain saw or backhoe. It's a good lesson spiritually. That flick of the wrist or pinch of the fingers is the simple word *no*. Learn to say it to fruitless things before they uncurl even one leaf.

SIGNS OF THE KINGDOM

We'll end where we started, in Luke 21, where Jesus equates summertime with his kingdom's arrival. It provides a surprising clue to how to recognize the advent of summer spiritually, and it explains why few of us taste the real thing:

"When you see Jerusalem being surrounded by armies, you will know that its desolation is near. Then let those who are in Judea flee to the mountains, let those in the city get out, and let those in the country not enter the city. For this is the time of punishment in fulfillment of all that has been written. How dreadful it will be in those days for pregnant women and nursing mothers! There will be great distress in the land and wrath against this people. They will fall by the sword and will be taken as prisoners to all the nations. Jerusalem will be trampled on by the Gentiles until the times of the Gentiles are fulfilled.

"There will be signs in the sun, moon and stars. On the earth, nations will be in anguish and perplexity at the roaring and tossing of the sea. People will faint from terror, apprehensive of what is coming on the world, for the heavenly bodies will be shaken. At that time they will see the Son of Man coming in a cloud with power and great glory. When *these things* begin to take place, stand up and lift up your heads, because your redemption is drawing near."

He told them this parable: "Look at the fig tree and all the trees. When they sprout leaves, you can see for yourselves and know that summer is near. Even so, when you see *these things* happening, you know that the kingdom of God is near."[15]

What things are "these things"?

These things, Jesus says, are signs of the kingdom breaking in. They announce God's coming reign. They usher in our summertime. Here are "these things":

Wars and revolutions
Nation rising against nation, kingdom against kingdom
Earthquakes, famines, pestilence, disturbances in the
    heavens
Persecution
Desecration
Siege[16]

When you see these things, the kingdom of God is near. Summer is at hand.

Jesus is speaking of last things. The apocalypse. The end of the world. Life as we know it coming to a cataclysmic end, and life as we long for it bursting forth in resplendent beauty. But the life we long for, the kingdom of God, cannot come without a storm.

That's true on a cosmic scale. And it's true on a personal scale: God's rule and reign are always preceded by an upheaval. Before beauty, ugliness. Before peace, war. Before order, chaos. When God's kingdom breaks in, whether in the heavens or in the nations or in one person's life, it arrives by way of disruption. Things that are meant to be must first plunder and displace things that are. The status quo must give way to God's rule and reign. The kingdom's *fullness* is the lion lying down with the lamb, swords beaten into plowshares, shalom in all and for all, but the kingdom's *advent* is affliction and upheaval, suffering and toil, loss and relinquishment, stretching and bruising.

And what we often do is everything possible to avoid it.

Here's why I think so few Christians experience the fullness of God's kingdom and the fullness of the summertime of the heart: because the path between here and there is unpleasant, to put it mildly. It is messy and costly and dangerous and hard. What God needs to do in the world to birth the kingdom is not pretty. And what God needs to do in our hearts and lives to birth the kingdom is not pretty, either.

So we run. We hide. We delay. We avoid. We return to what is familiar and safe, even if it takes us in the direction away from what is good and holy.

And we think we've avoided a catastrophe, when maybe all we've avoided is the kingdom. And, in doing so, foreclosed our own summer.

Is God doing big and messy and disruptive things in your life right now? Maybe you don't even know what season to call it. It feels not so much like a season as a tempest, an earthquake, a typhoon. And you're doing everything in your power to avoid it.

Maybe it would be better instead to ask God for strength to endure it.

Listen to what Jesus tells his followers to do when "these things" are happening: "Make up your mind not to worry beforehand how you will defend yourselves. For I will give you words and wisdom.... Not a hair of your head will perish.... When these things begin to take place, stand up and lift up your heads, because your redemption is drawing near."[17]

Summer lies the other side of wasteland.

Stand up, and lift up your head.

If this is what it takes for the kingdom to come, let it come.

TIME-IN 12

THESE THINGS

All hell breaks loose before all heaven does. According to Revelation and other Scriptures (Mark 13, for example), that's the shape of history. It's prelude to the second coming. Before it gets spectacularly good, it's going to get spectacularly bad.

This reality often works on a smaller and more intimate scale as well. I'm told by people who work in health care that unhealthy people who pursue health—better eating, more exercise, reduced stress—often go through a violent adjustment. Their bodies at first revolt. For a season, they are healthier being sick than getting well. There's even a word for this: homeostasis. All living entities—bodies, businesses, cities, countries—find their balance. Any correction to this, even if it's in the direction of greater health, knocks the thing off balance. It tries violently to recover.

I've seen that up close. I've seen it with crack addicts. I've seen it with messed-up families, dysfunctional committees, limping churches. Any move toward healing is a reeling blow. It's like trying to walk after spending a week on a whirligig: the world seems to spin precisely because you stopped spinning.

And so I often see a lot of quitting midway. I often see them climb back on the whirligig. I can no longer count the number of addicts I know who started their recovery and then bailed. I have almost lost count of the number of marriages I've seen that began a renewal and aborted.

It just gets too tough. The work, the sweat, the hassle, the heartbreak—it doesn't seem worth it. Egypt looks good when the desert gets hot and the menu hasn't changed in a while.

Yet Jesus said summer is preceded by all manner of disruptions, disappointments, violent adjustments—"these things," he calls them. He's saying, in effect, all hell breaks loose before all heaven does. In the years I've been a pastor, every season of flourishing in the church has been preceded by conflict, crisis, and a lot of people unhappy.

What are "these things" for you? What are the violent adjustments or deep disappointments or hard knocks or tedious stretches that you might have to endure this side of summertime? I'm convinced that I've forfeited more than one summer by an early exit. I'm convinced that some people never get to summer because they've developed the habit of an early exit—they leave their jobs, their churches, their friendships, their marriages when "these things" get too difficult.

Are you experiencing "these things" now? (One way to test whether it's one of "these things" is that your overwhelming reaction is to look for an exit.) Is it possible that the other side of "these things" is not disaster but summer?

Ask God for discernment. And if you believe you're in the midst of "these things," then ask him for strength to see it through.

And at some point, you'll also want to buy some pool toys.

The salmon
scattered down the ocean currents
    feel it
  a homecoming in their bellies
that can't be shaken or
    denied.
So they start out
  silver-bright and
  vigorous
still spoiling for a fight
to find the old wild waters
    and
beyond
  the place they began
  lucid and cold
    and deeply calm.
Do they know, heading
      back, they will turn blood red
  in the journey,
  and grow witch-nosed,
  and, jostling in shallows,
      be easy prey for bird and bear?
Or this: that when they arrive, if they do,
  all fight but one will have left them:
    to spawn the seed of
  children they will never meet,
  and then
    lie down
and turn swiftly
    into water?

                —M. BUCHANAN

CHAPTER 7

FALL

My wife and I, a few years ago, visited New Brunswick, that far-flung province of Canada where rocky earth and steely sea and windy sky all meet. We began in St. John, spent a few days in the Kingston Peninsula, drove through Moncton into the northwest corner of the province, stayed several nights on a remote lake whose waters were rimmed with massive boulders round as turtle shells. We crossed over into the state of Maine, drove down the coast, crossed back into New Brunswick, and ended, before looping back to depart from St. John, at St. Andrews on the Sea. This is an idyllic seaside village with a castlelike hotel dominating the landscape. We stayed here, eating lobster, wading barefoot in the icy Atlantic, waking each morning to shores washed fresh by sweeping tides.

The thing you need to know is that it was October. I live in British Columbia, another rock-ribbed province far-flung the other side of the continent, and we have our own wild ocean, and, besides, steep-shorn mountains, primeval forests, rivers that tumble from heights that turn them white in the tumbling. Few places rival its beauty. But New Brunswick in October comes close. New Brunswick's trees, especially, are hypnotically beautiful. The forests are mosaics of leaf. I'd round a bend of lonely highway, and the harrowing beauty of yet another hill aflame with color distracted me near to crashing.

Coming from coastal BC, I thought fall meant leaves turned yellow or brown, fell, and then winter, sodden and bleary, stumbled in, noncommittal. But New Brunswick, flaunting itself like Joseph in his coat of many colors, made me as jealous as Joseph's brothers, and I sulked because the Father hadn't given me one, too.

Biblically, fall captivates for a different reason: it's harvest time. In ancient agrarian society, harvest was reckoning. The window between bumper crop and famine was an eye of the needle, narrow sometimes as a single day. A good crop was cause for great rejoicing. A blighted crop, deep distress.

So harvest had a theological dimension to it. In its simplest form, harvest was an occasion for thanksgiving, a time to acknowledge God as provider: rainmaker, sun-keeper, storm-quencher. The season proved, yet again, God's enduring faithfulness. And it demonstrated, yet again, the utmost dependency of God's children on his faithfulness.

But even in the Old Testament, harvest began to take on a deeper theological significance, though that deeper significance becomes fully apparent only in the New Testament. To put it starkly, harvest is when we reap what we've sown. And we reap it unto a storing of it. Not only do we reap what we sow, but we store up what we reap. Our sowing has consequences in the present *and* in the future. It's for now, and for then.

That's good news, or bad. It all depends on what you sow, and how you sow.

But before that, what does the heart in fall feel like?

THE HEART IN FALL

The heart in fall is, in a word, expectant. If we've prepared well in spring, plowing and sowing and planting, then we wait in an expectancy of hope. If we have not prepared well, we wait in an expectation of disappointment, maybe dread.

"Land that drinks in the rain often falling on it and that produces a crop useful to those for whom it is farmed receives the blessing of God," Hebrews says. "But land that produces thorns and thistles is worthless and is in danger of being cursed. In the end it will be burned."[1] Hebrews alternates this way, between warning and encouragement. But it ties that warning and encouragement to several motifs. One minor motif running through the book is agricultural, the rhythms of planting and reaping. For example: "No discipline seems pleasant at the time, but painful. Later on, however, it *produces a harvest of righteousness and peace for those who have been trained by it*."[2] Or a few verses later: "See to it that no one misses the grace of God and that *no bitter root grows up* to cause trouble and defile many."[3]

Agriculture is about patience. And it's about anticipation: we *expect* something to come from our efforts. The heart in fall especially lives with this expectation. It feels the weight of it, the heft and tug of what's coming, in a way that it simply doesn't at other times.

Let me change the image somewhat to illustrate.

It just turned fall a few days ago, but only today does it *feel* like fall. Up until now, days were warm and languid, and bright with the last burst of hibiscus and geranium. Everyone wore shorts and T-shirts, even in the evenings, and some still swam in the rivers. It dawned this morning looking like more of the same. But by mid-morning, a greyness squelched the sun, a cold wind barreled down the sky, a chill spread through the house. And then a cold slathering rain began to fall.

So I started the season's first wood fire. The wood's been curing since last winter. I gathered an armload of it, plus a fistful of kindling, and started my fire. In a few minutes, it blazed hot and bright in the stove, the dry wood popping and sparking like firecrackers.

Then I went out and surveyed my woodpile. Just shy of three cords, I reckon. In a typical winter, I burn through three and a half. And if the spring is cool and wet, I'll push that close to four. I'm short of wood, then.

This was not a revelation. All spring and summer I knew this. I'd kept making, then forgetting, mental notes to myself to lay up more wood. I kept meaning to track down Michel, the French-Canadian guy with no fixed address from whom I usually buy firewood, simply because he has the gall to roll up in his battered truck, unannounced and uninvited, several times a year with a cut load of fir at an unbeatable price. Throughout the summer, whenever I'd see a truck loaded with firewood up to its gunnels and a number to call on its side, I'd call then and there.

The asking price was always, I thought, too high.

So I never got more. And today, estimating in my head the short-fall, I felt in my heart a weight of disappointment. Though I knew about this problem way back, I hadn't felt the weight till now, standing in my shed with the wind howling at my back, the rain pouring off the eaves. Now the time to do something about it has come and gone. Now, I pray for a mild, brief winter.

That's a long story to remake a simple point—that the heart in fall fills up with anticipation. And that anticipation—joyful, dreadful, eager, resigned—has much to do with how we have stewarded our other seasons.

I heard a friend, Jim, recently address an incoming group of Bible school students. He used the parable of the seeds and the soils. He quoted the popular aphorism, "You get out only what you put in." In the context—Bible students starting their school year—that sounded wise, if a tad cliché. But then Jim went on to say how untrue the saying is. In truth, we get out *much more* than we put in. We expect to. "Investors don't invest, bakers don't bake, farmers don't farm, expecting to get out only what they put in. They do it expecting to get out much more. Put it this way," Jim said, "you should expect to get out of this time and this experience much more than what you put into it. But you should expect to get out of it only the *same kind of thing* you put in. Put in gossip, or criticism, or fear, expect to get more out. Put in kindness, or encouragement, or love, expect to get more out."

I'm not sure how closely the students were listening. I'm not sure it changed any of their minds, altered any of their actions. I do know, though, that come "fall," come the end of their time at the school, their hearts will feel the weight of the truth Jim spoke about in a way none of them likely feels now.

WHAT YOU SOW

Here's a well-known biblical passage that speaks of these things: "Do not be deceived: God cannot be mocked. People reap what they sow. Those who sow to please their sinful nature, from that nature will reap destruction; those who sow to please the Spirit, from the Spirit

Peter, John, James, Paul, Jesus, sometimes Moses. A good company. The plan is this: when such impulses come, I make a split-second decision not to sow to them. They show up at the door, which is unfortunate. It doesn't mean I have to let them in. I can take every thought captive and make it obey Jesus.

That's half of the plan — the desperate, Hail Mary — pass half of it. The other half is this: in that split second when I refuse to sow to the flesh, I always hear, though often thin and far away, the Spirit speaking. I experience the faint pulse of the Spirit's invitation. "Come," he says, "and let me show you a more excellent way. Come take my yoke on you." What I've learned is that when sinful impulses abound, Holy Spirit promptings abound all the more. They just take some attuning to. But the more I practice this, the more I see that circumstances which trigger the flesh are even more opportunities to heed God. But I have to choose, in that moment that I choose not to sow to the sinful nature, to instead sow to the Spirit.

This is so important, I'll risk boring you by pushing it farther. So much of most Christians' battle against their sinful natures stops at the act of defiance or resistance. We just say no. That's a decent start. But it's only a start. To finish the race, there's another leg. Every temptation, every ambush by the flesh, comes also with a just-say-yes opportunity. We can sow to the Spirit. We can further the kingdom of God within us and among us. The Spirit asks us and empowers us not just to defeat sin but actually to displace it, drive it out. The Spirit doesn't want just to keep the darkness at bay but to flood the arena with light. The Spirit doesn't seek only to conquer evil; he fully intends to overcome evil with good.

Isn't that what Chuck Colson did? After a lifetime of sowing to the flesh, it caught up with him. He ended up in federal prison. But there he met Christ and learned a more excellent way. What's come of that, all these years later, is a worldwide ministry to prisoners. If all Colson had learned was to refuse to sow to the sinful nature, he would have become, I'm sure, a fine upstanding Christian. But because he learned also to sow to the Spirit, he became a holy saboteur, a kingdom insurrectionist, an agent of God's redemption in dark and broken places.

And all because he kept making a choice about which way he'd cast the seed.

Or there's James. James is in his midtwenties. His arms are embroidered with tattoos. He walks with a hitch, speaks with a stammer. He has visible scars on his head, like a broken vase hastily mended with glue. All these things—the tattoos, the hitch, the stammer, the scars—are mementos of his former life. James used to be in a gang. He trafficked drugs, and did a fair amount of them himself.

A deal went bad, and payback was a dogpile featuring a baseball bat. James was beaten black and blue, to a bloody pulp, to a sack of bones. He was not expected to live. That prognosis was revised, but he wasn't expected to talk again. Again, revised, but no possibility of ever walking again.

He walks and talks just fine. And he lives. By God's grace, he really lives.

When we baptized James, he shared from the water what Jesus has done and is doing in his life—the miracle of restored health and, even more, the miracle of salvation. The miracle of new life. The miracle of *walking* with God. The miracle of *talking* to God.

I love it when James comes Tuesday night to our church's prayer meeting. Each time he comes, he prays several times. It's always fresh, but keeps circling the same topics: "Thank you for what you are doing in my life, Jesus. Please keep doing it. And please do it in so-and-so's life, too." I could hear those prayers all night long.

But every day is a struggle. Put one seed between James's fingers, put a pile in his hand, give him a bucketful, give him a truckload, give him a whole granary, and James knows that unless he sows all of it, single seed or whole granary, to the Spirit, he'll raise a crop he doesn't want to harvest. So every moment of every day, he prays desperate prayers for strength to keep sowing to the Spirit.

Most of us live neither in the pressure cooker of a once-disgraced politician or the vice grip of a recovering addict. We live somewhere in the middle. Our opportunities are much plainer, our temptations much tamer. But the principle's the same. Our spirits and our flesh are at war. What we sow is what we grow. And many times every day, we are presented with a litany of invitations to sow to flesh or to spirit. Every interruption. Every criticism. Every temptation. Every glitch. Every driver cutting in on us. Every lineup at a cashier. Every dog barking in the night. Every gruff or bumbling or irritating person we meet. Everywhere in everything, there is the way of the Spirit, which is peace, joy, love, self-control, and the like. If we sow that seed, it enlarges, multiplies, sweetens. And there is the way of the flesh, which is rage, deceit, boasting, and the like. If we sow that seed, we can expect more of the same. It's both that simple and that hard.

HOW YOU SOW

The Bible also talks about *how* to sow. Its principal concern is, of course, *what* we sow. The best farming techniques on earth only worsen our plight if we've sown bad seed. All that good method does is multiply crop, increase yield; it doesn't change the genetic makeup of what's growing.

But let's assume we choose to sow good seed. The Bible tells us how:

Remember this: Whoever sows sparingly will also reap sparingly, and whoever sows generously will also reap generously. Each of you should give what you have decided in your heart to give, not reluctantly or under compulsion, for God loves a cheerful giver. And God is able to bless you abundantly, so that in all things at all times, having all that you need, you will abound in every good work. As it is written:

"They have scattered abroad their gifts to the poor; their righteousness endures forever."

Now he who supplies seed to the sower and bread for food will also supply and increase your store of seed and will enlarge the harvest of your righteousness. You will be made rich in every way so that you can be generous on every occasion, and through us your generosity will result in thanksgiving to God.[5]

Be careful how you sow.

Let me back up. This is the final chapter on the seasons of the heart. We began with winter, then moved sequentially through the other seasons: spring, summer, and now fall. Each season has a dominant mood. Winter is mournful. The mood of the other three seasons is, generally, joyful. But each season's mood of joy is in a different key. Spring is joy in the key of hope — getting ready for what's to come. Summer is joy in the key of satisfaction — delighting in what's now here. Fall is joy in the key of fulfillment — reaping what's been sown, and storing what's been reaped.

But the joy of fulfillment assumes we have sown abundantly to please the Spirit.

I want to convince you of this: sow generously, and sow to please the Spirit. If you sow to please the sinful nature, or even sow to please the Spirit but do so only sparingly, much regret awaits you.

TIME-IN 13

GET ON WITH IT

The statistics are overwhelming. Whenever surveys are done about spiritual growth, it's always those who give the most who grow the most. Those who give of their time, their talents, and their money consistently report higher levels of satisfaction in their lives, in their experiences with God, in the benefits they derive from and the loyalty they feel toward their churches.

The statistics also show the other side: those who give the least complain the most and are most often, by their own account, stuck. They're in an almost chronic state of disappointment. One statistic that always makes me laugh (which is a defense mechanism against crying or getting angry): the church's loudest critics are usually its lowest donors and least committed volunteers.

Now maybe all this is obvious: why would anyone give time and energy to something they thought wasteful, useless, heretical, etcetera? But as statisticians have attempted to tease the numbers out, they've found that giving (in all its forms) to a

I went past the field of a sluggard,
    past the vineyard of someone who has no sense;
thorns had come up everywhere,
    the ground was covered with weeds,
    and the stone wall was in ruins.
I applied my heart to what I observed
    and learned a lesson from what I saw:
A little sleep, a little slumber,
    a little folding of the hands to rest—
and poverty will come on you like a thief
    and scarcity like an armed man.[6]

Take care what you sow, and how you sow it. That's been the thrust of this chapter so far. In the next section, we'll look at what the heart in fall can anticipate if we've sown good seed generously.

---

church is not so much a consequence of being happy with the church as it is a primary cause of that happiness. People don't give because they love the church so much; they love the church so much because they give.

Jesus said, "Where your treasure is, there your heart will be also." The word order is all-important. Heart follows treasure, not the other way around. Passion tails commitment. First, the gift; then, the desire. This can be tracked in numerous contexts. The best way to renew a dying marriage, for example, is to put the effort in. Only then does love reawaken.

So I'm wondering if you need to get on with it. I'm wondering if some important thing in your life—a friendship, a marriage, a relationship with a parent or child, the church—is failing for your lack of getting on with it.

Choose one. And get on with it. Don't expect to feel deep feelings at first. The feelings will find you.

But before that, one last exhortation: make sure you sow something. That's the warning of the proverb just cited. It's also the warning of the parable of the talents, though in that story the metaphor shifts from agriculture to finance, from a field to a bank. But it's a story about a kind of sowing and reaping. Its principal lesson: do *something*.

Sunday after Sunday I look out on a fair-to-middling-sized congregation. I see three kinds of people. I see those who mostly sow good seed, some generously, some sparingly. I see those who often sow bad seed, in likewise proportions.

And I see those who sow no seed at all, or very little. They're not growing anything, good or bad. Their field's been fallow for years. Their lives are not vice ridden. But neither are they rich in virtue, crowned with wisdom, abounding in goodness. They're barren, by and large.

All that arable soil. All that rich pastureland. All that fertile ground. But no crop.

It's unlikely you are in that company. Most people who read books like this are "growers." But let's say you fit the third category more than the other two. I'm asking you one simple thing: resolve to sow *something*. Make it good seed, for sure, but even if you sow only sparingly to begin, just begin.

I heard a story years ago about a radio station with an evening program featuring live music by local musicians. One evening, the musical offering was from a small chamber ensemble, led by an elderly man. The man was a tad slow, a bit doddering. The airwaves opened but the man was unprepared. He fumbled through his score, trying to find his place. Dead space. Radio's great enemy. The radio host, unaware that his own microphone was still switched on, muttered, "Get on with it, you old goat!"

The entire audience heard. Included among them was a man, elderly himself, who'd been a Christian most his life. But he was fruitless. He heard the radio host's outburst as a direct word from God.

And he got on with it.

believe God loved me, that would make a difference. Pastor, do you think God loves me?"

Open your eyes.

Pray

And pray. That's what Jesus also asks of us. Pray God would send workers willing to join him in his kingdom work. Pray to God that this great moment isn't missed. That this little window of opportunity isn't squandered.

Prayer commits us at a heart level to what we endorse at a head level. Prayer mingles our tears and our longings with our observances and our assessments. *Looking* shows us the problem. *Praying* makes it our problem. Looking allows us to glimpse the opportunity. Praying requires us to seize it. It forces us to care about what we know about.

Which leads to the third thing Jesus asks of us. And here, as a friend of mine likes to say, Jesus stops preaching and starts meddling. "Look," he says. "Pray," he says.

Go

And now the meddling: "Go," he says.

You do it. You be the answer to your own prayer. "Even now those who reap draw their wages, even now they harvest the crop for eternal life, so that the sower and the reaper may be glad together. Thus the saying 'One sows and another reaps' is true. I sent you to reap what you have not worked for. Others have done the hard work, and you have reaped the benefits of their labor."[8]

"Even now." Even now, you could reap what you haven't sown. Even now you could taste the unearned privilege of rejoicing alongside those who have. Even now you could share the wages and reap the benefit of someone else's hard work.

Even now.

I honestly don't understand why we don't fall over astonished at this. To heck with meddling: *going* is the best part. And the easiest. I have never led a person to Christ who wasn't ripe for the harvest. There was no tugging and twisting, trying to get the fruit's stem to separate from the branch. There was no wrenching and pulling, trying to force the grain off the stalk. It all just fell into my hands at the slightest touch.

Every time that's happened, I've rejoiced. I've felt like I hit a jackpot. And every time it's happened, the person I've led to Christ feels I've done some heroic thing, some great act of daring and generosity.

I've done no such thing. I just reaped the benefit of someone else's hard work.

They toiled, lonely, dirty, in heat and cold.

I walked in, did the easy part, and got the paycheck.

What's not to like?

Look. Pray. Go. And then watch what God does with your simple act of saying yes.

A Harvest of Prosperity

There's also a harvest of prosperity. Paul says that if you give generously from your material wealth, you'll reap bountifully a *spiritual* wealth. "Whoever sows sparingly will also reap sparingly, and whoever sows generously will also reap generously.... And God is able to bless you abundantly, so that in all things at all times, having all that you need, you will abound in every good work.... Now he who supplies seed to the sower and bread for food will also supply and increase your store of seed and will enlarge the harvest of your righteousness. You will be made rich in every way so that you can be generous on every occasion, and through us your generosity will result in thanksgiving to God."[9]

Paul's not promoting here a health and wealth gospel, where God wants to make you drip with diamonds and put you behind the wheel of a Bentley. He is saying, simply, that generosity is good for your soul. The harvest the generous reap is a harvest of grace, good works, and righteousness. Generosity makes us more like Jesus.[10]

But that teaching is best paired with something else Paul says to the Corinthians. "If we have sown spiritual seed among you," he asks them in his first letter to them, "is it too much if we reap a material harvest from you?"[11] If we've given generously from our spiritual wealth, he's saying, isn't it fair that we should reap generously from your material wealth?

Generosity with material things creates bounty in spiritual things. Generosity with spiritual things invites generosity in material things. Each reinforces the other.

The simple, memorable principle in both these texts: be generous. Sow generously, whether it's spiritual giving or material giving. Don't be stingy with stuff or with truth. Be extravagant in both. In both, give as much as you can. Look for opportunities to do it. Stinginess in either area is self-defeating, because you'll reap what you sow, and then store up what you reap.

Sometimes I do funny little inventories in my head. I reflect on a Christian virtue—kindness, humility, love, compassion, wisdom, and so on. Then I tally all the people I know, or have met, or have heard about, who embody that virtue. I think of Linda's compassion, Brian's humility, Jan's kindness, Don's love. I thank God for that person, reflect a little on their "secret," and ask God to grow me to at least half their size.

Sometimes, I also take stock of another kind of person: the counterexamples. The bitter ones. The shriveled ones. The angry ones. The suspicious or proud or mean-tempered or foolhardy ones. I thank God for them, too: because they are live object lessons of what happens when someone misses God's grace, and so warnings about which roads not to travel.

I've discovered a pattern. Everyone in the first list has a generous spirit. They're all givers. And everyone in the second list has a stingy spirit. They're all takers.

True prosperity is not measured by how much anyone has. It's measured by how much they give. "Your life," Jesus said, "does not consist in the abundance of your possessions." And then he went on to tell the story of a man who took and took and never gave. The man dies alone, rich but impoverished. No one mourns his passing. He never let anyone get that close. He was rich all right, which might have been some consolation, but his prosperity was in all the wrong things, which is to say it was no prosperity at all.

Billy Graham in his autobiography gives a picture of two men, both old, but one who is generous, and the other, not:

Some years ago now … one of the wealthiest men in the world asked us to come to his lavish home for lunch [in the Caribbean]. He was seventy-five years old, and throughout the entire meal he seemed close to tears. "I am the most miserable man in the world," he said. "Out there is my yacht. I can go anywhere I want to. I have my private plane, my helicopters. I have everything I want to make me happy. And yet I'm miserable as hell."

TIME-IN 14

HOW RICH ARE YOU?

Ever since the fall—as in, the original rebellion—we've tended toward scarcity thinking. Indeed, the serpent incited humankind's rebellion by stirring up a crisis around the threat of scarcity. He distracted Adam and Eve from the abundance God provided and got them pining for the one thing God withheld.

"You haven't got enough," was his opening ploy. It's worked pretty well for him since.

Have you got enough? Or asked another way, How rich are you?

Take stock of your abundance. List obvious things—clothes to wear, a place to live, a chair to sit in, friends or family to have meals with, meals themselves. But then move to those things you rarely stop to appreciate:

> Air
> Water
> Bumblebees
> Hands and feet
> Ears and eyes
> The sound of rain
> A Bible verse that's been a lifelong companion
> A grandfather who taught you to tie a knot

You get the idea. A list like that can get very long. It can get so long, it can almost make you forget there's anything missing.

We talked with him and had prayer with him, trying to point him to Christ, who alone gives lasting meaning to life.

Then we walked down the hill to the small cottage where we were staying. That afternoon the pastor of the local Baptist church came to call. He was an Englishman, and he too was seventy-five. A widower, he spent most of his free time taking care of his two invalid sisters. He reminded me of a cricket— always jumping up and down, full of enthusiasm and love for Christ and for others.

"I don't have two pounds to my name," he said with a smile, "but I'm the happiest man on this island."

"Who do you think is the richer man?" I asked Ruth after he left.

We both knew the answer.[12]

To reap the first harvest, the harvest of souls, look, pray, and go.

To reap the second harvest, the harvest of prosperity, give generously, whether it's stuff or truth.

And now we turn to the third harvest, righteousness, and look at what we do in order to anticipate a bounty of that.

A Harvest of Righteousness

Righteousness, to put it succinctly and a little simplistically, is Christlikeness. It's where your thoughts, your desires, your attitudes, your actions, your character are more and more conformed to his. So this third harvest brings along with it the other two harvests. You cannot grow in Christlikeness, a heart after his, without also growing in evangelism and generosity, a heart to save and a heart to give. But the harvest of righteousness is also distinct from the other two. It requires two things: that we submit to God's discipline, and that we seek God's peace.

Submit to God's Discipline

God, according to the letter to the Hebrews, disciplines his children as a sign of his Fatherly love. The discipline is often painful, even misery-producing. It makes us want to quit or run. Let me quote the passage in full.

Endure hardship as discipline; God is treating you as his children. For what children are not disciplined by their father? If you are not disciplined—and everyone undergoes discipline—then you are not legitimate children at all. Moreover, we have all had parents who disciplined us and we respected them for it. How much more should we submit to the Father of spirits and live! Our parents disciplined us for a little while as they thought best; but God disciplines us for our good, that we may share in his holiness. No discipline seems pleasant at the time, but painful. Later on, however, it produces a harvest of righteousness and peace for those who have been trained by it.[13]

"No discipline is pleasant at the time, but painful."

So why bother?

Because, "Later on . . . it produces a harvest of righteousness and peace for those who have been trained by it."

But here's the verse that rocks my world: "Endure *hardship* as discipline. God is treating you as his children." Endure hardship as discipline. Hardship, in whatever form it takes, is all and sundry an opportunity to grow, but only if we allow God to use it that way. An act of endurance is required on our part. Every adversity, every disappointment, every setback, every affront is an opportunity to be conformed to the likeness of Jesus Christ. The painful trial you are going through in your (fill in the blank: marriage, finances, work, family, health) is something God can and wants to use to make you more like Jesus. Zig Ziglar says that a child who is not disciplined by his small world in love will be disciplined by the big world without love. Hardship is an inevitable part of life. Endure it as discipline, a sign that God is treating you as his child and is training you for holiness. In your small world, he is disciplining you with love.

It doesn't mean it won't be painful. No discipline is pleasant at the time. But it does mean that something good comes out of this. A harvest of righteousness and peace.

So submit to God's discipline.

THE JOY OF FULFILLMENT

The autumn of the heart is meant to be a season of joy in the key of fulfillment. What you've sown you now reap and store, no regrets.

I close with a story by my friend and fellow writer, Phil Callaway.

Ever since he was knee high to a Doberman, the boy was fearless. Take him to the ocean and he'd jump in looking for sharks. Take him to the mountains and he'd see how high he could climb....

In his first year of college he called one night.... "I scaled a 300-foot cliff today," he said, undaunted. "You'd have loved it."

Right. His father who contracts vertigo standing on a skateboard.

For years I've wondered what God would make of our son. Would he call him to be a crash-test dummy? A professional bungee jumper? Or would he fulfill every North American parent's dream by settling down in a huge house with a nice wife and providing us some grandchildren to spoil?

The unexpected answer arrived by email one day:

Dear Dad and Mom,

I just want you to know that I met a couple nice girls, and we're planning to be married. In Utah. Not really. But I did meet Lucy. You'll like her a lot. It's a surprise how quickly you can find a justice of the peace down here. Lucy owns a tattoo parlor, but seldom works. Her father won some money in a lottery, so she's set for life. I won't need to work anymore either. I've bought a Mercedes convertible and you'll be happy to know I put a chrome fish on the bumper.

If you haven't fainted yet, here's the truth. It may be more shocking. In the country of Uganda, the Lord's Resistance Army is committing atrocities against children that are too awful for me to put in this letter. Over the years they've abducted 50,000 kids and turned the ones they haven't murdered into soldiers. I'd like to work with street children in Kampala....

Dad, you told me once that Jesus came to comfort us, not to make us comfortable. I guess I've been comforted enough; it's time to offer some to others.

Your son, Steve

"Where did we go wrong?" I asked his mother. "Couldn't he just have a beach ministry in Hawaii? Maybe we blew it taking him to other countries and showing him what the real world looks like. Don't you just hate it when your son practices what you've been preaching?"

"It's what we prayed for all these years," she said with a grin, "that he would live life on purpose."[18]

Phil says that Steve sent "the unexpected answer." I don't think it was unexpected. They'd sowed this seed abundantly for years and years.

Perhaps, only, they were surprised at the size of the harvest.

CHAPTER 8

FALL ACTIVITIES

PART I

Fall is for reaping and for storing.

But it's also for feasting and for thanking.

In Canada, Thanksgiving comes in early October. It is a hundred times quieter than its American counterpart. A day or two before it's on us, we wonder who we might invite for dinner, and debate whether we should celebrate on Sunday evening, which is generally more convenient, or Monday evening, the day of the week our Thanksgiving always falls, thanks to the unbending rigor of government decree. If your children are at college, they're likely not to make the trip home. If your parents live out of town, they'll probably stay where they are, and you likewise.

I was once invited to celebrate American Thanksgiving with an American clan, and that was a hullabaloo—a pageant of eating and greeting, a festival of homecoming and down-home cooking. It was boisterous and extravagant. Canadians, typical to our nature, do things with much less fanfare, and less mess to clean up afterward: you do the dishes and go to bed.

But we do feast, and in much the same ways our southern neighbors do. We eat turkey or ham, or both. We drizzle the ham with sweet mustard sauce, and the turkey with silky gravy. We serve the turkey with cranberry sauce, and sometimes even make this from scratch, with little gratings of orange peel mixed in. And of course there's stuffing, great mounds of it at both ends of the table, the bread all glommed together with fat drenchings, and the really good mothers keep the gizzards out of it. We have all the requisite fixings: milky-buttery mashed potatoes, and Brussels sprouts (some sign of the *other* fall, the one in Eden, must be present at such meals, is my theory), and some intricate casserole made with vegetables and cream cheese and almond shavings. There are sweet potatoes, mashed or diced, slathered with brown sugar and topped with miniature marshmallows broiled to a toasty brown. There are several kinds of bread, too, at least one of them aswirl with great veins of cheese, and one that looks like it was rolled in a bird feeder before being baked.

And we all eat until we can't, until our stomachs ache with the muchness of it and we pronounce ourselves utterly full and completely satisfied, at least until the pumpkin pie, ruffled with whipped cream, is brought out, and we, heroically, mount another conquest.

If we did this every night, we'd soon die.

If we didn't do this once in a while, we'd soon die, too.

Fall is when we feast. We do it because we can—the food stores are full, if the year's been good. And we do it because, in some way hard to explain, we *must*. To refuse the feast is to refuse the bounty is to refuse the gift is to refuse the giver. Fasting when you should be feasting is sheer ingratitude. When some complained about Jesus' disciples not fasting, he responded, "How can the guests of the bridegroom fast while he is with them? They cannot, so long as they have him with them."[1] Sometimes asceticism is misplaced. It's just churlishness parading as holiness. It's just plain poor manners to refuse to eat at your friend's wedding. Likewise, in fall. There's no virtue in not coming to the festival when the season calls for one. There's no piety in the older brother standing in the field at gloaming, refusing to come in to feast and dance, wishing for goat meat when prime rib is on the menu. This isn't spiritual maturity. It's rank foolishness. This isn't self-control. It's rigor mortis.

As the father says to that older son, "We *had* to celebrate and be glad."[2] Sometimes, there is divine urgency, even necessity, to feasting. In fall, especially so.

In a page or two, I'll offer a spiritual equivalent to feasting. But before that, I want to make the connection between feasting and thanking. Autumn feasts are festivals of thanks. They're doxologies

and wise you are in the sowing, how well you've prepared the ground, how lavishly you've seeded it, what engineering innovations you've dreamed up to irrigate it. The enemy guarantees there will be no reaping. And what little you can scratch out, you must thresh in hiding places, no matter how awkward and inconvenient that is, no matter how unsuited winepresses are as threshing floors. It's that or starve.

So maybe Gideon's not a coward. He's a survivor. But the pressures of surviving have bred in him the traits of the coward—bellyaching, excuse-making, avoiding trouble at all costs, casting blame every which way.

He overcomes all that. He gets past his past—his sense of inadequacy, his deep-rooted grievances, his paralyzing doubts and fears. And most of all, his distorted perception, of God and self. Gideon claims "my clan is the weakest in Manasseh, and I am the least in my family." He sees himself as the runt of a litter of mongrels, the errand boy of a tribe of low-caste losers. This is more self-pity than anything. This is the voice of personal grievance speaking, the voice that inflates misfortune to massive proportions and downgrades advantages to uselessness, because soon we find out that Gideon has more than ten personal servants ready to do his bidding.[2] So much for his "weakest" and "least" status. At any rate, Gideon needs to triumph over all the skewed perceptions. And he needs to triumph over something else, the real source of his plight. But we'll come to that momentarily.

This is where Gideon's story plays into our theme of seasons: Gideon and his fellow Israelites have no harvest, or only enough to survive on, but not because they haven't sown in season. They've done all the hard and needed work. They've toiled, seven years running, at the back-bending labor of tilling and seeding, in the diminishing hope that this year, maybe, the Midianites will stay home. The Israelites have not been sluggards. If anything, they've worked harder than most. They've bent to the task, pushing against a mounting weight of sorrow and dread. They've watched, season after season, as their labor goes up in smoke. Then they've scavenged the fields, trampled and smoldering, just to glean a few handfuls of seed for next year's crop.

No, they're not sluggards. They just have no harvest. It's not because they've failed to do their part. It's because their enemies have destroyed the work of their hands.

I see this a lot. I see men, women, families who work and work, work harder than most, and never have much to show for it. Their sowing is abundant, but their harvest meager. And after a time, the constraints of survival, and the burning sense of unfairness, breed the traits of the coward. They become—most do, anyhow—sore, testy, cynical, blaming. Or merely passive, apathetic, resigned to their misery. They see themselves as jackpots in reverse, cosmic targets of unluckiness.

Half of this I have no way to explain. I can't account for it any more than I can give the right answer to Job's trials. It just is. There is a quotient of unfairness, a wild card of misfortune, in the tilt and whirl of life, and all explanations, theological and otherwise, fall wide of a real answer.

I think of Rishabh's mother.

Rishabh Gupta is a child in India my family has sponsored for the past ten years. We started when he was five. He's now fifteen. Not long ago, Cheryl and I were in India, and we traveled from New Delhi to Kanpur to visit Rishabh at his school. We spent the day with him, and an hour with his parents. His father is healthy but rarely works. His mother is beautiful—she could have been a prima donna in Bollywood—but the burden of providing for her son and husband has worn her thin. They spoke no English, and weren't inclined to talk much anyhow. Both were shy and wary. The father looked variously ashamed and contemptuous. The mother looked sad and world weary.

It was hard not to stare at her hands and arms, the mother's. They were delicate, thin-boned, with long elegant fingers. But her skin was scarred up to her midarms. Her hands and forearms were a welter of boils and pockmarks.

Later, I asked the director of the school what caused that.

"Mrs. Gupta provides for her family. She wakes before dawn and prepares three to five thousand sweet balls every morning. Then she sells them from a street stall throughout the day. She does that seven days a week, all day every day. She never rests. Rishabh helps her in the morning, and then comes here to school in the late afternoon until evening. The scars on his mother's hands and arms are from the hot oil she uses to cook the sweet balls."

"How much money does she make for all that work?"

"Less than five hundred rupees a day."

About ten dollars.

I can't tell you why Mrs. Guptah ended up here, threshing wheat in a winepress, barely reaping what she's sown. But in Gideon's case, and in the Israelites' as a whole, there is an answer. There's a reason they never reap what they sow.

IDOLS IN THE BACK YARD

Gideon has idols. That's his problem, and Israel's, too. The whole land has gone over to Baal, the ancient Canaanite god. The whole land is overrun with his image.[3]

Now this is funny, in a bitter kind of way. Baal was a fertility god. Worshiping Baal, and his consort Asherah, involved an almost crass commercial bargain: bow to him, he'll provide for you—crops, livestock, children. Deny him, he'll stick it to you.

Clearly it's not working—not for the Israelites, and not for the Midianites or the Amalekites. The Israelites are living hand-to-mouth and the Midianites are living on handouts, on the labors of others. They're all worshiping Baal, but he's sticking it to them anyhow, one way or the other. He's falling down in the simplest of exchanges. Still, both sides, Israelites and Midianites alike, cling to the myth of his potency and persist in their efforts.

The book of Judges, where Gideon's story is told, narrates a cycle in Israel's history: they prosper in safety; in their safe prosperity they grow complacent and forget God. In their forgetting God, they turn to Canaanite idols of one sort or another; in their turning to idols, God removes his hand of protection and blessing. In God's removing his hand of blessing, they suffer foreign oppression that marginalizes and impoverishes them; in their oppression, they cry out to God; in their crying out, God has mercy and rescues them by raising up a judge, a take-action deliverer who confronts the oppressor and throws off their yoke; in their deliverance, Israel turns back to God, and he restores them to prosperity and safety.

And then, in their safe prosperity, the cycle starts over again. Only each time, it gets a little worse, a little messier, and the judges themselves are little less heroic, less virtuous, more caught up in the habits and hang-ups they're trying to free Israel from.

Gideon is partway through this cycle, not the best of the judges, not the worst. But he does have a fatal flaw: he's a poster boy for all that's wrong with Israel. And this especially: his house is Baal headquarters. His dad, it turns out, is priest of the cult. The epicenter of idolatry is his own back yard.

Now here is where I need to exercise caution. I have, I said, seen the Gideon syndrome a lot—people who never reap what they've sown, never see the fruit of what they've worked so hard to get. And many times, as far as I can tell, there's no Baal worship going on with them. There aren't deep generational patterns of sin, rebellion, idolatry. They just have bad timing, a knack for being on the downside of an upswing, or the upside of a downswing. They're on the flight that gets canceled. They're in the house with leaky plumbing, the job that gets downsized, the town that gets forgotten. They just can't win for losing. But they're not *sinning*.

Most of the time.

But some of the time, hidden somewhere in their lives, there's a Baal—not of the Canaanite variety but a more modern one.

BAAL WORSHIP, THEN AND NOW

Baal was, to put is starkly, a sex god. The primary way his devotees worshiped him was through mimicry of his generative powers. Eroticism was worship. Orgiastic sex was a means of communion. One doesn't have to scour too hard to find equivalents for this all through history. Most recently, the worldwide and easy accessibility of internet pornography is enough to make Baal himself seem modest and prudish. Many men in our churches, and some women, go regularly to this altar. And, like Gideon and his fellow Israelites, they are sore oppressed because of it. All their efforts to grow a crop come up blighted.

But Baal, more precisely, was a fertility god. His luring power might be erotic pleasure, but his holding power was fruit. He *produced*, or so the mythos went. It would be one thing if mere pleasure was what he offered in exchange for your allegiance. That would simply require a feat of self-denial to trump. But Baal promised so much more. He promised life and life abundant. He promised all that was necessary for life—food, foremost—so that to deny him and so be denied by him would be a death sentence. What Baal did, if only he did it, was secure your life and well-being. He was guardian of your future. Without him, you were doomed.

Again, clearly the emperor, or the god, had no clothes. But neither Gideon, nor Israel, nor Midian seems to have noticed.

Baal worship is widespread in our day, and not just through internet porn. Our impulse to look to something other than God to secure our future is the very impulse that gripped the hearts of the Canaanites and, through them, the Israelites.

A church's budget meeting always reveals how much Baal worship lurks beneath the surface. We had one recently where many people—not all, for sure, but a sizable number—expressed views based on everything but faith. The economic forecast was bleak: layoffs, inflation, the shrinking of retail sales, a flattened real-estate market. We needed to exercise extreme caution, the argument went. All true enough, and I'm not here to argue for extravagance or foolhardy spending, but our church, like most churches in North America, has an average per-capita giving of about 3 percent. In a recent mass study of five hundred churches in North America of every size and shape, among those who self-described as "Christ-centered," fully 40 percent don't tithe.[4]

The majority of people in our churches are not staking their future on the steadfast goodness of God, who promises never to leave or forsake us. They're hedging their bets. They're seeking more prudent ways to secure their future. They're practicing not frugality (few North Americans could be accused of that) but plain old stinginess. And they're refusing to put God to the test in the single way the Bible tells us it's appropriate to do that—to entrust him with a full 10 percent of our income and watch him throw open the floodgates of heaven. The promise is explicit:

> "Will a mere mortal rob God? Yet you rob me. But you ask, 'How are we robbing you?' In tithes and offerings. You are under a curse—your whole nation—because you are robbing me. Bring the whole tithe into the storehouse, that there may be food in my house. Test me in this," says the LORD Almighty, "and see if I will not throw open the floodgates of heaven and pour out so much blessing that there will not be room enough to store it. I will prevent pests from devouring your crops, and the vines in your fields will not drop their fruit before it is ripe," says the LORD Almighty. "Then all the nations will call you blessed, for yours will be a delightful land," says the LORD Almighty.[5]

"I will prevent pests from devouring your crops, and the vines in your fields will not drop their fruit." You get to reap what you've sown, see the full fruit of your labor.

This is almost a reversal of one consequence of original sin. God told Adam, "Cursed is the ground because of you; through painful toil you will eat of it all the days of your life."[6] That was Gideon's curse. It was Israel's. The ground was cursed, in his case, by a very personal enemy, who breached the gate because of a very personal compromise: they had "exchanged the glory of the immortal God for images made to look like mortal human beings and birds and animals and reptiles. Therefore God gave them over in the sinful desires of their hearts."[7] The curse on the ground is removed not first by tithing but by what is underneath the act of tithing, or purity, or any other godly virtue: trusting God. Trusting produces tithing produces fidelity produces courage. Trusting produces fruit. It frees us to thresh on threshing floors.

Midian today is whatever it is in our lives that keeps us from bearing fruit. Might be a habit, an attitude, an addiction, a refusal, a demand. But Midian's power derives from a compact we make with Baal, and here's who I think Baal is today: whatever it is in our lives which we believe holds ultimate power over our future, and so which keeps us from trusting God. Baal is that which we believe secures our future. A job, a position, a relationship, a pension plan. It's not that these things, in their proper places, are not good. Most things that aspire to godhood—eros, mammon, and the like—make excellent house pets and gracious servants. Kept in a subservient role, they're great to have around. But when they rule us, and dictate to us what we can and cannot do, and lure us away from radical trust in God and obedience to him, they grow ugly and surly and brutish. A Baal indulged gives free rein to Midian, and the result is we thresh our wheat in winepresses.

BREAKING THE YOKE OF THE ENEMY, THEN AND NOW

Gideon is the man of God's own choosing. He is the one who, by divine strength and command, and with a small band of compatriots, will break the yoke of Midian. It's a famous story: God whittling down Gideon's already rump of an army to a measly three hundred, sifting out the cowards and the dullards, and then refusing to let them bear arms, sending them out with only jars and horns and torches. They win anyhow. They rout 135,000 Midianites and Amalekites, hands down. The days of threshing wheat in winepresses are over, and the days of reaping what's been sown have just begun. Let the good times roll.

But that great victory comes later. First, Gideon has Baal to deal with, Baal to overthrow, Baal's yoke to break: "That same night the LORD said to him, 'Take the second bull from your father's herd, the one seven years old. Tear down your father's altar to Baal and cut down the Asherah pole beside it. Then build a proper kind of altar to the LORD your God on the top of this height. Using the wood of the Asherah pole that you cut down, offer the second bull as a burnt offering.'"[8]

Midian's power—let me repeat—derives from Baal's rule. The extent that Israel, and Gideon with them, has bowed the knee to Baal is the extent to which they have forfeited Yahweh's protection from

Midian. Again, the irony of this is staggering: Baal, in exchange for your undivided devotion, was supposed to provide for you. He was a fertility god, after all. You swear allegiance, he brings home the mutton. That's the arrangement. That the arrangement is all one-sided in Baal's favor seems to have escaped both Israel, who keeps bowing the knee despite the famine, and Midian, who keeps having to raid the neighbor's pantry to eke out their existence.

Gideon is not just part of the general malaise; he's at the heart of it, the source of it. His father is a priest of Baal. He's keeper of the town's Baal altar and Asherah pole.

This is perhaps the high point of this entire story: God chooses the one most captive to be the one to end the captivity. God chooses the conduit for paganism to be the nemesis of it. He chooses the very one who signed the deal with the devil to be the one who revokes it. As the apostle Paul would later elaborate, and as Jesus clearly practiced, God is in the habit of choosing unlikely people to usher in his kingdom—not many wise or influential or noble but instead the foolish, the weak, the lowly, the despised.[9]

He chooses gang leaders to evangelize gangs, junkies to win junkies, prostitutes to announce good news to street walkers. Baal worshipers to destroy Baal altars. But first, the god who rules them must be toppled by them, by their own hands, and a proper altar to God must be built atop the ruins.

Gideon's willingness to tear down the Baal altar, to eradicate that which holds him and an entire nation in thrall, is a necessary condition of God's willingness to use him to defeat Midian. Midian is allowed to run amok as long as Baal is enthroned. Once Baal is toppled and burned, ridding the land of Midian is just a mop-up operation.

Gideon understands, though he's terrified: "So Gideon took ten of his servants and did as the LORD told him. But because he was afraid of his family and the townspeople, he did it at night rather than in the daytime."[10]

Here's how this episode ends:

> In the morning when the people of the town got up, there was Baal's altar, demolished, with the Asherah pole beside it cut down and the second bull sacrificed on the newly built altar!

They asked each other, "Who did this?" When they carefully investigated, they were told, "Gideon son of Joash did it."

The people of the town demanded of Joash, "Bring out your son. He must die, because he has broken down Baal's altar and cut down the Asherah pole beside it."

But Joash replied to the hostile crowd around him, "Are you going to plead Baal's cause? Are you trying to save him? Whoever fights for him shall be put to death by morning! If Baal really is a god, he can defend himself when someone breaks down his altar." So that day they gave Gideon the name Jerub-Baal, saying, "Let Baal contend with him," because he broke down Baal's altar.[11]

Don't Expect Applause

Ridding the town of Baal isn't immediately seen as good news by the townsfolk. It is seen as sacrilege, economic sabotage, a security breach worthy of grim punishment. This is worth some reflection. I think any Christian and any church that really, truly, fully practices radical obedience and surrender to God will be as much a threat as a hero. They will be seen, even within their own faith communities, as rabble-rousers, troublemakers, heretics. Blasphemers of the compromise we've made with the powers that be, contract-breachers of the middle position we worked out with the gods of the age. One of the most glaring examples we have of this in North American Christianity is a recent survey done of a wide cross section of young adults at Christian university. They were asked if they would consider a vocation in cross-cultural missions, and many said they would. But when asked what their primary obstacle to that was, most said their parents. Their parents want them to finish their degrees so that they can get good jobs so that they can be like everybody else. Don't expect that when you defy the gods of the age everyone in your town will come out cheering. Idols don't always fall to the hurrahs of the crowd.

Not that higher education or a good job are idols, at least not intrinsically. I have both. I see my education and my job as gifts of God and tools of God. But some things—almost anything—can take on idolatrous proportions when we cherish them at the expense of what God desires. We should be suspicious of anything that rivals our devotion to God, anything that distracts us from our pursuit of his kingdom. Anything. And we should subject all our evasions and rationalizations to the most thoroughgoing scrutiny.

I have a friend in the church whose son, soon after graduating from high school, moved to the Bronx to minister to children at risk. He gets paid a pittance — food money, basically — and gives himself body and soul to the task. Every day, he walks some of the most dangerous streets in the world, and loves some of the most abused and neglected children in the world. I asked my friend if this is what he dreamed for his son. "Couldn't have imagined it," he said.

"Does it bother you?" I asked.

"I couldn't be prouder," he said.

"Are you afraid for him?"

He looked pensive and answered slowly, "You know, I'd rather that my son died young on the streets of New York serving the kingdom of God than stayed safe, lived long, and died rich, but only ever served himself."

I could smell the smoke of burnt idols on him as he spoke.

Deal with It, for Your Own Sake and for the Sake of Others

Idol wrecking, it so happens, has a butterfly effect: one war of liberation in Gideon's back yard reverberates until the whole nation is living free.

And interestingly, the first person set free is Gideon's own father. The Baal altar and Asherah pole actually belong to his father, Joash. Gideon is the heir, the son of the man who presides over the cult. But it's Joash who belongs to the generation of those who hate the Lord. He's the architect of this mess, the tribal chieftain of this misrule. In a sense, Joash has the most to lose by Gideon's defiance. It puts him out of a job. He loses his status in the community. It's his altar that's destroyed, his bull that's sacrificed, his livelihood that's derailed.

But the man, it appears, couldn't be happier with the situation, or more proud of his son. I think he stopped believing in Baal a long way back, saw through the chicanery of his promises, but lacked the personal integrity or courage to do anything about it. He just kept on keeping on, going through the motions. Caught in the inertia of a false belief of diminishing returns that he thought was too entrenched to change. Until his son acted, he saw no way out of the status quo. Now that his son has acted, he sees no going back.

It has become standard fare, since Freud and probably long before that, to blame our parents for our sins. My father was an angry man, and my whole life I've battled anger. It's the easiest thing for me to pin the blame on him, to justify the way I am because of the way he was.

If the excuse works with others, it doesn't with God. God holds Gideon liable for his own sin and appoints Gideon to deal directly with it, regardless of its pedigree. I often hear from people with various besetting sins — pornography, waywardness, alcoholism, destructive gossip, violent temper — that they are merely repeating their mother's or father's behavior, as if that absolves them of any responsibility.

Gideon's story instructs us otherwise. It says deal with it. Deal with it for your own sake. And deal with it for your father's sake, or your mother's: they might just be the first people freed by your freedom. The whole creation, Paul says, waits in eager expectation for the children of God to be revealed. Others await our taking hold of liberty. Your own forebears might be waiting in such eager expectation, without even knowing it until they see it, but when you live out your glorious freedom under the fatherhood of God, walk in the authority and inheritance of your true adoption as sons and daughters, it will beckon them to freedom, too. I have seen this a hundred times: men and women come to faith in Christ, break their bondage to decay, throw off the idols of their childhood, and soon after their parents do the same.

Expect that when you defy the gods of the age, break and burn their altars, some will want your head, but many others will be set free — maybe first those from your own household.

God may be calling you to take a risky step of faith. That step may require more courage than you think you have. It may involve taking a stand against something, or someone, in your own household or workplace or social circle. It may take the moral support of a few good friends to carry it out.

But maybe it's a step you need to take, not just for your own sake but for the sake of the one whom at first you must defy.

Or maybe you're the father. Or the mother. Or the older brother. Or the foolish companion. Maybe you're the one being defied. Maybe there's someone in your household—a child, a sibling, a spouse—or in your midst—a colleague, a friend, a fellow church member—who seems too heavenly minded to be of any earthly good. You just wish they'd dismount their high horse and get with the program.

But maybe the program isn't the kingdom of God. And maybe God put that person in your midst, in your path, messing with your idols, for your sake as well as their own. Maybe he or she is a child of God, and God's revealing them so that you get to be set free too.

Embrace Your New Name

Gideon gets a new name, Jerub-Baal. It's an honor name, but not a name that honors Baal. It means "Let Baal contend with him." It means Baal ever after has a fierce opponent in Gideon. It means Baal should think twice before he makes another bid for president. Baal has a challenger and a nemesis in the land now. Baal beware.

James tells us to resist the devil and he will flee. That's impressive, because Peter says the devil's like a lion, seeking someone to devour. Our impulse with lions is to flee them, useless as that may be. It seems harebrained, and futile, to resist a lion, defy a lion, put a lion to the chase. But it's what James says. Neither the devil nor Baal is as powerful as they make themselves out to be. They're more shadow than substance, more growl and scowl than tooth and claw. Both Baal and the devil are easier to rout than they'd have you think, just as their minions—the Midianites, the townsfolk, the hosts of hell, whoever—are not half as menacing as they look.

It takes just one man, one woman, maybe with a few companions, to test the theory. It turns out Baal is a poor god and a weak opponent. But he makes for good kindling.

We often scare ourselves with talk of the devil—that if we take the devil on, go plundering in his realm, he'll come back at us with everything he's got. Well, let him. Mostly, we're just believing propaganda straight from Beelzebub himself. We fearmonger ourselves into inertia. That's a scandal. We should be out raiding his lair, like Jesus did, and his disciples after him. Be Jerub-Baals, demon hunters. Let Baal contend with us if he wants. Let him roar and growl and bare his teeth.

We're not going to do his bidding anymore.

TIME-IN 16

WHAT IS YOUR NAME?

In the movie *Monty Python and the Holy Grail*—an outrageous spoof on the legend of King Arthur—there's a scene in which Arthur and his knights have to cross a rickety bridge, all ropes and sticks, spanning a fiery gorge. An old man, blind, toothless, cackling, grizzled, stands at the entrance to the bridge and demands that each person seeking passage first answer three questions. If they answer all three correctly, they cross. If they get one wrong, they are hurled into the gorge.

Brave Sir Lancelot steps up first. "Ask me your three questions, old man. I am not afraid."

"What," the old man asks, "is your name?"

"I am Sir Lancelot of the Round Table."

"What is your quest?"

"I seek the Holy Grail."

"What is your favorite color?"

"Well that's easy—blue."

"All right, then," the old man says, suddenly amiable, "go across."

And on it goes, the joke turning on the old man's variations on the last question.

Silly movie. Silly scene.

Great questions.

What is your name? Who are you, really, beyond all pretense, all posturing, all self-effacement, all self-pity? Who is the person God knows and sees and calls forth? It's an identity question.

What is your quest? What is the desire in your heart that no diversion or disappointment has ever quenched? That thing you dreamed when you first came into the light? That vision of what God had for you to do and to be? It's a destiny question.

What is your favorite color? What makes you you? What are the quirks and intricacies of your personality, distinct as your fingerprint? What makes your heart leap? It's a passion question.

If you keep a journal, this is a good exercise to write down. God has designed us to live out of our true identities, to accomplish our truest quests, to do it in our unique personalities, fueled by our hearts' godly passions.

Crossing the bridge, getting from here to there, requires you to answer all three correctly.

***

I wrote this chapter for those who feel like all their spiritual efforts are wasted. I wrote it for those who feel fruitless, not for lack of trying but in spite of all their trying. Certainly, there are tough seasons in life, with low yields, and there's no accounting for it. But sometimes the fruitlessness has a cause: some marauder, some saboteur, that plunders or undoes us at eve of harvest. When that happens, season upon season, it's almost a given that the marauder found access through a door we left open. Almost always, that door is a Baal we keep, in some form or another.

Take him out, Jerub-Baal, and it's simply a matter of time before Midian falls, too.

After that, the next harvest is all yours.

PART 2
SPIRITUAL RHYTHMS

The first half of this book is a description of the heart's seasons and an exploration of how to steward them.

This next half is a collection of musings, eight in all, about spiritual rhythm. That's followed by a lengthy final reflection on four practices —worship, Word, prayer, and friendship—that nourish us in season and out, world without end.

The eight musings are not random, but neither are they entirely joined. They form a tapestry more than a quilt, an interweaving of themes rather than a juxtaposing of them. The thread uniting this entire half of the book, as I said, is spiritual rhythm: learning the art of moving with the Spirit, step for step, winter, spring, summer, fall.

This book is, first, a modest attempt to help you walk in grace in every season. But it also contains a modest proposal: that we rethink some basic premises about spiritual formation. We tend to measure spiritual maturity by the duration and strength of our attachments and commitments. In short, by how much we do. This yardstick has been serviceable up to a point. But it's seriously flawed. It's simply not biblical. The biblical measure of spiritual maturity is fruit.

My modest proposal: seasons are a better way to understand our spiritual lives. And each season has its own rhythm.

What follows are eight reflections about that.

CHAPTER 10

BALANCING
(OR NOT)

Seasons are inherently unbalanced. Where is balance in winter's bleakness? It is a deep crevice of darkness; it's a glut of cold. Where is the symmetry in spring's flooding downpours and bursting newness, in its heady mix of sweet fragrance and rank pungency? Where is the simple elegance in summer's wild wasteful profusion? Its blackberries alone are so abundant that even the birds that gorge themselves on them and the bears that turn their muzzles sticky in their blood eat their fill and still mountains of them go untouched. Where is the equilibrium in fall's madcap rush of colors, the urgency of its harvests, its sudden frosts and relentless winds?

There is none. All bends one way or the other and only rarely, if ever, sits still. In the ebb and flow of seasons, there is little slack tide.

Our age has its own cherished myths, and one of the most hypnotic is the myth of balance. I hear it everywhere, from old and young, city dwellers and country folk, carpenters and lawyers, students and homemakers. Everyone seeks balance. Everyone longs for that magical combining of rest and play and work that, once found, will make life simple, elegant, easy: balanced. Where is the perfect middle, they ask, the right proportion of duty and freedom, church and job, neighbors and family, time for others and time for me?

There is none. It is no more to be found than unicorns or perfect churches.

There are only seasons, seasons for everything, and seasons are inherently unbalanced.

The watchword for seasons isn't balance. It's rhythm. And rhythm requires a different approach. I seek balance when I stand up in a kayak. Staying in the boat depends on it. But I seek rhythm when I paddle the kayak. Getting anywhere depends on it. There's balance needed, too, but a balance that flows out of the rhythm, and often enough the rhythm forces me to extremes, a steep leaning one way or the other, so as to keep balance.

We crave balance but need rhythm.

For everything there is a season. There is a time, Ecclesiastes 3 says, for weeping. When Carol died, Cheryl and I (but especially Cheryl) wept long and deep and hard, and even most of our good days were interrupted, without warning, by flash floods. There was simply no balance to it. It was excessive and exhausting, oft times embarrassing. A month after her death, on a book tour, I spoke to a group of employees at a bookstore in Grand Rapids. In the middle of it, I came unstuck. I stood gasping and trembling, unable to speak, as twenty or so bewildered strangers with no context for my grief, no forewarning of it, looked on appalled, and then tried awkwardly to console me.

Or think of a lad in love. That's one of the four wonders of the world that boggled and astonished Agur, the speaker of oracles:

> There are three things that are too amazing for me,
>   four that I do not understand:
> the way of an eagle in the sky,
>   the way of a snake on a rock,
>   the way of a ship on the high seas,
>   and the way of a man with a maiden.
>   —PROVERBS 30:18–19

A convention of Hebrew wisdom literature is that the first three things in a list set up the fourth. Agur finds all four phenomena "too amazing" to understand, but especially the last one, the way of a man with a maiden. These first three wonders are mere prelude to the daunting strangeness and haunting beauty of this final mystery. One thing alone exceeds the holy enigma of any eagle soaring or snake coiling or ship pitching: a man courting.

I remember my own days of wooing well, and often see others in the throes of it now. Nothing is done by halves. A man in love is a fool and hero all in one, full of blather and valor. He's a spinning top. He's a show-off and an idealist, a warrior-martyr-dreamer. Truck drivers become poets. Cowards swell with courage. Bullies grow soft. And everything—vast mountains, towering forests, wild rivers, serene parkland—is only backdrop to stolen kisses.

There is no balance for a man in the full grip of infatuation. Soon enough, that same man will settle back into his old self—aloof or bragging, loud or timid, lazy or busy. He'll put on weight. Stop shaving. Snore. Watch too much television. She won't know where her courtier went. She kissed a prince; he became a frog. But in that season of madness, when first he spied her and wooed her, few of earth's many strange exotic things are stranger or more exotic than his way with his maiden. Not even cobras can compete.

There's no balance here.

We crave balance but need rhythm.

Spiritually, there are times for soaring, times for running, times for walking and trying not to faint. There are seasons of heady giddy romance, when Jesus seems more swashbuckler than shepherd. There are seasons of hard slogging, when Jesus seems almost a taskmaster, calling us to keep going when all we want to do is quit, cloaking his compassion under the guise of discipline. There are times to just hoist the sails and ride the wind, come what may. And there are times when all you can do is wait out the doldrums and hope you don't run out of fresh water before then.

All this needs rhythm. It needs leaning into, pacing yourself with, matching thrust with counterthrust.

An example would help. Carol's death altered the season for both me and, to a lesser extent, our church. We found out about her illness in spring, literally and figuratively. The church was abuzz with new ideas, fresh energy. Among other plans, we were preparing to plant a church. We laid out our strategy just before Easter. By fall, we'd be ready: the launch of New Life North.

Then Carol's crushing headaches and reckless clumsiness and mounting shrillness all got explained. Her head was crammed with sickness. And so the ordeal began.

At first, we held to our original plan. But very soon it became obvious that none of us, me least of all, had energy for this. Winter descended, cruel and abrupt, and all we could do was endure it. There would be no new church anytime soon. There were no daring ventures on the horizon. This next season was about surviving, not creating.

And it called for a different rhythm.

I had to change my pace. I started moving more slowly and cautiously. I tended my own soul with a care that in another season

---

TIME-IN 17

PLAYING BONGOS

My first time in Africa, I worked with a team of young adults from various parts of the world. One of the young men desperately wanted to play the African drum. Every church we'd go to, he'd plant himself in a squat, hug a big skin-drum between his knees, and start flailing away, to the infinite amusement of our African hosts and growing annoyance of his teammates.

The boy simply had no rhythm.

Try as he might, he whacked away with no more elegance than a bucket falling down a well. Gifted drummers would try to teach him, modeling how you feel the song in your bones, let it pulse up from the deep place in your belly, and then let it flow down your arms and through your hands. Drumming is just your inmost self dancing on a taut gazelle hide.

It was useless. He could no more drum than spit and swallow at the same time. It just wasn't in him.

But that kid could lift. He was powerfully built and helped himself along with a serious regimen of bodybuilding. He could pop up fence posts from the earth like most people pluck a tulip bulb. He could manage wheelbarrows of sloppy cement with the steadiness and endurance of a machine. He could dig all day and still want to play football after dinner.

would have been self-indulgent. Belly-button gazing. Cheryl and I spent inordinate amounts of time discussing in minute detail Carol's day, and our own. We gave ourselves more space. We gave ourselves more grace. We went for marriage counseling—a first in over twenty years of married life. We sought more time with friends, and spent the time both crying and laughing. We gathered our breath. We took a few holidays where all we did was read and sleep and stare at the rain. We ate fatty food once or twice a week without worrying about it.

There was no job too tough, too grueling, too menial he didn't jump in and perform it with simple competence and unfeigned joy.

Hard work was his bongos.

Part of good rhythm is knowing what your bongos are. A lot of our energy is squandered chasing things we'll never catch, pining for gifts we'll never receive. Meanwhile, the things we excel at, that we do with an ease and effectiveness that is life-giving to us and others, we devalue.

Has that happened with you? Is there a part of you that longs for a role or a skill or a gift that, if you're brutally honest with yourself, you lack, and no amount of trying or wishing will make it otherwise?

Sometimes our ambition outstrips, by a significant gap, our abilities. We watch the ten-talent people do dazzling things with their ten talents—accruing greater and greater wealth with every effort they put in—and it fills us with longing and envy. So instead of doing what we can with our single talent, we bury it.

And nobody wins.

Is there a skill, a talent, a gift—a rhythm—you have buried? Best you dig it up. You may not be a brilliant bongo player, but can you lift fence posts? This, too, the kingdom needs, maybe even more than bongos.

It would have been harebrained to try during that wintertime of my heart to keep the rhythm I had before it. As I shared at the beginning of this book, I had already attempted that a few times in my life when the season changed abruptly, and paid dearly for it. It would, likewise, be harebrained in my heart's current springtime to keep the rhythm I developed during Carol's illness. The rhythm was life-giving, or at least life-preserving, in winter; it would be death-dealing, or at least life-sucking, in spring.

Have you got rhythm?

CHOOSING
THE RIGHT WEARINESS

Part of good rhythm, in every season, is choosing the right weariness.

Let me explain. In Isaiah 43, God accuses his own people this way: "You have not wearied yourselves for me, O Israel." The context is God's invitation to Israel to love and serve him, the one who created them, rescued them, ransomed them, provides for them.

But they won't listen. They won't come. They want their own way. God has put them at the heart of his concern, yet they have put God on the periphery of theirs. So they are busy with many things. With idols. With vanities. With complaints. With sins. They are so busy with these things that they have grown weary in them and of them. Indeed, they have wearied God with it all.[1]

But they've not wearied themselves for God.

They've poured themselves out on things that have poured nothing back, and they are empty and spent as a consequence. The one pouring out that would refill and replenish them as they did it—a passionate pursuit of God—they spurn. They are not making themselves weary for the only one who can refresh them in their weariness.

Life is inherently wearying. Seasons are inherently unbalanced. The sooner we accept this, the less disappointed we'll be. We're just better off to abandon the false hope that, with enough money and time, we'll arrive at some ideal state of existence, a place unscathed by burdens and pressures and disappointments and trials. That place

GLORIOUS LOPSIDEDNESS

Life is about pursuits, and something always has to give. "Run," Paul says, "in such a way as to get the prize."[3] Chase what matters.

Often our pursuits are trivial. They might masquerade as great dreams, but it's by their fruit that you know them. We gain things that perish only to lose things meant to endure, things we were to guard with all our hearts: we get a big house, but estranged children; we win the applause of strangers, and lose our friends; we acquire wealth and status, but grow cold toward God; we acquire much and spend much, but give little and—really—get little. The Bible tells us to seek the Lord. It tells us to seek peace and pursue it. It tells us to seek the kingdom of God and his righteousness. We can know all this, and even do it, but lose our way along the way and end up chasing things we'll never catch or, if we do, wish we hadn't.

But here's what I keep trying to say: it's impossible to pursue anything without forsaking other things. It's impossible to live in the grip of a pursuit and manage it in some balanced way. By their very nature, grand pursuits demand sacrifice. They require that we live gloriously lopsided. Magnificently obsessed. The pursuit may change season to season. (And here I speak of seasons of life—raising children—but it applies equally to seasons of the heart.) Or the particular way of engaging a pursuit may shift season to season. (I have many times preached the Word "out of season," but nonetheless preached it—maybe with more urgency, or less, more fire in the bones, or the sentence of death in my heart. But woe to me if I do not preach.)

But I can't say I've ever had balance. The only times I've come near are when I've forsaken my pursuit, and this I don't recommend. Those have been times, in my case, when I've been waylaid or wayward: pulled by distractions so hypnotic I wandered in a dark wood, or laden with apathy so thick every desire lay muffled beneath it, or wracked with disappointment so jagged it made everything inside me ache. I got unbalanced in such times anyhow, but the tilt was askew—toward self-indulgence, self-pity, self-protection, some *self*-thing. Excess marked me out, only I exceeded at that which, mostly, I should have shunned or, at least, done by halves.

My whole life has been an exercise in lopsidedness.

I'm guessing yours has, too. It's just the nature of the thing, and there's no helping it. What we can help is whether our lives are *gloriously* lopsided, tilting toward light, in pursuit of Jesus through hill and dale.

My friend Brian Doerksen wrote a song during one of the darkest times of his life, after he lost nearly everything. It's called "Now Is the Time to Worship," and it became a worldwide anthem. Brian wrote it as a declaration, a resolve: now, right now, here and now, in the midst of loss and confusion and humiliation and anger—*now* is the time to worship. Now is the time to press into the hope of the kingdom. The situation wasn't about finding balance. It was about finding a rhythm to negotiate and sustain a cockeyed, headlong swerve toward the light.

I recommend we abandon the dream of balance. Maybe you can attain to balance fleetingly, in Zenlike moments of personal bliss, but generally the kingdom of God permits us no such inner quietude and windless poise. The kingdom of God since the days of John the Baptist, Jesus said, has been forcefully advancing, and forceful people, violent people—unbalanced men and women, I take that to mean—lay hold of it.

Seek ye first the kingdom of God.

In season and out.

CHAPTER 11

ABIDING

I am the vine; you are the branches. If you remain in me and I in you, you will bear much fruit; apart from me you can do nothing. If you do not remain in me, you are like a branch that is thrown away and withers; such branches are picked up, thrown into the fire and burned. If you remain in me and my words remain in you, ask whatever you wish, and it will be done for you. This is to my Father's glory, that you bear much fruit, showing yourselves to be my disciples.

—JOHN 15:5–8 TNIV

Most doctrine hangs by the fingernails of small words: *of, with, from, for, as, by, through, while, to.* Prepositions, they're called. Whole theological counsels and camps, entire denominations and movements, the line between heresy and orthodoxy—all this, often, dances on the pinheads of prepositions. Prepositions are the eye of the needle that the camel of dogma must squeeze through. An example: the battle to forge the Chalcedonian creed, written to clarify the nature of the incarnation, raged over a single preposition: whether Jesus was "from" two natures or "in" two natures.

The power of tiny words is everywhere. Many of the conversations I have with leaders turn on a single question: "Are you leading *up* or leading *down?*" I assume the person is exercising leadership. That's their gift. They influence others whether or not they want to or think they are. My question has to do with the direction of their influence. Up or down. Two radically different outcomes, yet separated only by the paper-thinness of a single word: a preposition.

IN CHRIST

Biblically, every preposition is important. It shades or tilts meaning one way or another. But if one preposition surpasses all the rest, I think it's *in*. You must abide *in* me, Jesus said, and I must abide *in* you. The reality of *in*-ness, of being in Christ and Christ being in us, is the essence of the loving, transforming relationship Jesus invites us to enjoy. In the end, when it comes to knowing God, we are either in or out.

Over the past few months, as I was memorizing the letter to the Philippians, greater clarity about all this came to me. In that letter, Paul uses many prepositions to articulate the nature of our relationship with Christ. We do much *through* Christ, *for* Christ, *with* Christ, *by* Christ. But especially, our life is *in* Christ. In Philippians alone, Paul uses the phrase "in Christ Jesus" or "in the Lord" eighteen times, and means by it everything from who we are to what we have to what we're called to be and do. *In*-ness defines the shape of our Christian identities, abilities, destinies. We are saints in Christ. We are confident in Christ. We are called heavenward in Christ. We stand firm in Christ, rejoice in him, hope in him, agree in him, glory in him, are found in him, are guarded, heart and mind, in him, have all our needs met in him, and welcome others in him.

Pondering that, I reckon this: the deep and simple answer to all of life lies here, hidden in plain sight. If we could fully embrace this life of *in*-ness, all would be well, and all manner of things would be well. Right now, I'm no better than halfway there. Much of my confidence, my rejoicing, my hope, my agreeableness, my efforts to stand firm, my attempts to guard my heart and mind—much of it is in something other than Christ. I agree in things going my way. I rejoice in my health. I am confident in my proven ability to ride a bike without tipping, mostly. I hope in the strength of the local economy. I guard my heart and mind in the maintenance of carefully delineated boundaries.

And the extent to which any of these things rests in something other than Christ is the extent to which they are rickety. My health could fail without warning. Things don't always go my way. I can't even always stay upright on a bike—this summer, navigating around a fallen tree, I fell and injured myself. The local and global economies are shaky. My boundaries shift beyond my control, and the buffers and barricades I've erected, and decorated to look like something else, get breached.

And so life becomes precarious. In the face of that precariousness, I find myself lapsing into the very thing Paul wants to spare me from —anxiety. I become anxious about everything.

Life in Christ is the only life that bears fruit, or at least fruit that lasts, and that you want to last. Every life, true enough, bears fruit. We all produce something. But it's either fruit that doesn't last— good things we can't sustain—or it's fruit that does last, but we wish it didn't—bad things we can't be rid of.

I think of Lester, who's had one relationship with a woman his whole life, only repeated seven times. They all start the same: a heady attraction, a sexual frenzy, a trumpeting of, "Finally, the One!" a decision to move in together. And they all end the same, though they're becoming, mercifully, shorter and shorter in duration: a growing irritableness, fights that intensify and lengthen, finally one wild blistering row that often concludes with the neighbors phoning the police and restraining orders being issued. Lester sits in my office weeping, asking, "Why is this happening to me?"

Where do I start?

Of course, I want to moralize. I'm good at this, gifted even. My mouth drips stern lectures with minimal prompting. I heap guilt and, subtly, enshrine my own example of "virtuous living" to be emulated. But the problem is always deeper than this, and the solution always other than this. Anything done without faith, Paul says, is sin. On that score, much of my virtue is just a gimcrack disguise for my sin. Because—well, I've already said it: I hope and agree and rejoice and stand firm and etcetera and etcetera *in* many things other than Christ.

The only fruit that glorifies God stems from abiding in Christ, and he in us. It's a life of faith and faithfulness. It's a life of utter dependency and yet, strangely, daring initiative. Put another way, much and yet nothing depends on me. What depends on me is my tenacious dependence on Christ. I must do that thing which exposes the utmost bankruptcy of all my doings. Apart from him, he clearly said, "I can do nothing." I depend on him for exactly everything. If I fail in this one thing, this tenacious dependency, I fail entirely. And yet the other side of this is what Paul proclaims in Philippians, the secret, he says, of being content in any and every situation: "I can do everything through him who gives me strength."[1] I can do everything, or nothing, all hinging on one thing: being in Christ, or not.

I have a small confession: this kind of language — *through* Christ, *in* Christ — drives me a little crazy. Not because I don't believe it, but because I struggle to know what it means in practical terms.

I find this helps: abiding in Jesus is almost identical to doing things in Jesus' name. Over and over, the Bible tells us to pray, to ask, to heal, to speak, to worship, to have faith, to be baptized, to give thanks in the name of Jesus. Paul sums it up this way: "And whatever you do, whether in word or deed, *do it all* in the name of the Lord Jesus."[2]

The name of Jesus is his nature. It is his essence. It is his inmost self. When I speak or act in his name, I speak in his stead. If I'm to do that with integrity, not duplicity, then I must take pains to make sure my actions and words align with his actions and words, that there's a clear, unambiguous correspondence between the two. Otherwise, I usurp his authority. I use his name in vain. Otherwise, my body language gainsays my words, my tone betrays me. To be *in* Jesus is to act and speak in his name, which means it is to align my acting and speaking with who he is. It is to conform my life to his life.

I know there's more to it than this. There is the mysterious inworking and outworking of the Holy Spirit. But as we've seen elsewhere, life in the Spirit involves a likewise alignment of my thoughts, my words, my deeds with the heart of Jesus.

It's that alignment, the *in*-ness, that produces fruit that lasts.

ROOTS AND BRANCHES

This is where this theme of seasons is so hopeful, at least to me. Seasons mean that I can nurture fruit, God-glorifying fruit, even in those times when there's nothing to show for it. The result of all four seasons is, hopefully, fruit. But only one season bears it. The necessary conditions, in season and out, are root and branch.

Clarence is a good example. Clarence died full of years and short of breath. He never had any meat on him. He was a long sack of sharp bones. In his last years, his lungs grew shallow and swampy, and he toted a canister of oxygen, shouldered on his back like a papoose, with tubes running to other tubes that looped under his nose and fed him a constant stream of air. He showed up every Sunday for church. We tend to be noisy as a collective—drums abanging, guitars awailing, fiddles afiddling, and the like. Some older people run for cover, and once or twice I've thought of it myself. Clarence never did, nor did his lovely wife, Erna. They smiled always, complained never. They were simply happy to be in a church "with so many young people."

I only ever knew Clarence in this state, or thereabouts, and never knew him when he was hearty and deep-voiced. I'd missed him most of his life. Erna tells me it was a life of tireless vigor. He ran things, built things, went places, knew people.

But I met a man who wheezed and shuffled and stooped, and spoke in a voice like a ghost telling you a secret. His body was frail and shivery. Sometimes his breathing got so labored you could hear the gears clanking inside him, metallic things shaking loose. His eyes had that rheumy weepy look, like dew on a spiderweb.

But I panicked, personally, when it was clear Clarence was going to die.

He didn't panic. He was ready to die. He awoke every morning and wished out loud Jesus would come fetch him. Erna, though deeply sad, didn't panic. They'd had fifty-five good years and told each other every day that they loved each other. Their children, distraught in their own way, didn't panic: they all gathered to say goodbye, full of stories and gratitude, but no unfinished business.

Deaths don't come much cleaner.

But I panicked because Clarence, thin, bent, breathless Clarence, spent most of his days praying for the likes of me, and I wondered who God had lined up to step into this role once he was gone. In all the time Clarence attended the church where I pastor, he never *did* a thing other than show up, which by that time was a feat in itself. Oh, and I'm pretty sure he gave faithfully. But he didn't usher, teach Sunday school, evangelize anyone, disciple anyone, sit on any committees. We built in that time a shiny new building and set things up so anyone could pitch in, but Clarence never did. Erna, she bustled about with many tasks, and still does. But Clarence, he walked slowly in, slowly out, oxygen tank at his heels like a loyal poodle.

But the roots ran deep, and the branches stretched sturdy and long, and oh, the fruit. That man was clasped up to heaven, I think, in midstream of an intercession. He learned the secret of abiding. He practiced a tenacious dependency on Christ. So in the long winter of his life, when nothing else was growing, he experienced his greatest closeness with Jesus. (And with Erna, for that matter. He arranged for flowers and a love letter to be sent to her soon after he died, a kind of wink from heaven.)

The season Clarence found himself in late in life didn't matter. The roots and branches did. There was nothing spindly about spindly Clarence's relationship with Christ. An earthquake could not have uprooted what a lifetime of slow steady growing had created. And the fruit of that was, I think, the sweetest fruit of all, like grapes picked at the first kiss of frost: his life took the shape of a prayer. If prayer, as Revelation 5 tells us, is incense in the throne room of God, then Clarence's last days were pure fragrance.

I still haven't found whoever it is to whom God assigned Clarence's work after Clarence retired. On bad days, I wonder if God ever did make that reassignment. The upside of that is it impels me, freshly desperate, into a more tenacious dependency.

Which is what I'm learning to say to men like Lester (after I've fought down my temptation to harangue them). Haranguing can, sometimes but only for a time, get people to behave themselves. But the Pharisees were all about behaving themselves. And Jesus, by my reading, was seriously underwhelmed with that.

I'm learning to do as Jesus did with men like Lester, and men like myself, for that matter: invite them, invite myself, into deeper rootedness. That's what grows sturdy branches that, abracadabra,

CHAPTER 12

SEEKING

I recently had an epiphany: about half the Christians I know love the King but are almost oblivious to the fact that he rules a kingdom, and that he calls them, in season and out, to seek his kingdom and to advance it. They are intimate with the King, or at least say they are, but they're not about the King's business. And this: that about half the pagans I know have some inkling there's a kingdom—that life is meant to be other than it is, more joyful, hopeful, peaceful, fruitful, just; less segregated, paranoid, dismal, violent—and to varying degrees they are stumbling toward the kingdom, groping for it. But they are mostly oblivious to two things: first, that what they dream, however blurrily, is really the kingdom of God rather than some political utopia or socialist paradise or retooled version of the American dream, and second, that this kingdom has a King. They intuit the kingdom, and in some remarkable cases are doing the King's business, but they shun or remain aloof from or outright ignorant of or openly hostile to its King.

I think of Harold, a friend of mine. He's a big, tall, handsome First Nations man with long black hair that he shakes like a rock star's mane and with arms brocaded with tattoos. He dresses mostly in black leather. I call him the Indian Bono. He's a rough sort—his language, his ways. He always smells of cigarettes.

And he's a moviemaker. He's making several movies at the moment. One of them is about breaking racial barriers. It's about gangs. It's about the roots of violence and despair. I'm not sure, exactly, what it's all about, except that it's about the kingdom of God, and Harold seems the mostly likely man to make it.

And that's because Harold made another movie about the kingdom of God. It's called *Broken Down*, and it was a huge local blockbuster. It was screened the first night in a theater that seats 738, and hundreds of people were turned away at the door. They showed it the next night to a packed house, and ever since, Harold's been traveling to nearby communities who hear about his movie and want to see it, too.

Harold wouldn't tell you that *Broken Down* is about the kingdom of God. He made it as a documentary on the homeless in our community, the men and women who live in tents, in shipping containers, in stairwells, who scavenge bottles for enough money to buy beer and cigarettes. He made it to tell the story of drug addicts in Vancouver's east side, the pale and skittish junkies who'll do anything, *anything*, for their next fix.

But the story he ends up telling is the story of the humanity of people whose humanity most of us forgot a long time ago, when we were signing petitions to keep them off our streets and lobbying governments to step up policing their presence. He tells the story of the child who still lives inside each man, each woman, who still wishes they were home safe, with mom and dad. He tells the story of the longing in each person that someday, one day, maybe soon, they're going to turn this around, get off this stuff, get a job, start a family, reconcile with parents.

Maybe next month.

I wept through most of it. Especially, I wept for Lilly. Lilly's a First Nations girl, maybe twenty or twenty-two, nearly incoherent from her heroin addiction and her sexual trauma. She does whatever a man wants for as much as he's willing to pay, and only occasionally uses any of the money for food. She sleeps wherever she can scrounge up warmth and dryness, but that's a rare find in the back alleys of a rainy city. In the movie, Lilly rocks back and forth, looks away from the camera, mumbles, lamenting and cursing, laughs without joy. She shows the bruises on her legs, from beatings, from needles. She hates men and fears them. (Harold told me that when he approached her to ask if he could talk with her, she cowered and groveled, told him she'd do anything he wanted if he didn't hurt her.)

Why is this the kingdom? Well, in some ways it's the opposite. It's the desolation the Prince of Darkness has wreaked. It's an unrelenting display of his deceitfulness and ruthlessness and corrupt power. But here's why *Broken Down* is, at its heart, about the kingdom of God: because in the pin-drop quiet of that theater, as we watched Lilly, and Red and Brenda and others, all those watching, those who knew and loved Jesus and those who didn't, yearned for the world to be otherwise. And most of us, at least for the brief moment of our watching, were willing to do our part to make it otherwise. In us all a prayer took shape, however inarticulate: "Your kingdom come, your will be done, on earth as it is heaven."

Most of us walked away from that, shook it off, went back to signing petitions and buying big TVs on credit.

But for a moment, eternity intersected us, the kingdom brushed us, and we ached for a world of shalom.

The other movie Harold's making is about the teenage gangs in our city that make the streets a dangerous place on certain nights after midnight or so. People, innocent people out walking their dogs or getting off a bus or coming home from watching a movie at a friend's house, sometimes get accosted by eight, ten, a dozen kids with sticks and chains, and many of the victims end up in hospital. Some go straight to the morgue. A young boy, barely into his teens, recently got a whole mouthful of teeth kicked in just for being in the wrong place at the wrong time. Another young man, early twenties, the son of a good friend of mine, narrowly averted the same fate by offering, without resistance, the two hundred dollars he had in his wallet. He got away with only having his face spat upon like a cuspidor. Another young man, all of fifteen, got a knife in his belly and didn't live to see daylight.

Again, this doesn't seem like a ripe subject matter for the kingdom, except that every time one of these incidents happens, it shakes the whole town, if only a little, out of our apathy and lethargy, and makes us long for something different. In our worst moods, which hit us often, the difference we want is retaliation, vigilante forces, massive police strike-forces bearing down on the evildoers. We want higher, thicker walls on our gated communities. We want more surveillance cameras.

But in our best moods, the difference we seek is shalom, where everything is as God intends it to be: streets are wide open and safe; the generations bless each other, learn from one another; every tongue and tribe and nation is present and honored; no one lies and no one steals and no one lacks for anything.

We want shalom, though no one but me and a few of the crazies I hang around with call it that.

What Harold's been doing is interviewing gang members, especially the leaders. He's chasing a hunch that, beneath the bravado and bloodlust, nobody wants to live this way. That underneath the cockiness and brashness and cruelty is someone just wishing they mattered.

The way Harold puts it: "No kid when he's five dreams of beating heads in with baseball bats as a career. I'll tell you what puts them there: fear. They're afraid that it's this, or nothing."

And he openly wonders what the alternative to *this* and *nothing* might be.

That would be the kingdom.

TAKING HOLD OF THE KINGDOM

I'm captivated by the kingdom of God. Jesus came announcing it. He said it is near, and here, and within us. He said that the first and most urgent item on the agenda is to repent and then take hold, with both fists, of this kingdom, and not to look back for anything.

Somehow, somewhere, for some reason, we domesticated this. We latched on to the Born Again theme and made that Jesus' principal concern. That is important, no question, but Jesus said it only once, to one man, in a private conversation, and almost as a rebuke. What he said repeatedly, to all who had ears, in the most public way and as the essence of good news, was the kingdom is at hand. And you can join. Just believe and repent.

So all these years later, we're doing remedial work in theology and from pulpits, trying to make the good news good again. I'm not saying being born again isn't good news. It is, and of the highest order, to anyone, which is everyone, who needs to know that life can start fresh and be lived on God's terms. (This, in the root sense, is *hilarious*: a great merriment through an outpouring of grace secured by a costly appeasement.) The problem is that *born again* has become more of a slogan and a formula than the immodest proposal Jesus meant by it. He meant, preposterously, that anyone—anyone at all—can become a new creation. We've reduced that to anyone can go to heaven. No small thing, for sure, but Jesus had other things in mind as well. The remedial work, then, is to unleash the gospel in all its wildness, its topsy-turvy, inside-out, subversive force. It's to proclaim a gospel that has both this-world and the-world-to-come implications. If forced to pick, I'd take the world-to-come implications. But we're not forced to pick. We get both. We're invited to enter the kingdom *now*, and stay forever. The kingdom makes the gospel good news to the poor and the broken, to prisoners and prostitutes. And the kingdom makes the gospel bad news to Caesars and Rich Young Rulers. It disturbs the dreams of Pilates and wrecks the parties of Herods.

Jesus came announcing the kingdom.

A DIFFERENT KIND
OF SUCCESS

Maybe I'm claiming too much, but if Jesus wants us both to bear much fruit and to pursue the kingdom of God first—if to do one is, indeed, to do the other, and vice versa—then one of the best shifts we could make in our churches is to dismantle the model of spirituality that equates busyness with faithfulness and replace it with the simple idea that fruit alone denotes faithfulness, and fruit requires seasons. Seasons as a model for spirituality accords with kingdom life in ways that shine light on both the kingdom and the seasons.

Let me put it this way: we have adopted a view of the spiritual life and church growth that is a variation on free-market capitalism. In capitalism, the economy, in order to be strong, must constantly grow. A 3 percent shrinkage in the Gross Domestic Product for two or more quarters is a recession. (A 10 percent shrinkage is a depression.) Three percent. Governments fly into panic, banks stock the moat, corporations start to implode. It's wolves. It's bubonic plague. It's the sky falling.

Where else is constant growth an unequivocal sign of health? In human bodies, it's a sign of obesity or cancer. Yet we've applied the standard of constant growth to our churches and to our spiritual lives. We applaud every sign of getting bigger, and fret every sign of getting smaller.

This is bizarre.

And it's not the kingdom. The kingdom is mysterious, Jesus says. It's hidden as much as visible, underground as much as manifest. It's not something about which you can say, "Here it is," or, "There it is." It's within us, but it turns out it belongs to the least of these, and its secrets are revealed to children. Tax collectors and prostitutes are more likely to enter it than Pharisees and seminarians. It's hard to measure by the gauges and scales we use to measure, say, success. Like the Spirit, the kingdom moves where it wills, and no one knows where it comes from or where it's going.

Let me speak plainly. What I'm discovering is the kingdom's presence in places where all normal touchstones of success fail. Recently, I spent the day with my friends Pete and Marnie Mitchell. Pete and Marnie are Salvation Army church-planters working in two areas very inhospitable to the gospel—Vancouver's east side, an inner-city slum of flop houses, crack dens, brothels, watering holes, strip clubs. It has the highest incidence of heroin users in Canada, and the highest incidence of HIV/AIDS cases in North America. The other area they work is Vancouver's Commercial Drive district, which is about as close to ancient Corinth as a place can get—decadent, amoral, teeming with sexual license and vice.

When I visited, we started the day in a tumbledown walk-up on the east side. The stairwell smelled of urine. The room we met in had holes kicked into the walls. The light in the bathroom didn't work, which might have been a mercy. The furniture was moldering and tattered. Marnie taught at the War College, the in-house training the Salvation Army does for those who have signed on with the mission. Her topic was spiritual warfare, and the importance of making sure we are clean vessels in God's hands. The class was made up of a handful of students. Some were suburban kids who sought a life in Christ that would be more than attending youth group movie nights and playing games with Jell-O. But most of the students were people who, not long ago, were living on the streets, turning tricks, making deals, scoring drugs, hustling, busking, panhandling. They were, altogether, the most unlikely troop of warriors you've ever set eyes on. Their kingdom disguises were perfect, the camouflage flawless: no one anywhere would ever suspect them of subverting evil, putting the devil on the run.

Then we walked Commercial Drive. Here, the sex shops don't hide their wares behind tastefully frosted windows. It's all displayed like fruit in a market stall, like rugs and water jugs at a Turkish bazaar. And everywhere—in the windows of clothing stores and music stores, restaurants and coffee shops, plastered up and down power poles, emblazoned on the sides of bus-stop shelters—everywhere posters and handbills advertise all manner of strange erotic diversions. There's nothing you can't get down here.

And it's here, right in the middle of all this, that Pete and Marnie are planting a church. The audacity of that is stunning. The beauty of it is captivating. They call it Cross-Culture. What pluck!

Is it successful?

Yes.

No.

Depends what you mean. They witness miracles of transformation that most people rarely see. And they have their hearts torn in two more than most mortals can bear. They've learned not to despise the day of small things but to find the kingdom in faith sometimes no larger than a mustard seed. I don't think success is the right criterion for this.

They're bearing fruit, in season and out, and whether that's success or not doesn't matter. It's the kingdom.

Maybe you don't spend a lot of time with crack addicts and prostitutes. As my New Zealander friends like to say, "No worries": the kingdom is still in your midst. The kingdom shines through the mundane and the quotidian. The everlasting flits at the edges of the everyday. It can show up in a conversation you get into at the grocery checkout with the cashier who's just broken your eggs. It can happen with your child, who needs a little more attention just now than you think you have patience for. It can happen with a coworker who irritates you. It happens at those times, in those places, when something of God's goodness, kindness, justice — God's shalom — is chosen over the alternatives.

I listened last night to one of my favorite podcasts, *The Moth*, which features "true stories told live without notes." This one was a story by Ellie Lee on the wisdom of her father, Ming. Ming is a Chinese immigrant who succeeded in America by selling groceries to other Chinese immigrants at prices just mere percentage points above cost. One day, a nine-year-old boy came into Ming's store and began shoplifting. Ming followed the boy, who didn't know he was the store owner and so brazenly carried on with his thievery. Then the boy sat down, in the middle of the aisle, devouring the stolen food.

Ming watched. When it seemed the boy had eaten enough, he asked, "Are you full?"

"Almost."

"Where are your parents?"

"They work."

"Why aren't you at home?"

"There's no food there. I'm so hungry."

"My friend," Ming said, "I own this store. You have just stolen from me, and that's not a good thing. I don't want you doing that again, okay?"

The boy, frightened, nodded.

"What I'm asking is this: whenever you're hungry, you come right in here and tell me. I will make sure you have enough to eat."[1]

For years, Ming's little friend ate well.

The kingdom, right there, and from a man who, as far as I know, may not even know there's a King.

Just think what could happen on your watch.

TIME-IN 19

STUMBLING ON THE KINGDOM

Most of our evangelism consists of trying to get people into church. Good as that is (I firmly believe that the church is Christ's body, Christ's bride, God's family; therefore, flawed as the local church is, it makes no sense to say you love Jesus and God and not care about the church), it's not enough.

Jesus' standing invitation is not to come to church but to enter the kingdom. Most churches are bricolages of all kinds of things more than they are panoramas of the kingdom come in power. They're composed of shards of social agency, scraps of country club, skeins of gossip, and, scattered throughout, a handful of kingdom, unobtrusive as pieces of painted macaroni. Churches, even the best of them, contain the kingdom but can hardly be described as the fullness thereof.

And here's the funny thing: most of the world looks roughly the same: a bit of this and a bit of that and, scattered throughout, the kingdom, quiet and unobtrusive, easily missed.

I suggest our evangelism remain inviting people to church. But I suggest we also include inviting people into the kingdom. And the great thing is, though your neighbor or coworker may right now have zero interest in coming to your church, she already may be stumbling around in the kingdom.

In my town, non-church people care about the homeless, single mothers, the high level of malnutrition and illiteracy among low-income families, the problem of gangs, the enduring legacy of racial animosity, and a hundred other things. I chaired a community committee recently that helped gather funds and create a vision to refit a school bus to take learning resources to Native reservations. As I write this, it's at one of the most remote and impoverished reservations in the province.

God cares about all this. His kingdom of shalom speaks to all this.

What I've found is that an equally effective way to help people meet Jesus is to help them see that, though they haven't been in church in years, they've been crisscrossing the kingdom on a daily basis.

Just as people can sit in church for months, maybe years, and miss Jesus, they can be in the kingdom for a long time and miss him too.

Which is where you come in. You likely know a person or two who's not ready to come to your church. But they're already brushing up against the kingdom. Maybe God put you beside them to help them find the King.

CHAPTER 13

WALKING
(IN THE LIGHT)

Last summer, two friends and I went for a walk that became a hike that became a climb. The trail started at one friend's house, crossed a road, skirted a park, meandered up a gentle slope. We entered a forest, dense and coastal, canopied with cedar and fir, bedded with salal and fern. It was a hot sky, but those trees sifted sunlight down to cool shade, and the trail, crisscrossing the hill's wide flank, climbed so gradually, so innocently, that we talked without breaking stride or sweat or the rhythm of our breathing. And then, abruptly, the trail veered sharply and went straight up. The trail widened here as well, and faced south, so that the sun fell on it, and us, with cruel and mocking triumph. As we walked, then hiked, then climbed, my body grew heavy and my breath grew short. Sweat thickened on my neck and back. My legs burned.

And then Rob, one of my friends, told me about walking lockstep.

Rob had led several youth snow camps. Snow camps take place in wintertime and require steep and long climbs above a mountain's treeline, into its crevices of ice, up to its narrow ledges of rock, its jagged ridges of snow, its pinnacles, where cunning winds try to push you from dizzying heights. Somewhere up there, you make camp and endure for three days, battling frostbite and hypothermia, risking long free falls to your death. It is supposed to be fun.

It was on one of these trips that Rob learned, from an experienced climber, how to walk lockstep. The man who taught him was ten years older and forty pounds heavier than he was. Rob ran two or three miles daily, played squash several times a week, ate healthy food in moderate portions. But the climb brutalized him and barely scathed the other man. So Rob asked him how he was managing to stay fresh.

Walking lockstep, the man told him. It's a technique that forces your weight onto your bones. It has the added benefit of slowing you down, so that you conserve energy and even out your breathing.

And it's simple.

You just straighten out your downward leg an extra inch or so on every step. You lock, or almost so, your knee. This, as I said, slows you down a pinch and lets you catch your breath. But the greater benefit is it shifts your body's girth and heft from muscle to bone. You make your skeleton carry you.

Rob explained this, and I tried it: immediately my breath settled, my muscles relaxed, and the strain of climbing eased.

I reached the top refreshed, not exhausted.

LOCKSTEP IN THE SPIRIT

Is there a spiritual equivalent to walking lockstep? Is there some simple way to carry ourselves that might dramatically increase our spiritual strength and endurance? That would allow us to go farther up, deeper in? To arrive refreshed, not exhausted?

The answer is obvious, though not easy. The spiritual equivalent to walking lockstep is walking in the Spirit. It's to learn the art of what Paul describes to the Colossians: "I labor, struggling with all his energy, which so powerfully works in me."[1] The strangeness of kingdom life is that it's both easy and arduous, agonizing and invigorating. It's a labor and a struggle, but also a tapping of a powerful energy not our own. Paul lays out the principle behind this easy arduousness: "Since we live by the Spirit, let us keep in step with the Spirit."[2] This would be the same Spirit Jesus talks about: windlike, blowing wherever he pleases, unseen but deeply felt. The Spirit is capable of everything from cooling our hot heads to plucking and flinging our whole houses skyward. One day he's a breeze, the next a typhoon.

Just keep in step.

But how?

That is a variation on the very question Jesus was once asked by Nicodemus, a man of the Pharisee sect. He comes to Jesus at night for a theological tête-à-tête.[3] Jesus says to him, "The wind blows wherever it pleases. You hear its sound, but you cannot tell where it comes from or where it is going. So it is with everyone born of the Spirit."

Nicodemus responds, "How can this be?"[4]

Of course, Nicodemus isn't asking "how" in the way I am. He means, to paraphrase, "What on earth are you talking about? I can't make head or tail out of this born-again stuff, this Spirit and water and wind talk. Speak plainly."

Jesus rebukes Nicodemus for his lack of understanding; he's supposed to be "Israel's teacher," capable of handling heaven's mysteries, yet here is fumbling earth's rudiments.

But frankly, I'm glad he asked. Because Jesus' teaching puzzles me too, and I'm happy a literal-minded, maybe slow-witted man was stumped enough to tease from Jesus an explanation of sorts. In that explanation, Jesus not only answers Nicodemus's question—How can this *be*?—but he answers mine as well—How do we *do* this?

How can this *be*?

This can be, Jesus says, only through the Son of Man, the one who has gone into heaven and come from heaven: when Jesus, the Son of Man, is lifted up, *everyone who believes* in him may have eternal life.[5] Jesus connects his being lifted up with the episode in Numbers 21, where the Israelites were spared certain death from snake bites when Moses lifted a symbol of a snake on a pole and the stricken gazed upon it. Jesus' cryptic remarks here—being lifted up, snakes on poles in deserts—refer to his death on a cross, something which John and, indeed, Jesus make explicit elsewhere.[6] So the mystery of being born of the Spirit is accomplished when the Son of Man is lifted up. In that moment, he becomes sin *for* us, and when we turn to him, sin *in* us loses its power. Its venom is drawn. At that moment, something breaks in hell, and something opens in heaven, and the impossible becomes possible: old and young, men and women, girls and boys, Africans and Asians and Caucasians and Latinos and Aboriginals, the rich and the poor—anyone anywhere anytime can start life anew.

You can be born again.

But how can we *do* this? That's my question: how do we, once we're born of the Spirit, move like the Spirit? "The wind blows wherever it pleases. You hear its sound, but you cannot tell where it comes from or where it is going. So it is with everyone born of the Spirit."

So it is with everyone who's born again.

Everyone.

Now I'm stumped. I've been a pastor for twenty years, in two congregations. The churches I've served, both of them, and the many more I've visited, have been made up of the usual culprits: quirky saints, limping sinners, hungry pilgrims, hair-splitting dogmatists, shout-at-the-devil charismatics. They've been a ragtag of mystics and sticklers, zealots and tax collectors, recovering addicts, recovering fundamentalists, recovering liberals. I've had those who suspect my every word and move, and those who see in the same divine oracle, sacred gesture.

But few evoke the wind. Few elicit the response, "Ah, what a strange and wondrous breeze blows there. I hear it, I'm just not sure where it comes from or where it's going."

And those who do, who evoke the wind, I often dismiss as, umm, questionable. Unstable. Flaky. I don't invite them to sit on committees. I don't recruit them for key leadership posts. I don't even, usually, let them hand out bulletins. Because, well, I don't know where they've come from. I don't know where they're going. They seem, in fact, to go wherever they please, and I like people with a little more "accountability structure" than that.

How does Jesus intend for us to keep in lockstep with a windlike Spirit? That is, I think, the question Jesus answers implicitly in what he says next.[7]

In a phrase: live in the light.

LIGHT

CHOOSING TO LIVE IN THE LIGHT

Jesus says he came as a sign of God's love, and that love radiates. It's light. "Light," Jesus says, "has come into the world." This light he equates with truth. This light implies a judgment—a verdict, Jesus calls it. A rendering of final decision, condemnation or pardon. So this light calls for response. It calls for faith—choosing to believe in Jesus, to put your full weight in the gift of God—and it calls for facing up—choosing to come into the light, to bring your whole self into the wide searching brightness of it.

The light exposes, and the light heals. It's the healing, the promise of it, that draws some in. And it's the exposing, the threat of it, that keeps most at bay, that, indeed, keeps most *loving* the darkness.

To love the darkness. It's a strong word, love. In the Greek, it's none other than the word John made famous, *agapao*. It's the same word he uses in John 3:16 to describe God's self-giving, sacrificial love for us—"For God so loved [*agapao*] the world that he gave his one and only Son, that whoever believes in him shall not perish but have eternal life." God loves us this way, unconditionally, against all odds, despite the pain.

And we love darkness the same: unconditionally, against all odds, despite the pain. It's what's kept me, even as a pastor, from always bringing all I am into the Light—the fear that *this* sin, *this* grievance, *this* grudge, *this* crimp in my soul, will hurt more to fix than to keep.

This is the condemnation, Jesus says: light has come to you, but you won't come to it. Staying where you are when something else, something infinitely better, is offered, is its own condemnation. You can't get well in the dark. You doom yourself by trying. But we try anyhow. The perpetual delusion of humanity is thinking we're better off hiding than confessing, avoiding rather than facing, clinging to our sickness instead of taking the remedy that's freely given and readily available.

Keeping in step with the Spirit, windlike as he is, is (at least) about walking in the light, and living there.

I believe that in every circumstance, there's light and dark. There is truth and there is untruth. There's the leading of the Spirit, and there are the temptations of the flesh. When I drive, or speak with someone, or look at a woman, or spend money—everywhere, in everything, there's light and dark.

Take driving, for instance. This has been a battlefield for me since before I drove, when my father treated every trip as a chariot race. Other cars with other drivers were our rivals. I sat long hours in the back seat as he fumed and cursed behind the wheel, and that stamped me deeply. I often felt tremendous irritation with him—I can't remember once ever feeling admiration for how he drove—but somehow I failed to convert my irritation into a resolve to be otherwise. I mimicked him down to the smallest detail, and even magnified his example.

When I became a man, I did not put away childish things, not in this matter. I had, as though genetically bestowed, a lead foot. I had a quick temper. I had a range of gestures, reserved and specially cultivated only for behind the wheel. The minute I sat there, the world became a contest for road space, right of way, lane mergers. The world was populated with rivals and obstacles.

This is not, as you can see, an edifying story, especially since my behavior behind the wheel persisted for many years past my conversion, past my call to ministry, past the birth of my three children, past many milestones that should have killed it in its tracks. What finally brought me to my senses was, a few years back, a rapidly approaching date: my own son's sixteenth birthday. I realized he'd grown up under the shadow of my poor example, and suddenly I was deeply repentant and genuinely desperate to change.

So I did.

And it was easier than I thought. I applied to driving what I had discovered about the rest of life: there is a way to please God in each and every moment, and to receive the strength of God for just such a thing. And there is a way to disappoint God in each and every situation—by our actions, words, thoughts, attitudes—and to refuse his strength to do otherwise. With driving, I was consistently and willfully forgetting and rejecting virtually every time I sat behind a wheel what I was consistently and willfully remembering and embracing virtually everywhere else. My father set other poor examples for me (and, for the record, many good ones) that I learned not to imitate. His example of poor driving, almost alone among the other poor examples he set, had me in its grip. Which is another way of saying that this wasn't his problem. It was all mine.

I had been driving, and driving poorly, for almost thirty years. I did it right up until the day I resolved to walk in the light—and drive in the light, too. That was all it took.

So here's how it works. I'm coming to an intersection. There are more cars, I can see, than will get through at the next light. My well-ingrained habit is to fume, mutter, feel a vague sense of blame toward the driver immediately in front of me. This irritates my wife and children (when they're with me), dishonors God (who's Lord of time), erodes my health, wastes the moment, and doesn't do a single thing to speed things up—in fact, it heightens my sense of delay.

I chose the darkness.

Same red light, same lineup. This time, I choose the light. If I have passengers, I relish the moment for more conversation. If I'm alone, I "redeem the time": talk to God, ponder a problem, listen more intently to the teaching CD I have in, sing along more lustily with the music CD I'm listening to. And here's where it gets really subversive: I pray for and bless the driver in front of me.

It's where the Spirit's moving, and I just try to keep up, follow the light while I wait for the light.

LIGHT WAXES AND WANES

You're wondering, maybe, what any of this has to do with seasons. Not much, yet maybe everything. One of the most distinctive characteristics about the seasons, where I live, is the varying duration of light season to season, and the varying quality of it. The dead of winter has a very short day, and high summer a very long one. In the dead of winter, the light is brooding and grey or thin and pallid. In high summer, the light is tapestry-like, richly hued, dense with shadows. And between the two, winter and summer, each week rings yet another change in the light's duration and intensity.

I think this observation can be applied, almost directly, to the seasons of the heart. Season to season, light waxes and wanes. It thins and thickens, lengthens and shortens. In Canada, sunlight in winter is a rare bird, skittish and shy, easily put to flight, and so we crave it, hunt it, hold it tightly to ourselves whenever we lay hold of it; we find the trapezoidal patches of sunlight that fall slantwise through our windows, the beams of dusty gold that splash up against the far wall, and stretch out in them like felines. But in summer, light is so profuse, so predatory, so prolonged, we often avoid it: seek shade, wear wide-brimmed hats, sport sunglasses, duck into cool dark rooms, skulk along the shadow sides of buildings.

In spiritual matters, I think the observation holds true: we are more apt to seek the light in hard seasons than easy ones. I've observed in another book that the famous scene where Peter says to Christ, "Depart from me, Lord, for I am a sinful man!" may be a true moment of Isaiah-like revelation, when Peter sees the sordidness and shabbiness of his own life in light of Christ's glory; but it might just be an evasion ploy, a diversionary tactic, a rash outburst to buy himself some time. After all, Peter says those words while standing knee-deep in fish. The catch of a lifetime. His biggest windfall ever. And I think he had an inkling—maybe it was sheer gut feeling, or it was some wild glint he saw in Jesus' eye—that Jesus had no intention of letting him enjoy it. It was a test. Jesus was about to up the ante, to find out if Peter loved him more than *these*. "Follow me," Jesus says. And he means *now*.

That boatful of fish would have cashed out nicely. It would have paid a lot of bills, bought a lot of upgrades, provided a few luxuries. It would have made Peter's hardscrabble existence not so hard and scrabbly. Summer's about to break. "Depart from me, Lord." With the prospect of an easy season right under his nose, and with the alternative that Jesus is about to offer, the life of a holy vagabond, Peter's first instinct is to dodge the light.

Compare that with the companion story in John 21, where the risen Christ appears on a beach across from where Peter and his crew are fishing. It's been a long night, and unproductive. Jesus hollers from the shore a fishing tip: cast your net on the other side. Maybe he can see, from his angle of vision, some sign that bodes fish, a ruffle on the lake's surface, a gleam just beneath it. Or maybe he just *knows*. Anyhow, they do as he says, and once more the catch is on. This time Peter acts in the opposite way of last time: he strips, plunges into the water (he tried walking atop that lake once, with mixed results), and comes up panting and dripping, hoping with everything in him that Jesus will reissue the call, the hard call to follow him.

Jesus does not disappoint.

Why such a different reaction this time around?

The season Peter's been in. Those three denials, and all that surrounded them—the arrest, the trial, the beating, the *Via Dolorosa*, Golgotha, the cross, the death—have plunged him hard and fast into winter. Life has never been darker for him. Peter knows this time that the fish are not for keeping. "Do you love me more than these?" He's so starved for the light, so overjoyed that Christ would shine his face upon him again, that he's the first to show up.

TURNING TOWARD THE LIGHT

Go back to the early chapters of John's gospel. The light has come into the world, John says, and his life is the light of all people; Christ is the true light that gives light to every man, every woman, every everyone. That's chapter 1. Chapter 3 picks up the theme: light has come into the world, but many people do not come into the light. John says that's because their deeds are evil. They fear exposure.

But John also equates light with three other things: truth, grace, and the Holy Spirit. And in other places, John further explains those terms: truth is discovered through obedience.[8] Grace is an uncommon word in John's writing,[9] but there's no reason to think he didn't use it in a way similar to Paul: divine power that liberates us to live in and for God, no longer defeated or enslaved by sin. The Spirit is at work in the world to bring conviction concerning sin, righteousness, and judgment.[10]

When I put all that together, I arrive here: that every gesture toward truth, every twinge of genuine conviction, every flicker of grace is a turn toward light. Likewise, every distortion or suppression of truth, every act of hardening one's heart against conviction, every act of yielding to sin is a turn toward darkness. "This is the message we have heard from Him and announce to you," John says, "that God is Light, and in Him there is no darkness at all. If we say that we have fellowship with Him and yet walk in the darkness, we lie and do not practice the truth; but if we walk in the Light as He Himself is in the Light, we have fellowship with one another, and the blood of Jesus His Son cleanses us from all sin."[11] John's first letter is complicated. To oversimplify it for clarity's sake, the principal sin he speaks about is a denial of Christ's incarnation — that Jesus has come in the flesh — and the chief symptom of that denial is a failure to love the person right in front of us. That's why when we walk in light, we have fellowship with God and, in turn, "fellowship with one another."

I know the imperative of love. I know its specific weight, its texture in my hand, its tug on my shirtsleeve. I know that my chronic impatience is defiance of that imperative. I know that the times I'm prideful, lustful, envious, hoarding, and all the other many ways I enjoy being miserable, I'm refusing the way of love.

And in each case, I'm choosing darkness over light.

We're most light starved, and so most hungry for the light, in winter, or in any grey and difficult season. It's why Jesus said some of the most sinful people are closer to the kingdom of God than some of the most righteous: the adversity of their lives, the damage they've done to self and others, the clear evidence that their lives aren't working on their own terms make them (at least some of them) desperate for a way out. Their deeds are evil, but it makes them long for daylight.

Zacchaeus, that wee little man, is a perfect example. His story is told only by Luke, lover of the misfit. Zacchaeus has lived, we gather, most his life in the dark. He was a tax collector, which in the eyes of his community made him a collaborator with evil, a thief and predator and traitor. But when Jesus, the light that had come into the world, came to his town of Jericho, Zacchaeus couldn't come into the light faster. He wanted to stare straight at the sun. He climbed a sycamore tree to compensate for his runty stature so that noth-

If you want to steward every season and derive the full benefit of each, give thanks *in* all things, and give thanks *for* all things. Train yourself in this. It doesn't mean pretending everything in your life is good. It means trusting God, trusting him always, that he is able and willing to work all things, even the worst things, together for good.

Start small, if you must. As Anne Lamott says, when you're learning to forgive, you don't start with the Nazis. Well, when you're learning to give thanks, you don't start with the Nazis either, or 9/11, or global warming, or the AIDS/HIV epidemic, or the war in whatever part of the world war rages. Start with the things you can genuinely be thankful for, but which you may take for granted. Like your shoes. Your clothes. A car that, at least most of the time, runs. A fridge that, at a minimum, keeps the milk cold. And thank him for the milk, for that matter. And thank him for a device—almost for certain one of these is mere steps from you as you read this—that with the simple flick of your wrist gushes clean water, hot or cold, or a lovely mingling of the two. Thank him for your church. Thank him for your neighbors—yes, even *that* one, who at least, and without even trying, has deepened your prayer life. Thank God for your mother. And your mother-in-law. Thank him for green grass and blue skies and pizza and good coffee, and for any friend who knows you well and still likes you. Thank him that you can thank him— that you have sufficient breath and sanity, and that he's the kind of God who listens. The list of things to be thankful for is very long.

Make a daily practice of that, and what will happen is you will start to see the world differently. More light. More of your life will look and feel like pure gift—the clouds that bring the rain, the wind that sweeps the clouds, the cat that wakens the wolf inside your dog, who in turn wakens the lion inside the cat, the food you ate today, the step machine that helps you burn the calories from the food, the way your wife arches her eyebrows at you in playful rebuke, the semi-interesting sermon your pastor preached last week, the pew you sat on to hear it.

Gifts, all of them.

And once your world gets bigger, more light-saturated, it will become easier to thank God for things that do not look or feel like gifts: sicknesses and recessions and wintertime and sitting in a prison with a bleeding back.

You might get so good at this, even then, even there, you'll sing. Never know who might be listening.

TIME-IN 21

WHAT'S THE WORST THAT CAN HAPPEN TO YOU?

My wife's uncle had a poster in his house. It read:

What's the Worst That Can Happen to You?
If you party all the time, what's the worst that can happen to you?
You might live, or you might die.
If you live, there's nothing to worry about.
If you die, what's the worst that can happen to you?
You might go to heaven, or you might go to hell.
If you go to heaven, there's nothing to worry about.
If you go to hell, you'll be so [insert expletive] busy partying with all your friends, there'll be nothing to worry about.

Funny.

Sort of.

Not.

Jesus said, "Do not be afraid of those who kill the body but cannot kill the soul. Rather, be afraid of the One who can destroy both soul and body in hell."[16] I have a friend who paraphrases it this way: "Fear the one who, when you're dead, ain't done with you yet."

The worst that can happen to you is to die without Christ. It's to suffer what the book of Revelation calls the "second death."[17] That's the one to be avoided. That's the soul-destroying death.

I keep thinking about Paul and Silas in that prison cell. I keep asking myself if I believe the good news and the bad news deeply enough that I would care at all about that jailer and those prisoners. I wonder if I really believe that the worst thing that can happen to you is the second death, that it is so horrific that I'd be willing to go to impossible lengths in order for some to be saved.

I'm asking here a personal question and also a much larger one: is the diminishing confidence we seem to have in the good news related to the lack of conviction we seem to have about the bad news?

Do I believe in hell as much as in heaven?

We're not living in an era or a culture that nurtures a belief in either heaven or hell. And certainly not the latter. Yet the reality of hell (and heaven) is clearly part of Jesus' teaching. It's been core church doctrine throughout history. And it powerfully motivates evangelism. God wants us to join him in a desperate rescue mission.

This may seem an odd exercise, but spend some time thinking about hell. Thinking about what it means to have a destroyed soul (and still be conscious). What it means to be eternally separated from God.

Salvation gets people to heaven. Just as important, it spares them from going to hell.

That might be worth singing in a prison cell for.

*** Light

In C. S. Lewis's *The Voyage of the Dawntreader*, a company of adventurers makes a journey to World's End, where the Kingdom of Aslan begins. The closer they get, the more intense the light becomes. Yet as they drink from the ocean, which is not salty but sweet, and hearty as a meal, its properties strengthen their eyes so that, though the light is increasingly brilliant, it doesn't hurt them. "They could look straight up at the sun and without blinking. They could see more light than they had ever seen before. And the deck and the sail and their own faces and bodies became brighter and every rope shone. And next morning, when the sun rose, now five or six times its old size, they stared hard into it and could see the very feathers of the birds that came flying from it."[18]

Lewis must have been thinking of the writings of the apostle John, which I've leaned on almost exclusively in this chapter. John wrote a gospel and three epistles in which he talks much about the Light. And he also wrote the final book of the Bible, Revelation. His final vision is of the New Jerusalem, the city on a hill—in fact, on a mountain. "The kingdom of the world has become the kingdom of our Lord and of his Christ."[19] Here's what John sees: "The city does not need the sun or the moon to shine on it, for the glory of God gives it light, and the Lamb is its lamp. The nations will walk by its light.... On no day will its gates ever be shut, for there will be no night there."[20]

That's a lot of light. And how blessed we are that even now we walk by it. And one day, we'll look full into it and not blink.

CHAPTER 14

BEING
(A TREE)

I've been thinking a lot about trees, and reading a little about them, too. I've lived with trees my entire life and missed them most of the same—though I derive small comfort from biologist Colin Tudge, who probably knows more about trees than anybody living, and whose definition of a tree is "a big plant with a stick up the middle."[1] That's about all I know, even though I live in a province world-renowned for its trees, especially its towering Douglas firs and thick-girthed coastal cedars. The sale of timber from our forests is one of our primary sources of wealth, and when Asians or Americans aren't buying, or aren't paying what we're asking, things get lean around here.

And I live in a part of that province—southern, coastal, temperate —where trees grow big fast. A combination of things makes it so. It rains torrentially for weeks at a time, but when the sun comes out it gets right down to business. There are mountains all around, and they hold, fall to spring, dense snow packs on their crowny heights, and then send, spring to fall, meltwater down their sides, down into streams, into rivers and lakes, out to ocean, so that few trees have to work very hard to find rich moist soil to bed down in. Temperatures are mild all year round, though usually every winter serves up one week of biting cold that kills nasty insects that otherwise might burrow under the bark and stunt or kill a tree's growth.

When I first moved here, I had little money and a yard bereft of vegetation. I bought sixty dollars worth of mail-order plants, including a maple tree that, in the catalog photo, reached to the sky and stretched to the horizon, and that all summer cast a vast canopy of shade and each autumn massed with flaming red leaves, each as big as a kite. It cost me $1.99, plus shipping and handling, so I could hardly believe my good luck.

The day the delivery truck pulled up to deliver my order—a big moving van with a wide and long box trailer—I was giddy with anticipation. I signed the delivery order, and the delivery man solemnly rolled up the door on the back of his trailer to, well, deliver my instant garden that would, in turn, deliver me from the shame of my yard's nakedness. I waited for him to deliver, to pull down the ramp so he could forklift out my pallets of trees and shrubs and ask, "Where should I put 'em all?"

This didn't happen.

He simply handed me a packet, a cardboard oblong box about two feet by six inches, and light as bubble wrap, which it was mostly full of. Inside were several tiny boxes, labeled with their contents. The contents, stapled to the inside of each box, consisted of plastic bags with a fistful of black earth in each and, poking up from this, a frail and curling sprout. I had about ten of these boxes, and then one thing else: my maple tree. That was different. That was a stick. It was about eight inches long, branchless, with a thin skein of roots bundled in a small purse of burlap and held together with an elastic band.

I was crushingly disappointed. I was sorely humiliated. I felt like sending the whole thing back. I thought I was the laughingstock of whatever shell company existed out there to take my hard-earned money and send me this ridiculous and worthless pile of junk in exchange. I felt like Jack must have when he sold the cow for magic beans, only to be told by his mother that he'd been duped and now they'd starve for his folly.

But just like Jack, I planted it anyhow.

And I could not have been more surprised than Jack when, not overnight, but soon enough, those sprouts grew into flourishing shrubs and perennials that, if I do not dutifully hack them back each spring, long ago would have taken over my entire yard.

Most amazing was the maple tree. When I got it, I cut out a little graft of lawn in my front yard and planted the eight-inch stick there.

ties; in the second, the death of a friend, Carol, that plunged me into a climate that was soul-withering and created a sense of futility in the very idea of priorities.

I'm not exactly sure why similar seasons produced dramatically different growth rates. Indeed, I'm disturbed by it. Looking back on both years, I note some differences between them that partially explain why pain was a good environment in one instance, almost inhospitable in another.

One difference was that in 1997, I was just launching my writing career. That was exhilarating—the much-dreamed-of, little-expected moment when someone was actually going to pay me to write a book and was going to go to all the trouble themselves to make it snazzy and profitable. It sounds petty and vain—it *is* petty and vain—to be so easily pleased, but there it is. All writers I know, despite their protests to the contrary, long to be published and to sell well, and not for all the right motives, either. At any rate, in 1997, I was on the cusp of all that, so my pain had a happy companion, a circumstance that could usually cheer me just by thinking about it.

In 2006, I was writing my fifth book (this is my sixth), and it met with disappointing sales, and though I didn't know that at the time—that it would disappoint—I knew in my bones, and didn't much care. Writing a fifth book—and a sixth, if you want the truth—is much like having a fifth (or sixth) child (I imagine): you love it, are committed to it, but you're so very, very tired. And in 1997, we were just moving into a season of rapid growth at the church where I pastor, and making plans to build a bigger building. Again, it sounds petty and vain, and likely is, but that pleased me, too. But in 2006, the church where I pastor—same church—was carrying a cumbersome debt for the building we built. And, besides that, I had a lot of people unhappy with me. I remember (vaguely) an elders meeting in which one of the elders looked at me, told me not to take his next remarks personally, then told me he felt our church was adrift in a fog, going nowhere and likely to end up on the rocks.

And all I thought was, "Yeah. So. Tell me something I don't know."

So the climate was different. The crisis of 1997, in retrospect, seemed a patch of wild cold weather, an unseasonal ice storm, in

TIME-IN 22

GROWTH RINGS

Get a piece of paper out (or find a fresh page in your journal). Write down a chronology of your life, starting with birth and moving to this very day. But write it as a series of concentric circles, like the cross-cut of a tree stump. Birth is the core, or pith. Each ring around the core is an "era" of life—childhood, adolescence, early adulthood, and so on. Note as points between the rings of the eras the life-shaping events that happened within that era—when someone close to you died, or you first moved out, or the dates when you had children, that sort of thing. Many of those life-shaping events will signal for you the beginning of a new era, which you will mark by a new circle. And then (and I realize you may have to use several pieces of paper to get this right) estimate the thickness of each ring, using thickness to denote how much you grew spiritually and emotionally in that era.

My tree rings look like this:

Dendrachronology for Mark Buchanan

I've divided my life into thirteen eras, from birth (June 3, 1960) to the present. The eras are as follows:

1 Early childhood in Calgary (1960–65)—happy, healthy.

2 Midchildhood in Kamloops (1965–67)—same.

3 Childhood to early adolescence in Prince George (1967–72)—same.

4 Midadolescence in Prince George (1972–75)—dark, lonely, frightening.

5 Late adolescence in Vancouver (1975–78)—feels like new life; God hunger awakens.

6 Early adulthood in Vancouver (1978–81)—crisis and confusion.

7 Adulthood in Vancouver (1981–89)—come to faith; marry; get two degrees.

8 Begin pastoring in Vernon (1989–90)—crisis.

9 Continue pastoring in Vernon (1990–95)—begin to go deep in my faith.

10 Move to Duncan to pastor (1995–96)—crisis.

11 Continue to pastor in Duncan (1996–2005)—struggles and joys.

12 Carol's sickness and death in Duncan (2005–2007)—crisis.

13 Recovery and new season of growth (2007–present).

Which areas are thickest, and which thinnest? Can you correlate that at all with that era's defining events? Can you remember what your relationship with God was like in each era? Who was there for you? What got you through the thin eras? What do you long for the most from the thick eras?

Glean any insights that might help you.

what otherwise was shaping up to be a lovely spring and long hot summer. The crisis of 2006, in retrospect (of which, at this juncture, is brief), seemed a prelude to a long dark winter, like waking up one day in September to a chill in the air that bodes storm, and you know summer is decisively over and autumn will be short.

What's your dendrachronology?

If someone took a core sample of your soul, which years would have a thick girth of meatiness, which a papery thinness? It's not a bad exercise to take stock of that. I learned a few valuable lessons comparing those two years—lessons about the nature of pain, and the power of circumstances. But the best lesson I derived from my reflection is the lesson of sustainability. It's so important, the next chapter's devoted to it.

CHAPTER 15

SUSTAINING

Everyone who cares about natural resources—air, soil, water, forests, fish stock, and the like—concerns themselves with sustainability. In logging, you can't log faster than the forests can regrow, even if that means we plant most of the new trees ourselves. In fishing, you can't fish more than the fish can spawn, even if that means we create spawning plants. And so on. So where I live, heavily dependent on timber and wild salmon, every summer, armies of hale young men and women clamber up the steep sides of mountains freshly logged, plugging tree seedlings in earth they just spiked to make a socket. They get paid per seedling, so the game is to plant whole forests in a day, and the next day do it again. And along many rivers are fish plants where fry are hatched, grown to a few inches, and released into the waters to replenish the fish stock that trawlers and seiners have pulled out to put fresh on meat counters and, canned, on grocery shelves.

They're sustaining what we have so that, the theory goes, there will be something left—a net equivalent—for the next generation, and the one after that. And there's more. In those two examples, forestry and fishing, and many others I could use, the lack of sustainability doesn't just mean we'll have less timber and salmon for the next generation. Because deforestation causes collateral damage—soil erosion, the flourishing of nonindigenous plants, the loss of habitat for wildlife, the alteration of weather patterns, and more—its destructive effects are cumulative. Likewise for depleted salmon stocks—it affects, at minimum, the welfare of other creatures—orcas, bears, eagles—who depend on salmon for food.

A lot depends on sustainability.

I began to ask myself, What is my plan for sustainability in my spiritual life? If some seasons deplete me—if they clear-cut the hillside, empty the ocean—what can I do to begin regrowth?

A PSALM I LIFE

My own sustainability is grounded in a Psalm 1 life:

> Blessed are those
>> who do not walk in step with the wicked
>> or stand in the way that sinners take
>> or sit in the company of mockers,
> but who delight in the law of the LORD
>> and meditate on his law day and night.
> They are like a tree planted by streams of water,
>> which yields its fruit in season
>> and whose leaf does not wither—
>> whatever they do prospers.
> Not so the wicked!
>> They are like chaff
>> that the wind blows away.
> Therefore the wicked will not stand in the judgment,
>> nor sinners in the assembly of the righteous.
> For the LORD watches over the way of the righteous,
>> but the way of the wicked will be destroyed.
>
> —TNIV

Old Testament scholar Bruce Waltke calls this the gateway of the Psalms. It is not merely the first psalm but the entire Psalter's plinth and portal, its bedrock and keyhole: it anticipates and summarizes the other 149 psalms. Psalm 1 works as a kind of interpretive grid for everything that follows. If the Psalms, in sum and substance, train us how to serve and love a holy God (just as Proverbs, in sum and substance, trains us how to serve and love fallen people), Psalm 1 provides basic orientation. If the Psalms, in sum and substance, teach us how to pray, to shape our grief and rage and joy and loneliness, and everything else besides, into holy communion, then Psalm 1 lays the foundation. Miss this, you'll get it elsewhere, only it will take longer. Grasp this, you'll have the field guide for identifying what the rest of the Psalms show in vivid detail.

Psalm 1 is about choosing where to take root. That's a choice no actual tree gets: in the wild, wherever a tree takes root is decided by a series of serendipitous events—the way the wind is blowing the day the tree casts *that* seed, the distance the bird flies who eats it, the quality of the soil its stool falls upon. And under cultivation, wherever a tree is rooted is decided by the gardener.

But we're not trees. We're simply *like* trees. So we have the privilege and the responsibility to choose where we set our roots. The epigraph of this book is a stanza of a poem, "The Sun," by David Whyte:

> Sometimes reading
> ... I look out
> at everything
> growing so wild
> and faithfully beneath
> the sky
> and wonder
> why we are the one
> terrible
> part of creation
> privileged
> to refuse our flowering

"The one terrible part of creation privileged to refuse our flowering." That line haunts me.

Our "privileged refusal" stems from a basic choice about where we set our roots. Psalm 1 presents two contrasting choices: draw our nourishment from "the wicked"—the world—or draw it from the "law"—the Word. Of course, there are many gradations between these stark choices. (Psalm 1 tacitly acknowledges this, with its imagery of *walking* in the counsel of the wicked, *standing* in the way of sinners, *sitting* in the seat of mockers; the arc of motion here is from curiosity to interaction to conversion. It's from eavesdropping on the wicked's talk to absorption in it.)

Psalm 1 asks of us (or commends to us) both a choice and a refusal. It pronounces blessing on both—blessing, first, on the refusal, on those who reject the counsel of the wicked, the way of

---

TIME-IN 23

PRIVILEGED REFUSAL

During the Vietnam War, the United States bombed bridges in remote areas of the country to disrupt movement of their enemy, the Vietcong. The Vietcong simply built submerged bridges. They strung their bridge cables six or so inches under the muddy water. In this way, they obscured the bridge from aerial view and continued their ground movement unabated. American attempts to find and destroy those bridges became more work than it was worth.

There are a few submerged bridges in all of us that give the enemy access, free and unhindered movement in us.

All of them are worth finding and destroying.

Maybe the hardiest of those bridges, the one you can destroy and find it rebuilt overnight, is pride. Pride contributes the mother lode to our "privileged refusals."

Pride is the sneakiest of the seven deadly sins. Like philosopher Blaise Pascal, I'm so prideful I'm even proud of my humility. There's a story about the renowned New York preacher whose friend accused him of pride. He vehemently denied it. So the friend challenged him: demonstrate your professed humility by standing all day on the busiest New York street corner wearing a sign, front and back, announcing "The End Is Near! Repent!" The preacher took him up on the challenge. He went to New York's busiest street corner, donned the sign, and stood all day. Passersby, if they noticed at all, heaped derision on him. Some recognized him, and that was even worse. That night, drifting off to sleep,

day and night. The Hebrew word for *meditate* (*hâgâh*, if you need to know, with both vowels elongated: *haw-gaw*) means, literally, "to murmur." It connotes total preoccupation, being fixated on something so that we repeat it over and over, the thought of it laced with every other thought, mingling with our breath. People *hâgâh* when they're delighted or angered or worried. A man smitten by love does it, murmuring his beloved's name, her many virtues; a man smitten with rage does it, muttering his enemy's name, his many vices; a woman fretting does it, mumbling her anxieties, the many things that might go wrong.

We naturally *hâgâh* when we're in the grip of an obsession.

So obviously, when it comes to meditating on the law of the Lord day and night (there's that obsessiveness again — day and night, hovering over the hours, stalking our steps, haunting our sleep), the delight needs to come first. How can we murmur day and night about that which has failed to ignite our imaginations, capture our hearts?

But that's where Psalm 1 gets things slightly askew, a little backward. For Psalm 1, I think, meditation *creates* delight, not the other way around.

Some things we meditate on — we *hâgâh* — because we delight in them. Our obsession is simply the spillover of our desire. I see a fly rod that seems in every way superior to the one I own, and I desire it. I imagine the feisty trout, the indomitable steelhead, the stubborn char that will take it and shake it like a divining rod. I see myself by my favorite fishing hole, early morning, clear and cool, mist rising off the river. I see that place where the whitewater slows, darkens, whorls with deep backward arcing currents. Fish are always there, playing the edges of those currents, looking for food. I will oblige them.

Well, desire takes hold, and wells up as obsession. The pleasure of the thing, just the thought of it, gets me muttering.

But other things we learn to desire by obsessing over them. We know we should care about the HIV/AIDS pandemic, especially the desolation it's causing across sub-Saharan Africa, but there's little pleasure in thinking about it. There's no delight. It's the World Bank's and the UN's and Bono's problem. I'm going fly-fishing instead.

But if I train myself to care—if I make myself meditate on the problem, *hâgâh* it—after a time, the desire to do something about it, to make it my own problem, grows. If I *hâgâh* enough, I soon find myself in the full grip of an unconquerable obsession.

The law of the Lord is like that. We first ascribe to it great value and discipline ourselves to study it. But it's when, as a sheer act of obedience often, we meditate on it day and night that delight becomes the real thing.

I have certainly seen this in my own life, and get to witness it up close often in my line of work. I was told "in the early days of my acquaintance with the gospel," as Paul calls it, to make a daily habit of reading the Bible. Nothing was more foreign to me. I enjoyed reading back then, but not daily, and not ancient holy books. I read mostly fantasy fiction—brawny heroes swashbuckling their way to rescue damsels and slay villains, and save the world along the way.

I believed the people who told me that the Bible is fascinating and life-changing. I became, by an accident of circumstances, a Baptist, and haven't yet repented of that, and so I got steeped in the Baptist creed about the Bible—it's my guide for life and faith. So I did as I was told. I read it daily.

It was dreadful at first. I liked very much the Gospels—I'd actually come to faith reading them—but my instructions, distinctly, were to read "the whole counsel of God."[7] Genesis proved strange but, mostly, compelling. The opening bits of Exodus equally so. But it slowed down considerably after that, and I wondered if I'd been misinformed. More than once I had the uncharitable thought that perhaps those who prescribed this medicine weren't taking it themselves. Large swaths of Exodus and Numbers and Leviticus and Deuteronomy nearly made me lapse into paganism—if the Bible wasn't narrating genocidal policy carried out with ruthless efficiency, or enforcing what I saw as bigoted or misogynistic rules, it was boring me to tears with the rigmarole of priestly vestments and dietary laws, or the bewildering array of offerings to atone for an equally bewildering array of sins.

It was stunning to me that it was these books, largely, that Psalm 1, and Psalm 19, and Psalm 119, referred to as "delightful." It was even more stunning to me that it was these books, largely, that comprised Jesus' "Bible." Neither the psalm writers, those great extollers of the Word, nor Jesus, who told us to live not by bread alone but by every word that comes from the mouth of God, had the Gospels or the epistles in their scope. They had Leviticus and Numbers and the like. The psalmist in 119 actually says he desires God's law—his statutes, ordinances, decrees, precepts, and so on—more than he desires silver and gold. *Really?* I thought. I pictured, at his invitation, "much pure gold," which I take to mean a great mound of wealth. I imagined what all that gold could buy. (The fly rod!) I imagined how nice it was to look at all on its own. I set all that alongside, say, Leviticus 15:8 ("If the man with the discharge spits on someone who is clean, that person must wash his clothes and bathe with water, and he will be unclean till evening"). And I wondered, given a straight and honest choice, with no terrible eternal things hanging in the balance, would I really pick this selection from Leviticus over almost anything else?

But I was told the Bible, all of it, was good for me, and though my confidence wavered, I still believed, and pressed on.

I meditated on it. And then I began to notice something. It didn't happen all at once, but something was growing. I was delighting in the Word. I found myself, on my yearly pass through the entire Bible (another thing I was told to do), excited about all those parts I used to dread. Every year, I find some new treasures. The fact that more and more I see the Bible whole—the history and theology and cultural development underneath it all fitting together, top to bottom, start to finish—means that even those parts that remain, well, a bit tedious I see in a new light. I see them as integral to the whole story like the plumbing and wiring of a house are integral to everything else in it, necessary for its full functioning, even though they're not the parts we care to look at often.

I have many favorite things about being a pastor (and a few loathsome things), but ranking in my top three is watching a Christ-follower, young or old, wake fresh to the Word of God.

It happened only recently with Bill.

Bill had been reading, and not reading, the Bible for decades. He read it mostly out of duty, and with almost no benefit. When he didn't read it, he felt a vague pervasive guilt. He complained a lot, about his kids, his wife, his job, the church. He was tedious.

We sometimes practice in our church an ancient exercise called *lectio divina*—Latin for "sacred reading." *Lectio*, as my wife describes it, is "listening to the Word with your heart." We usually do a *lectio* in small gatherings, though I've done it on my own, and attempted it in larger groups. A reader chooses a short passage of Scripture and reads it three times, slowly, without much inflection. The others listen. They listen for a word or phrase that, we like to say, "sings, rings, or stings." Often on the third reading, we ask a question: "In this story of the man who fell on the roadside, where do you see yourself? Whose company are you traveling in?" Or, "Imagine Jesus is washing your feet in the upper room. What are you seeing, thinking, feeling?"

Bill happened to be sitting in one of these. It changed something in him. The Scriptures began to convict and console him. He started to *hear* God. He started to obey God. And, hearing and obeying, he wanted more.

Delight gave way to meditation, meditation to further delight.

I like being around Bill now. He's interesting. He's humble. He inspiring.

He's rooted.

***

Let me sum up this chapter.

We, like trees, grow seasonally in our spiritual lives, a cycle of growth and dormancy.

Unlike trees, we can choose where we set our roots.

The best choice is to set them near water—to delight in the Word of God and meditate on it day and night.

Delight starts when we ascribe to that Word great value, even before we discover that value personally. On the basis of our conviction, we meditate on the Word—we *hâgâh* it.

In time, what we do in duty we continue in devotion. Our delight in the Word, at first chosen but increasingly spontaneous, draws us to *hâgâh* the Word more and more, not because it's good for us but because it's good. The meditation in turn deepens the delight.

And then this: you are "like a tree planted by streams of water, which yields its fruit in season and whose leaf does not wither. Whatever [you do] prospers."

Even winter can't destroy you.

CHAPTER 16

KNOCKING
(ON HEAVEN'S DOOR)

Some days, writing, I feel like Jack Torrance, Jack Nicholson's character in the movie *The Shining*: deranged beneath the guise of charm, playing a game of brinkmanship with madness. My wife graciously brings me lunch from yesterday's leftovers. I wanly smile at her, too bent to my task to interrupt myself with speech. I labor over a manuscript, reams thick, that never seems to get closer to being finished. She understands. She supports me. But if only she knew: I work and work, hunched over my keyboard, to say only one thing, repeated line by line, page by page, chapter by chapter. Torrance's line was "All work and no play makes Jack a dull boy."

My line might be this: "Be so heavenly minded you're of great earthly good."

There is nothing in this world that infuses me with hope, joy, and strength—so wild and pure it can intoxicate with a single sip—like the thought of the next world. I don't mean our insipid versions of the next world—the plump cupids, the pillowy clouds, the tapering shafts of shimmery light, the droopy-winged harpists, the cherubim and seraphim that neither provoke dread nor inspire awe, and a god who looks vaguely like Heidi's grandfather. That depiction of heaven bores us on earth, so it's hard to imagine it inflaming raptures of bliss for us in the hereafter.

I mean the heaven that, as Paul describes it, cannot be described: no eye has seen it, no ear heard it. It transcends imagination, just like life outside the womb defies the understanding of an unborn child. Even if an infant curled inside its mother were capable of thinking grown-up thoughts, could it possibly imagine what anyone meant by just the word *dog*? The loping shedding Labradors and mincing pampered poodles and gaunt sprinting greyhounds and jowly howling blood hounds, and all the sleek and furry and yappy and growly and playful and fearsome creatures in between?

You have to see them all to figure it out, and even then you're just beginning.

Well, heaven's that—this splendid and varied wonder that every effort to portray with earthly categories is doomed to caricature. You'll have to see it to get it, and even then you're only starting.

And yet, we long for it.

GRASPING AFTER HEAVEN

Heaven is in our hearts. God has "set eternity in the human heart."[1] We bear some knowledge beyond our knowing.

Neuroscientists point to the grasping instinct in infants—the inborn impulse to clutch upward when falling—as clear evidence of evolution: a vestige of every human's essential monkey business, a throwback to our tree-dwelling, vine-leaping days when falling was measured not by inches but by dizzying heights. Thus, evolution favored the primate that could hang on, and those genes kept replicating and, in the case of humans, never got eradicated.

Well, maybe. But it seems a stretch to me. Humans have cultivated a thousand acts of grasping, most of which have nothing to do with recovering from a fall, and a few that are precursors to one. It is telling that the first word a child usually speaks—beyond the iconic *mama* and *dada* and the all-purpose monosyllable *no*—is not *help* but *mine*. Our grasping instinct, I think, has a root not exclusive to primates.

But all that is to say this: we have more than a grasping instinct. We also have, and more potently, more enduringly, a longing instinct. We all wish, to varying degrees, to be somewhere else, or to be someone else, or to be doing something else. How often do you hear a comment like this: "I'm so restless, and I can't figure it out. I've got a good job, a good marriage. My kids are great. We just moved into a new house six months ago. But it hasn't taken away my restlessness. In some ways, it's made it worse. I'm trying to figure out if I'm really in the place I'm supposed to be right now."

Most of us misinterpret our longing instinct. "He has also set eternity in the human heart," the full text of Ecclesiastes 3:11 says, "yet no one can fathom what God has done from beginning to end." We fail lifelong to understand the true source of our restlessness, the sense that we are not in the right place right now. And so, misdiagnosing our discontent, we seek remedy for it in things that, at best, provide temporary relief, and more often bring deeper frustration. We divorce, move, quit, leave our church. We blame the restlessness on the boss, the spouse, the pastor, the town we're in.

Whatever.

When all along it's God's fault. It is God who set eternity in your heart. Restlessness is not the vestige of some long evolutionary process. It's the prank God pulled on us from the first day until now. It is God who stuck a homing device right in the middle of you, so that every pulse triggers it. It's God who, knitting you in your mother's womb and numbering your days before one came to pass, left a gaping hole inside you that only he can fill, and only fully when you see him face-to-face. Heaven is the strange memory infusing your drive to battle upriver toward spawning grounds, to fly whole continents just to return to the rocky cleft you came from.

Jared Diamond, in his book *Collapse*, tells about the woebegone inhabitants of Easter Island, a half-starved little huddle of survivors from a once-thriving civilization, who in 1838 sent a tiny delegation of ten men on five canoes, tippy and leaky, to trade with a French cargo ship anchored offshore. The captain later wrote, "All the natives repeated often and excitedly the word *miru* and became impatient because they saw that we did not understand it: this word is the name of the timber used by Polynesians to make their canoes. That was what they wanted most, and they used every means to make us understand this."[2]

As Diamond shows, none of these islanders would have ever seen *miru*. *Miru* had disappeared centuries before—earlier generations of Easter Islanders had stripped the island's once lush and dense forests down to lifeless barrenness, no trading partner or scouting expedition from another Polynesian island had come near in hundreds of years, and the Easter Islander's tippy, leaky, tiny canoes could barely manage the trip across the bay, let alone navigate hundreds of miles of open ocean to make landfall where big trees still grew.

Miru was a memory that stirred a longing. They knew what they wanted, "wanted most," even though not one of them had ever seen it with their own eyes.

That's heaven. That's eternity. It's our *miru*. It's the "memory" God himself planted in our hearts that now stirs our deepest longing. It's what we want most. It's the memory of a tree we once desired but were forbidden, but which one day will feed us and heal us.[3] Only, most of us spend our lifetimes never figuring that out. We actually think a new spouse or house or SUV or month-long cruise will subdue our deep restlessness, when only God, face-to-face, can do that.

SEASONS AND SEEDS OF ETERNITY

Biblically, heaven and seasons closely join. The writer of Ecclesiastes, either Solomon or some chastened dissolute just like him, connects our longing instinct, this seed of eternity in our hearts, with seasons. The verse I've been working off of—God sets eternity in our hearts—comes on the heels of the verses with which I began this book, Ecclesiastes 3:1–8—for *everything* there is a season. The writer further distills this insight: "He has made *everything*"—there's that word again—"beautiful in its time. He has also set eternity in the human heart; yet no one can fathom what God has done from beginning to end."[4]

He has made *everything* beautiful in its time. For *everything* there is a season.

Each season has its beauty. And yet each season's beauty has a bait-and-switch operation at work within it: it draws us in only to draw us out, to take us elsewhere, to get our hopes up only to set our hopes on something else, something better, something bigger. That something else and bigger and better is heaven. Miss this, you'll waste your life chasing that which no season can create but only hint at, only beckon us toward.

For everything there is a season, and in every season there's enough beauty to awaken your longing instinct. Something awaits you that highest summer can only, at best, give a fleeting glimpse of. Something beckons you that bleakest winter can never, at worst, entirely eclipse. The seasons awaken in us the "memory" of *miru*, of some great thing we've never seen, that which we had but lost but that one day we'll have again. By God's design, every season whispers to us, if we'll listen, of that place at the center of which stands a tree, a great *miru*, and that tree produces fruit twelve months of the year.

TIME-IN 25

HEAVEN-BENT

I never used to think about heaven. Earth has always captivated me. I'm in no hurry to leave. Once I ran out of air forty feet under the water on a scuba dive. I misread my gauge and sucked my tank dry. The panic in my heart showed me, despite all my claims otherwise, that I am very attached to this mortal coil.

But I think about heaven a lot now. I think about it for the usual reasons. I've lost a lot of people I love, and I want to see them again. I have increasing aches and pains and strange shadows passing through me, and it's harder and harder to hide that outwardly I'm wasting away. Some days are, frankly, miserable, and the idea of heaven is a powerful tonic for that.

But I also think of heaven because it helps me love this earth and this life more. It energizes me for the grind and the battle. It lights my days, whether they're hard or boring or fun and easy.

In fact, I'm trying to be so heavenly minded I can be of some earthly good. That old dictum to the opposite effect is hokum. The most effective people who have ever lived on the earth have been the most heavenly minded ones. They simply had nothing to lose in giving themselves wholly to the kingdom of God. It's those with no hope of heaven who often end up both bitter and useless on this earth.

List seven things that make you look forward to heaven. Over the next week, spend time each day thinking about one of each of the seven things.

At the end of the seven days, see if everything around you doesn't shine in a different light.

***

I'm wondering if you might be mistaking a heavenly desire for an earthly one. I'm wondering if the restlessness you might be feeling somewhere in your life—your marriage, maybe, or your work, or your church, in anything you once found beautiful but which has since grown dull—is really your inbuilt yearning for heaven. It's your homing device triggering. You fantasize that moving on, finding some beautiful new thing to console you or amuse you, might remedy your ache. Well it just might, for a spell. But it will age you faster, and leave you aching more and with a sour taste in your mouth.

Eternity is in your heart. God's planted a seed of heaven in you, an acorn from the *miru*. The hope of heaven, real as hunger, is what keeps stirring. If you try to fill that hope with things that only hint at its true fulfillment, you'll be disappointed. But when we "set [our] hearts on things above"[5] and "fix our eyes ... on what is unseen,"[6] then even if "outwardly we are wasting away," still "inwardly we are being renewed day by day."[7]

I don't think anyone's in danger of being so heavenly minded they're of no earthly good. I think most of the world has gone the other direction and become so earthly minded few are useful to heaven or earth.

But by now, you must know what you're really missing.

CHAPTER 17

PERSEVERING

Today is Canadian Thanksgiving, early October, cool and grey. We invited good friends over last night to feast with us on turkey, and all that comes with turkey—fat-drenched things, sauce-laden things, sugar-laced things—and then pumpkin pie and blackberry pie, mounded with whipped cream. The power went out just before we sat down, so we lit candles everywhere and dined in golden light and shadows, almost wishing the power stayed off. It came on just in time to make after-dinner coffee.

I slept well, and late. It rained overnight and the boughs of the cedars outside my windows are silvery with the damp. A lone bird walks the pathway beside the garden, plucking fallen berries. About half the leaves on my fruit trees still cling, parched and wizened, to their branches. The rest of the leaves lie scattered across lawn and garden, a thickness of moldering parchment that mocks my sloth for not gathering them earlier when they were still light and dry.

Behind me, a fire of maple wood and fir burns hot and loud. I stacked that wood on a sweltering day in June, to season it, and the heat through the summer made its end bead with sap so that now, pushing a length of it into my open grate, I must take care lest my hands gum with pitch and my palms the rest of the day bear dark stains.

The chair I sit in has, strapped to its back, a gift my wife gave me for Christmas last year: a massage pad. Inside are two balls that move in elliptical circles, up and down, in and out. The ellipses are designed to create a pulsing, digging motion, and if I press my back

into it, the rollers grab and knead my muscles until even the snarliest knot unravels. It's like having a masseuse at my beck and call.

I'm trying to tell you I'm happy. Not shout-it-out-loud, stand-on-my head, cartwheel-the-lawn, dance-on-the-rooftop happy. Just happy: simply content, satisfied in some deep-down indescribable way. The silver cedar boughs and the turkey still digesting in my stomach and the fire warming my house and my back are not the cause of this happiness. At best, they're the expression of it. They announce, quietly, and they celebrate, modestly, my happiness.

But they didn't cause it.

Jesus did. Jesus does. I honestly believe that I'd know and taste this simple happiness without the turkey, the fire, the cedars. I believe I'd know it even in the distinct absence of these things.

The seed of this book, you might remember, was my discovery of winter. The death of a close friend and colleague, Carol, led my wife and me into a bleakness we'd not known before. It was a lonely place, and dark. It was cold. It was fruitless. Yet it was there, of all places, in the "fellowship of sharing in his sufferings, becoming like him in his death,"[1] that we both discovered an intimacy with Christ we had not known before, either.

We met the Man for All Seasons. We met the man of sorrows, familiar with suffering. We met the man who, for the joy set before him, endured the cross, scorning its shame. In meeting Jesus here, even here, we also experienced a similar joy set before us. It didn't make the sorrow any less—the Man for All Seasons, after all, gives life *to the full*, nothing muted, nothing watered down, nothing by halves—but it did impart a peace beyond our understanding.

One fruit of that meeting is this moment, this deep and simple joy I feel. I don't think this joy is immune to downturns. Another loss would wound it, maybe grievously. A decline, sudden or gradual, in health, would force it to recoup. Any number of things could disrupt or damage it.

But not, I think, permanently. My discovery of winter was even more a discovery of the Man for All Seasons, who never leaves us nor forsakes us.

And a light came on. I've been a pastor long enough that the light

should have come on long ago, but nonetheless it came on lately. The light was this: that joy hinges only thinly on circumstances. Its true source is the Man for All Seasons. Of course, I knew this from way back, but only in the Greek way, in my head. I could preach lengthy, even eloquent, sermons about it, but only winter gave me firsthand experience with it. Winter made me safe for, I'm guessing, half my congregation, that half who had been or were in deep suffering. And my genuine testimony of meeting Christ in winter made me a herald of good news for prisoners. I became a watchman announcing a great light for "people walking in darkness."[2]

But there's more. The experience gave me a touchstone for understanding something that's perplexed me most my life: why suffering either sweetens and softens people, or sours and hardens them, with scarcely any in-between. I can think of dozens of people I know, many in my church, who have gone through bitter travail. Theirs have been trials of Job-like proportions. But they bear no ill will, indulge in no self-pity, and miss no opportunity to pour out grace. They laugh with pure mirth. They are tender with others, and humble of heart. They are generous with the little they usually have. And, contrariwise, I can think of a handful of people, some in my church, who have suffered trials, hard but not always bitter, that have nonetheless turned them bitter, wary, prickly, surly. Their laughter is sardonic or cynical. They often are harsh with others, and proud, and stingy with the much they usually have.

How is this? Like Dr. Seuss's Grinch, I would "puzzle and puzzle 'til my puzzler was sore" and still not crack the thing open.

But wintertime did it.

We steward choices, in season and out. We take every thought captive and make it obedient to Christ, or we don't. What I'd missed before winter was simply this: I can take my thoughts captive and make them obey Christ only if Christ is with me and for me in all things and at all times. If Christ isn't with me in the loneliest places, then there is no one in such places to help me capture my thoughts and no one to whom those thoughts must submit. But if he is here, even here, then even here I can live out this command.

And so what was obscure for me became clear: the people I know

for whom suffering has been a deepening and a softening are people who've held tight, in season and out, to the Man for All Seasons. They have a holy stubbornness, like Job. They keep believing that, someday, God will show up and explain it all, or maybe show up and refuse to explain any of it but make it all okay anyhow. Or they're like Paul. Beat him, stone him, shipwreck him, half starve him, and he finds some back door to the God whose strength is made perfect in his weakness.

The people I know for whom suffering has been a thinning and a hardening saw their suffering, their winter, as a sign of God's abandonment, and let go. They may remain in the church — a few do — but they sit back like Michal watching David dancing, disdaining the God-hungry.

Writing all this trivializes it. I see that. I'm not saying it well. There are infinite variations in everyone's wintertime — differing stages of life, scales of pain, histories of woe, the company we keep, the temperaments we landed with, how healthy or sick our churches are. I know that. But there does appear to me, amid all those variables, this one constant: wanting to know Jesus not just in the power of his resurrection but equally in "the fellowship of sharing in his sufferings." That passage, from Philippians, more than anywhere else uses the language of "holding on" and "pressing on." Best I quote it in full: "I want to know Christ — yes, to know the power of his resurrection and participation in his sufferings, becoming like him in his death, and so, somehow, attaining to the resurrection from the dead. Not that I have already obtained all this, or have already arrived at my goal, but I press on to take hold of that for which Christ Jesus took hold of me. Brothers and sisters, I do not consider myself yet to have taken hold of it. But one thing I do: Forgetting what is behind and straining toward what is ahead, I press on toward the goal to win the prize for which God has called me heavenward in Christ Jesus."[3]

"This one thing I do." This one thing is really two things, or two things joined in one seamless, indivisible act: holding on and pressing on.

HOLDING ON,
PRESSING ON

Which brings me to a word which has taken on deep resonance for me: *perseverance.*

Let me tell you Sam's story. Sam started coming to the church where I'm pastor around eight years ago. He was in his early thirties then. He immediately caught my attention. Sam had an obvious gift, raw and undisciplined, of leadership. I love that kind (perhaps a weakness of mine). He'd kissed the Blarney stone, so could talk a storm, a rapid-fire barrage of persuasion, invitation, admonition, personal testimony, biblical insight. It was quite a thing. At an inter-church service for Palm Sunday, when I was appointed with the task of finding someone who could give a "riveting personal testimony," I thought only of Sam and sought out only Sam. I recommended to his pastor at the time that he invite Sam to speak. Sam did, and he did not disappoint.

Not then.

But Sam, it turned out, lived his whole life under a cloud of disappointment, and so lived his whole life disappointing others. He was a flash in the pan that only left the pan charred, and flavored everything else with a bitter aftertaste.

There were reasons for this. Sam nursed a wound of rejection. He had been given up as a toddler into foster care, and spent the first twelve years of his childhood in a home that was cold and unloving. He had to fend for himself. He learned to trust no one.

His giftedness, ample as it was, was not only bearing little or no fruit. It was actually causing harm. It had become a decoy and disguise, less and less plausible, for a life empty at the core.

So he came and he went in people's lives. Always, in his coming, it was for "real this time."

It never was. He'd get bored, or things would get hard — disappointments would accumulate — and he would disappear again.

When he showed up for the sixth or seventh time at church, my own disappointment in him was at the point where I was ready to give up. He filled out a pew card and put it in the offering: "I'm back and want to get serious about my faith and ministry. When can we meet?"

I called him and met him in a coffee shop. I asked him where he'd been, why he was back. The news took me off guard. He'd gone to Vancouver to pursue another relationship that ended in disappointment. But he was back because a girl here was pregnant with his child.

"Oh. Okay. So you've come back to marry her?"

"No. She's not right for me. But I thought I had a responsibility, and so I'm here to do what I can."

I asked Sam, then, to tell me his whole story. The foster homes. The many women who'd been in and out of his life. All the jobs he'd had and lost or quit. All the churches he'd attended and left.

It took a while.

When he'd finished, I said, "Sam, as you told all that in one go, did any theme or themes emerge for you?" He thought a moment, shook his head.

"One theme emerged for me," I said. "Can I tell you?"

He nodded.

"You're a quitter. You've never seen anything through. It always gets hard or boring, or both, and then you beg off, often with a pious excuse: it's not God's will, or the Spirit 'led' you. But the result is always the same: you finish nothing."

That stung him into silence.

"Sam, I didn't come to accuse you. That's the devil's work. But I do hope to be a voice in your wilderness. And like John the Baptist, I want to say to you, 'Prepare the way of the Lord. Make straight paths for him.' Sam, here's how I understand that: do what you need to do to simplify God's work in your life. If you need to fill in valleys and level mountains to make it work, do it. I'm asking you to resolve things this time and not to quit. Resolve to see this through to the end. Why don't you start this way: over the next week or so, study everything the Bible says on perseverance. Journal it. Pray it out. Wrestle it through. Find the meaning of the word, its substance. Find how to persevere, by what strength, in what hope. Leave no stone unturned."

Sam was sullen by now, darkly silent. I was uncertain whether he'd do as I suggested.

I didn't see him at church again for four months, though occasionally I'd see him walking around town, stooped, head hung, grizzled and blotchy, looking like he was living in the bush.

Then he showed up at church one Sunday. With Johanna, the girl who was carrying his child.

Really serious this time, he said.

It went up and down. They were going to get married. They weren't. The baby came. They moved in together. He drank a lot. Then one day the police had to come to the house to break up a physical fight.

That gave me and another pastor the moment, yet another one, to get down to brass tacks. Sam this time seemed genuinely broken. Willing to do what needed doing. He moved out of the house. He quit drinking, and began a regimen of spiritual practices and practical steps to keep it that way.

A few weeks later, he asked me to marry him and Johanna.

I refused.

I told them that the only way I would even remotely consider it was if they underwent rigorous preparations. Rebuilt their relationship from the ground up. And since I was the one making the demand, I made the offer to help them do that.

They accepted, and then began many months of personal discipleship. Around month two, we hit a wall, and I asked to meet just with Sam for a few sessions. I suspected he was ready to pull his old worn-out trick, his Houdini routine, and disappear. He was. He felt, he told me, that he just couldn't go through with this. It was too hard. There were too many problems.

And then I reminded him about perseverance.

"Sam, did you ever do that study I asked you to do on perseverance?"

"No."

"Well, you need it now more than ever. But here's the good news. Remember I said the pattern I saw in your life was quitting?"

"Yeah."

"You haven't quit yet. Not on this. You're actually persevering. Sticking to your post. You gave up the bottle and stayed off. You moved out of the house and stayed out. You stayed in the relationship despite disappointment. You're becoming a good father to your daughter. Do you see that?"

"Yeah."

"Tell me what difference it's making."

"Well, I'm closer to God. I have to be. I can't do this without him. And some of the ways I've handled situations in the past—getting angry, blaming, hiding—I don't do that as much. I'm calmer. I'm able to see the big picture. I'm able to discover joy on the other side of hardship."

"Ah, you know what you just described?"

"What?"

"The fruit of perseverance. Paul says that suffering—when life doesn't work the way you want it to but makes you groan—suffering produces perseverance. Determination grows best in the soil of pain. And perseverance, he says, produces character—something deep down inside you starts agreeing with God and so looking more like God. And then character produces hope—you actually begin to believe, in your bones, that this will turn out for good, no matter how bleak it looks now. And hope—listen—doesn't disappoint.

"Sam, you've lived your whole life disappointed and disappointing. You've believed that a life without disappointment would mean you got everything you wanted when you wanted it. But that's just fed your disappointment. God's life without disappointment is the fullness of his presence—his "love poured into our hearts by the Holy Spirit," is how he puts it. But that life is the gift the far side of perseverance.[4]

"Do you want to hear more?"

"Yeah."

"That was Paul on perseverance. James says perseverance is developed by the 'testing of your faith,' by trials, hardships, misery, disappointments. It's another way of saying what Paul says: suffering produces this. Then James says that perseverance must 'finish its work' —in other words, you don't just work on persevering; persevering works on you—so that you may become mature, complete, not lacking anything. Again, that's almost shorthand for character, hope, and a life without disappointment. The reward of perseverance is fullness.

"James also warns about the fallout when we don't persevere. We get tossed around by life. We stop living in expectancy toward God. We become 'unstable' in all we do. Sound familiar?"[5]

Sam laughed. "Yeah."

"You want more?"

"Yeah."

"Peter weighs in on the subject. Peter lists perseverance as the middle virtue in a list of seven virtues that we must 'add to our faith.'[6] What he promises if we possess perseverance, plus six other virtues, 'in increasing measure' is that we will 'participate in the divine nature and escape the corruption of the world.' You'll be godly and not worldly. And he further promises that we will be effective and productive in our walk with Christ. Another way of saying all that: perseverance produces character—participation in God, noncompliance with evil—which produces hope, and hope doesn't disappoint—we become fruitful for the King and his kingdom. That's fullness.

"Peter, like James, also warns us what happens when we lack perseverance. He says we'll be 'nearsighted and blind,' and we will forget that we've been 'cleansed from past sins.' We'll see our lives only up close, never the big picture, never from God's perspective, and largely we won't see it at all: the things that matter most we'll be blind to. And the life we've been freed from we'll keep going back to because we'll forget we've been freed from it.

"Sound familiar?"

"Yeah."

Well, it was a good lecture. But I'm replicating it here not to impress you (or bore you) but for this reason: something changed that day for Sam. Something very deep and very real. A month later, I married him and Johanna.

A year later, through ups and downs, they're not disappointed.

Perseverance will do that, every time.

A CONSTANT IN THE MIDST
OF SEASONAL TRANSITIONS

The nature of our lives is seasonal. Winter, spring, summer, fall, but hardly ever in that order. I've watched men and women and boys and girls go with dramatic suddenness from one to the other. Tomorrow, I attend two funerals. One for a man whose death was "in season"— he was eighty-something, had lived well, loved deeply, said what he needed to say by way of thank you and goodbye. His wife misses him terribly, but her heart is buoyant with hope and anticipation. It's not wintertime for her, at least not deep winter, and already there abound signs of spring.

The other funeral is for a woman whose death was "out of season"—she was fifty-something, mother to two young adults, in prime health, who contracted some rare strange virus and went away without a proper leave-taking. Her family is bewildered, angry, dismayed. They are so stunned they have not even begun to grieve.

Winter is hard upon them, and it likely will be a long dark season.

I've seen the suddenness of seasonal change. And I've seen its gradualness. I've watched this past year my dear friend and colleague and mentor, Joy Brewster, go from high summer (and that in her seventies) into a long deep winter, but slowly. Her kidneys are failing, and the illness and its remedies have sapped her energy and muddled her brain. There are hopeful signs. They come with a doctor's upbeat report or a few days of feeling that old pluck and strength coming back. And then they're gone, chased away by a doctor's grim report or several days of debilitating weariness.

And I've seen, both sudden and gradual, similar movements between seasons: a man who, because of childhood abuse, walked in the gloom of shame most his life, then one night had a dream and woke up walking on sunshine, and it's lasted; a girl who, from a nasty drug habit, reaped ten years of bad harvests, then went to rehab and got serious about God, and now is reaping good things; a couple who struggled in their marriage for twenty-five years but who went to a counselor who called them to bone-deep repentance and heartfelt obedience, and who now are in a summertime so abundant and sweet and warm and full of light that other couples are getting healed by just their shadow falling on them.

But always, in season and out, young and old, single or couple, the constant is one thing: perseverance. But not just persevering in that grueling, teeth-gritting, sweat-of-my-brow sense. Rather, persevering with the Christ who walks with them everywhere and always.

"Where are you?" That was God's question to Adam back in Eden, when he came to walk with Adam and couldn't find him. God often asks me that question. Me, I'm usually in the middle of something. I'm long past the exhilaration of beginning. I'm a long way from the satisfaction of finishing. I'm somewhere in the middle: fifty years old, twenty-five years married, twenty years in pastoral work, perpetually renovating my house.

And what I need most days, in this wide stretch of land, is perseverance. To keep moving, or stay put—whatever persevering means in each case. To stay the course or stand my ground. And it is strength to me that God finds me here and wants to walk with me.

Where are you? When God comes to walk with you, where does he find you? So excited, he has to run to catch up? So weary he has to lift you to your feet?

Or in the middle somewhere, just putting one foot before the next? Know this, he's come looking for you, to walk with you. He wants you to finish this course. He has good things along the way, and very good things awaiting.

TIME-IN 26

WHERE ARE YOU?

God is inquisitive. He's always asking questions: "Where are you? Who told you that you were naked? Where is your brother? Is it lawful to heal on the Sabbath? Where is your faith? Why are you so afraid? Why do you call me good? Who do you say I am?" Some of these questions—most, in fact—don't feel rhetorical, asked in the cool posture of the academic or politician setting herself up for dazzling oratory or clever commentary.

God genuinely seems to want to know.

It's not that he doesn't know the answer himself. It's more, I think, that we don't—that we haven't paused to sift and ponder our own motives and actions. We're just barreling on ahead, blithely living the unexamined life. The question stops us mid-breath, midstride.

Who *do* I think Jesus is?

Why *am* I so afraid?

Why *do* I call him good?

Who *told me* I was naked?

Where *am* I?

Let me ask you God's original question: where are you? Can you locate yourself within God's proximity? Can you identify where you're drawing near, and where you're pulling away? Can you identify what you're trying to hide from him?

"It is a dreadful thing," Hebrews 10:31 says, "to fall into the hands of the living God."

Agreed.

Only one thing is more dreadful: not to fall into his hands. So let us heed the counsel, also in Hebrews 10, to "draw near to God with a sincere heart in full assurance of faith, having our hearts sprinkled to cleanse us from a guilty conscience and having our bodies washed with pure water."[7]

***

Why am I happy? With Christ by my side, summer doesn't distract. With Christ by my side, winter doesn't destroy. With Christ by my side, the hard work of fall and spring does not overwhelm. I get knocked down, but I get back up. I forget for a moment, but I live mostly in remembering his faithfulness, anticipating his goodness.

I persevere.

I'm not disappointed.

The Man for All Seasons will do that for you, every time.

CHAPTER 18

IN SEASON
AND OUT

When life gets tough, have a beer.

That's my advice. Only, I'm speaking in a biblical sense, with a biblical language: *beer* is the Hebrew word for *well*, a place you draw not fermented hops but water. So let me put it in straight English: when life gets tough, have a well.

Or two.

Or three.

When you dry up, have a place that replenishes you.

I live in the wetlands, so to speak, where almost every tree is planted by streams of living water. Most of our water problems stem from having too much: roots get waterlogged, culverts engorge, storm drains overflow, rivers spill their banks, mountains give way, cherries burst their skins, mold breeds in basements, rainwater finds every broken seam on every rooftop and turns gyprock into mush. A drought means I'm not allowed to soak my lawn more than twice a week in high summer, and a severe drought means I'm not allowed to do that at all. But not once in my life has drought meant I might not drink. It's never even meant I might not shower, or water my peonies, or wash my clothes or my car. Not once has my life ever grown tenuous, fragile, marginal, for lack of water. There's always been enough, and more.

But a *beer*, a well, was the lifeblood of ancient Near Eastern people. It still is. A tapped source of sweet cool water flowing beneath sun-scorched earth could turn wasteland into homeland. A well was hidden life in a world of sudden death, or not so sudden, prolonged and agonizing death, a withering from the inside out.

You could live without many things—markets and livestock, entertainment and ease of transport. What you couldn't live without was a good *beer*.

Which is also true spiritually. We need a place of replenishment. We need a place to quench our thirst, to water our dryness. We need a place that gives life when all around us is desert.

BEER LAHI ROI

Hagar was the Egyptian handmaiden of Sarai, wife of Abram (later to be named Sarah and Abraham). Life had gotten tough for her, if ever it was easy. Handmaiden was just a polite way of saying that Hagar was Sarai's personal slave. Her chattel. And Sarai took full advantage of that: first, forcing Hagar to bear Abram's child on her behalf, then despising Hagar and mistreating her for the very thing she was commanded to do. Hagar's attitude doesn't help any.

> Now Sarai, Abram's wife, had borne him no children. But she had an Egyptian maidservant named Hagar; so she said to Abram, "The LORD has kept me from having children. Go, sleep with my maidservant; perhaps I can build a family through her."
>
> Abram agreed to what Sarai said. So after Abram had been living in Canaan ten years, Sarai his wife took her Egyptian maidservant Hagar and gave her to her husband to be his wife. He slept with Hagar, and she conceived.
>
> When she knew she was pregnant, she began to despise her mistress. Then Sarai said to Abram, "You are responsible for the wrong I am suffering. I put my servant in your arms, and now that she knows she is pregnant, she despises me. May the LORD judge between you and me."
>
> "Your servant is in your hands," Abram said. "Do with her whatever you think best." Then Sarai mistreated Hagar; so she fled from her.[1]

In a strange way, Hagar is a reverse image of a distant future:

generations later, the Hebrew people, Abraham's descendants, will en masse be slaves to the Egyptian people, chattel to Pharaoh, brutalized and hard pressed. The roles will be inverted. But here, the father and mother of our faith come off as taskmasters. They sow to the wind a cruelty that, centuries later, their offspring will reap in the whirlwind. And like the Egyptian Hagar, the Hebrew people will seek the refuge of the desert.

But any desert without a *beer* is a death trap. So Hagar goes to a spring in the desert. She finds a *beer*. Here's what happens:

> The angel of the LORD found Hagar near a spring in the desert; it was the spring that is beside the road to Shur. And he said, "Hagar, servant of Sarai, where have you come from, and where are you going?"
>
> "I'm running away from my mistress Sarai," she answered.
>
> Then the angel of the LORD told her, "Go back to your mistress and submit to her." The angel added, "I will so increase your descendants that they will be too numerous to count."
>
> The angel of the LORD also said to her:
>
>> "You are now with child
>> and you will have a son.
>> You shall name him Ishmael,
>> for the LORD has heard of your misery.
>>
>> He will be a wild donkey of a man;
>> his hand will be against everyone
>> and everyone's hand against him,
>> and he will live in hostility
>> toward all his brothers."
>
> She gave this name to the LORD who spoke to her: "You are the God who sees me," for she said, "I have now seen the One who sees me." That is why the well was called Beer Lahai Roi; it is still there, between Kadesh and Bered.[2]

The angel of the Lord is not prone to long speeches. He's not given to either harsh scoldings or tender consolations. He deals in tough questions and stark truths, which can be their own form of scolding and consolation. He begins with a question—or two, to be precise: "Hagar, where are you coming from, and where are you going?"

Hagar can answer the first. She is fleeing. She is doing anything, even a rash and hopeless thing, to get away from a bad situation. She simply fired up the old Ford in the middle of the night, with its engine that won't hold idle, its rusty panels and bald tires, its one window that rolls up cockeyed to the frame; she tossed in a suitcase with a few tatty clothes, a grainy photo of her mother, and a stick of salami and headed out for anywhere that's not here. No plan at all other than to get out of Dodge.

I often ask people in distress, "Where are you coming from, and where are you going?" And I usually find they can answer, easily, the first question (though often they want to evade the question all the same), but rarely the second. Most people who are overwhelmed by circumstances know where they've come from. They can name in vivid detail the situation, person, job, town, marriage—whatever—from which they're desperate to get away.

They just can't say what's next. The recent past, and then some, they see as in a sideview mirror: objects appear closer and larger than they actually are. The past looms huge. But the future is opaque. A whiteout. A black hole. A vanishing point. They have hopes, thin and tentative, or thick and obsessive, but little clarity.

The angel of the Lord asks the two questions at the heart of the matter. Many hundreds of years hence, Jesus will have virtually the same conversation with another lonely and evasive woman at another well: the Samaritan woman, escaping at high noon to a spring in the desert. She too has a clear idea where she's come from (five husbands, and the man she lives with now is not her husband), but no idea where she's going—what's next, how to dial out, how to backpedal to innocence, how to mend a life broken into a thousand little pieces. Jesus helps her with all that. He offers her a different kind of *beer*, a deeper well, where living water flows, nourishing and replenishing always.[3]

In the case of the angel of the Lord and Hagar, as with Jesus and the Samaritan woman, he just sends her back. The angel tells Hagar to return to Sarai, to step back into submission. This would be bleak news, except Hagar doesn't appear to receive it as such. Our parting glimpse of her is of a woman deeply hopeful, freshly resolved, maybe even cheerful. She almost, it seems, whistles and skips her way home.

Why?

Well, for one, the angel makes a promise: she will have a child, a son. Only, it's a promise that's more bad news than good: he will be a "wild donkey of a man," hating and hated by everyone. I know parenting standards have shifted over the generations, but it's hard to imagine any mother relishing news of this kind: "Little Ishy is going to be churlish and stubborn and have no friends and get into fights his whole life." Even a much tougher breed of mother than our age is producing could hardly have been cheered by this.

I don't think she derived much consolation from the promise. That's not what the story suggests. The story suggests that her consolation derived not from God's promise but from God's presence. "I have seen the One who sees me," she says. And God does more than see her. The story tells us he's the God who also hears her (v. 11) and speaks to her (v. 13).

So she names the place. She names it after the spring, the well: Beer Lahai Roi. "The Well of the God Who Lives and Who Sees Me."

That's a good *beer*. That's a good well. She finds in the desert a well that heralds a God who finds her in the desert. A God who listens and speaks—words that may console, but mostly that just tell it like it is. A God who promises, but whose promises are not unmixed blessings—for Israel, his promise includes warnings of slavery and struggle; for Isaiah, it includes the certainty of hardship and failure; for Mary, it includes a sword piercing her own heart; for Peter, it includes a brutal death. And for Hagar, the promise means a son of trouble.

The promise is mixed blessing, cold comfort in some ways.

It's not the promise but the presence that changes everything.

It's knowing there's a Man for All Seasons, with you in the palace and with you in the desert, abiding with you, in tents and in caves, in lonely places and in crowds, when you're prince and ruler, or when you're slave and handmaiden, when the child you bear is golden, destined for greatness, or troubled, destined for pain. Or when the child is not coming at all.

Still and all, there's a God, a living God, who sees you, and hears you, and speaks to you. Who loves you. A Man for All Seasons.

You just need to find the *beer* where you find the God who finds you.

Getting there sometimes involves a journey—maybe not of miles but of effort. And sometimes, like Hagar, we find our Beer Lahai Roi looking for something else, some other well, some other *beer*. In pastor Tim Keller's book *The Reason for God*, he tells about a woman who approached him in his church one day and told him her story. For years, she was angry and disappointed with God. She had searched for him high and low, done everything she was supposed to do—all the right disciplines, the whole regimen—and still she hadn't found him. Then one day, someone suggested she stop trying to find God and, instead, ask God to find her.

So she did.

And he did.[4]

My sense is that, for most of us, as I think it was for the woman in Keller's story, it's a bit of both: we go to the well, and God's already waiting. In the rest of this chapter, I want to look at four very reliable wells.

FINDING YOUR *BEER*

There are four wells—three I've found, one I've dug—where I find God, or he finds me. I need these wells in season and out; I need them lest I stop seeing the God who sees me, stop speaking to the God who hears me, stop hearing the God who speaks to me. Lest I forget that he is the Living One. Lest I forget where I've come from, and where I'm going.

Here are the four *beers* I believe are for in season and out: worship, the Word of God, prayer, and community.

Worship

Worship is the *beer* to which Jesus draws the woman at the well. She, we saw, is a kind of Hagar, fleeing a situation she can't stand but can't change. The conversation she has with Jesus shifts, at her prompting, to questions about worship. Does God like old or new, this place or that, one tribe's brand over another's? Is God charismatic, classical, liturgical, emergent? Does he listen to Wesley or Redman? Does he prefer smells and bells, shouting and clapping, genuflecting or back-sprawling, solemn procession or a wild-eyed free-for-all?

Jesus cuts through all that tired debate with a clear word about what God is really looking for: not a kind of worship but a kind of worshiper. "A time is coming," Jesus tells the Samaritan woman, "and has now come when the true worshipers will worship the Father in spirit and in truth, for they are *the kind of worshipers* the Father seeks. God is spirit, and his worshipers must worship in spirit and in truth."[5]

"The kind of worshipers the Father seeks." God seeks something *in us.* He desires not a given style (though, in my view, there's no question that country and western is beyond the pale) but a kind of person. If ever there were an opportunity for Jesus to resolve, once and for all, our entangling and exhausting debates about musical and liturgical preferences, this is it. This is the perfect moment for the Spirit to superintend a declaration from Jesus himself that establishes for all eternity God's likes and dislikes in such matters: "Well, woman, the truth is, God will only really warm up to our worship several centuries from now, when white Europeans in cathedrals built in the late Middle Ages whose transepts enhance the human voice will wear formal dress and sing hymns written by academic theologians and set to Bach." Or, "Matter of fact, lady, it's not until the emergent church arrives on the scene, late twentieth century, and gets the right combination of free-form grunge-tinged music and high church pomp, set in converted warehouses or British-style pubs, that the Father will say, 'Ah-ha! That's what I was thinking all along!'"

Jesus doesn't do this. He shifts the basis of the conversation away from the kind of worship God wants to the kind of worshiper he seeks.

One who worships in spirit and in truth. That's as close as Jesus gets to answering what kind of worship God wants. Simply, worship in spirit and in truth.

Meaning? *Spirit* here refers not to the Holy Spirit but to our inmost selves — the human spirit within which the Holy Spirit dwells, with whom the Holy Spirit communes, to whom the Holy Spirit speaks. The soul of you. Jesus is saying that God seeks people who seek him in the inmost places. Their seeking is beyond mere gesture. It's more than a fidelity to creedal statements or a proficiency in ecclesial postures. It may, in fact, be less than obvious on the surface: no hand-waving or hand-folding necessarily, no leaping up or kneeling down as a matter of course, no long stern faces or radiant upturned ones as a sure sign of God's presence. Instead, it's a stirring down in the root cellar, a hunger and an aching in that part of us that no one but God and we can see, and sometimes only God.

And God seeks those who worship in truth. Jesus is clear enough about what he means: "You Samaritans worship what you do not know, we Jews what we know." Worshiping what we know — the God we can name rather than the God we guess at — is better. Yet the next thing Jesus says pushes what he means even beyond this: "Yet a time is coming and has now come when [we] will worship in ... truth."

Worshiping in truth includes worshiping what we know, but it transcends it. Such worship begins in theological precision but moves quickly to impassioned adoration. It builds off of not a rubble pile of wishful thinking, ill-sorted superstitions, anecdotal evidence, wild speculations, but biblical revelation tested by centuries of theological reflection. It starts there, but if it stays there, it becomes merely an exercise in academic correctness.

Worship in truth (and this is something we do corporately, as the church, but also individually) is theologically sound *and* intellectually engaged *and* emotionally connected. It names God, then meditates on and celebrates the name. Is God good? To declare that is to worship what we know. It is indisputable creed. But to engage it intellectually and connect with it emotionally, we must also remember, recite, and anticipate the goodness of God. We must reflect on his acts of goodness, throughout history and the earth and to us personally, recite them (speak them out) and anticipate them (expect that God will now and always act according to his goodness).

Worshiping thus, in spirit and in truth, spells for me the difference of whether I live or die, spiritually speaking. To merely go through the motions of worship for the sake of appearances, without engaging my deepest self, and to worship in either theological vacuity or rigidity, empty-headed or all-head, only makes me worse. To worship in spirit and truth is to meet afresh the God who lives and who sees me.

This is a well I go to in season and out, in good times and bad. The corporate part is simple enough. I'm a pastor. That brings its own claptrap of hazards—the Uzzah syndrome, for one, where I get so distracted with all the rigmarole, making sure the ark of the covenant arrives on schedule, no glitches, no stumbles, that I end up meddling when I should be dancing.[6] But at least I have unhindered access to holy ground, and a built-in expectation that, at a minimum, I'll show up. The individual part takes more discipline. No one but God waits for me here. None other rewards my attendance or punishes my truancy. I can stay as long as I like, but also leave as soon as I wish. But it's when I'm alone, like Hagar, that I meet God most profoundly. So even though I've come to the well many times and left with not much more than a cup of water, I've seen the God who sees me enough times, too, that it's always worth the wait.

I'm finding I need this well as much, maybe more, in good times as in bad. I don't know why, but good times often have a spiritually numbing effect. Ease is a breeding ground for complacency and mediocrity. My spiritual life, like everyone else's, is imperiled by adversity, but not nearly as much as by prosperity: the times I've been most spiritually shallow have been the times I've been materially flush, and started to indulge that and expect that.

When life gets tough, and when life gets easy, I need this *beer*, this well in the desert where I recover my sense of the aliveness of God, and the sure knowledge of his watchcare.

There is no season when worship is unnecessary, the wrong activity. We've seen: pruning is ill-timed in summer, harvesting futile in spring, planting foolish in fall. But worship is good in season and out. Each season may change the visage of worship, its outward form. Summer may catch us worshiping in the mode of play or rest, spring in the modes of industry and expectancy. In fall we might worship in exuberant thanksgiving, in winter brokenhearted lament. But never should a season find us bereft of worship.

The way Jesus' encounter with the woman at the well ends says it all. When she realizes who he is, what he gives, she runs to town to tell everyone. Whatever barrier of estrangement has arisen between her and the townsfolk, a single encounter with Christ is enough to pull it down. "Come and meet the man who told me everything I ever did," she tells the others. "Could this be the Messiah?"

Come and meet the man who knew where I was coming from, and who told me where I am going—who offered me a whole new destination. Come see the God who sees me, and loves me all the same.

The well of Jacob has become her Beer Lahai Roi. The place of evasion has become the place of encounter.

God found her. It changed everything.

The Word of God

When it comes to *beers*, I cannot overstate how important the Word of God is. This sounds like an old preacher's harangue, and I guess it is. I feel I've joined the ranks of all those Jeremiahs, those prophets of doom, decrying the famine of the Word of God in our day.

Except, they're right.

If "people do not live on bread alone, but on every word that comes from the mouth of God," then many in our churches are starving to death. I have reached a point of holy impatience about this: when someone comes to me and tells me their marriage is crumbling, or their anxiety is skyrocketing, or their addiction is spiraling, or (fill in the blank), I first say, "Tell me what God is saying to you in his Word." Most times this elicits a blank stare, then either an apologetic scrambling or a testy push-back. Either, "Well, you know, I should be reading the Bible, I know, but life is just crazy right now, you know." Or, "Are you not hearing me? I'm telling you I'm in a three-alarm emergency, and you're telling me a little Bible reading is going to make it all go away?"

Which is not what I'm telling anyone. What I am telling them, without apology or accusation, just straight up, is that a steady practice of Bible reading, in season and out, is going to give them strength beyond themselves and wisdom above themselves and courage bigger than themselves, all the things they need when the crisis comes.

That's Jesus' promise and warning both. He said that the community gathered around him divides in two—those who hear "these words of mine" and put them into practice, and those who hear "these words of mine" and don't put them into practice. Everyone's a builder, Jesus says, building something. Two builders can build with equal skill, both using the right materials. The difference is not in how they build, what they build, with what they build. The difference is what they build upon. That difference, literally, is foundational: rock, or sand. That which endures, or that which erodes. That which can permanently secure whatever rests upon it, or that which eventually destroys whatever's set upon it. Christ's words practiced are a foundation of rock. His words ignored are a foundation of sand.

But from the outside, on a bright spring morning, no one can tell which house is which. It's possible—this happens often enough—that the sand trap is bigger, better, and brighter by all accounts, bar one. It's the eye-catcher in the real-estate flyer. It's the house you slow down to look at when you're driving by. It may be composed of higher quality materials—slate tiles on a complicated roofline, cedar post-and-beam in the entrance, real shiplap beneath the siding, actual river rock in the fireplace, hardwood floors from Brazil, marble countertops from Italy, nickel-plated door handles, solid fir window casings. The other place, by comparison, is drab and boxy: asphalt shingles on a single-crown roof, cheap laminate on the floor, particle board cabinetry, door handles that feel like empty tin cups in your hand.

The lasting value of each house is disguised until a storm hits.

And storms do come. Not all houses, not all lives, of course, are built in the hurricane corridor or the typhoon alley (though we can all think of people we know whose houses are built in such precarious places), but no house is immune, lifelong, to a tempest. Storms do come. Illnesses. Betrayals. Church splits. Corporate downsizing. Financial setbacks. Divorce. A child, or two, gone tragically astray. An old temptation firing up after years of dormancy.

Storms do come. The rain falls, the wind blows, the river rises.

And then even best-built houses, if the foundation lacks integrity, collapse. And even modest houses, if the foundation is solid, stand.

Jesus speaks to the community gathered around him—this is not a word directed to the world but to the church—and Jesus distinguishes *within that community* between those who practice what he preaches, and those who don't. But Jesus assumes in both cases that all have heard "these words of mine." Jesus doesn't even consider the possibility that someone within the community of faith might be ignorant of "these word of mine." Hearing's a given. The only option, in his mind, is obeying or not obeying.

Which worries me. There are people in my church who've been sitting there a very long time, decades in some cases, who've hardly an inkling of what Jesus says. I don't think their ignorance is from a serious deficiency in our preaching, or from a scarcity of classes and resources readily available through our church. They just have no appetite for the Bible. They are entirely dependent for their scriptural nourishment on the rations we hand out Sunday mornings and Wednesday nights. Like the Syro-Phonecian woman Jesus speaks with, they eat the crumbs falling off the table.[7]

Storms reveal it. Adversity tests foundations. And if those are inherently unstable, all we build—regardless of how hard we worked to build it, what skill and diligence we applied—collapses.

But I see the other side of this, too. There is a woman in our church who, as I write, is caught in a perfect storm. It's converging from several fronts: financial, medical, familial, marital. It's a conspiracy of earth and sky and sea to shake her to the bedrock. Which is just the point: her life *has* bedrock. After all those things have done their worst, there is a point where they can do no more, and when all has been shaken, the house still stands, not by virtue of the house, but by virtue of what the house stands upon. Her life, in season and out, has been an immersion in God's Word, and a faithful heeding of it.

It's rock all the way through. When another piece of hard news crashes in, she anchors deeper to God's promises and God's charac-

---

TIME-IN 27

STONE OF DESTINY

I was scheduled to preach in twenty minutes, and I was still down at the river, scrambling along the bank to find smooth rocks that fit snugly in my palm. I needed a bag of them. And I still had to get back in time to wash the mud and grit off them.

I hate it when I get a good idea with little time to pull it off. This was one of those. I was preaching on "Only let us live up to what we have already attained," from Philippians 3:16. Driving to the church, the notion struck me to collect stones, hand them out, along with a felt pen, to each person as they came into the service, and instruct them to write one word on their stone. The word named something they had once attained but since lost.

Peace.

Hope.

Purity.

Joy.

Fear of the Lord.

Or whatever.

I got to church on time, cleaned the stones and had them handed out with the pens, and had each person write their word on it. Then I preached the sermon. I closed with an illustration from a movie I'd recently seen (which is what prompted the idea). The movie's called *The Stone of Destiny*. It's based on the true account of a few Scottish nationalists who travel to Westminster Abbey in London and steal back Scotland's Stone of Scone, or the Stone of Destiny—a massive slab of nondescript rock that

ter, all of which she learned, precept upon precept, in quieter times. Her heart is breaking. Don't misunderstand me. But she won't break.

The Word is a good *beer*. But — please — don't wait until the storm hits to go there. Develop a habit of drawing from it in season and out.

---

is Scotland's symbol of freedom and sovereignty. The English had the stone under the royal throne in Westminster Abbey. The symbolism of that is obvious: Scotland's freedom and sovereignty are subjugated to British control.

Against all odds, the Scottish conspirators steal the stone back.

I then asked people to look at their stones. "Look at the word you've written on it," I said. "It is a symbol of your freedom and God's sovereignty. Whatever you wrote there is God's gift to you.

"Somehow, you let your adversary take that gift from you and put it under his throne.

"Just go get it back."

Then I pretty much forgot about the whole thing.

Several months later, I found a stone among my wife's things. Two letters were written on it — AW.

I remembered the sermon. I asked her what her letters mean.

"Alive Word," she said. "I used to love reading the Bible. It was so alive to me. And then joy went missing, and I never chased after it. I just plodded through, getting little out of it. But after your sermon, I asked God to make his Word alive to me again. And he did. My times of Bible reading have been amazing since then.

"I guess I took back my Stone of Destiny."

What would you write on the stone?

Now go get it back.

And don't just hear the Word. That's dangerous. Better not to know what God requires than to know and not heed. The Word demands a response. Do what it says. Someone who only hears the Word, James says, and doesn't put it into practice is like a man who looks at himself in the mirror and then walks away, forgetting what he looks like. Egg on his face. Seed husks in his teeth. Hair tousled. Tie crooked. Dandruff on collar. Mustard stain on lapel. He thinks, *Before I go meet my fiancée, or present to my clients, or interview for a job, or argue a case in court, I should do something about how I look.*

Then he walks away, straight to where he's heading.

James captures the subtle but huge difference between hearing God's Word under an "I should" clause and hearing it under an "I will" clause. Our churches throng with the former, are sparse with the latter. The former hear the Word of God and say, "I should." I *should* tithe. I *should* stop looking at porno. I *should* spend more time at home. I *should* care for the oppressed. I *should* give to the poor. I *should* make God first.

And so on.

I should is the watchword of the damned. Only, with the damned, there's a single verb added to the clause: I should *have.*

I will is the salute of the redeemed. God's Word compels them. For them, the distance between hearing the Word and heeding it is a single step. The time delay between the audio and the audition, the hearing and the doing, is no more than the time lapse between pulling a trigger and firing a bullet, turning a tap and drawing water, flicking a switch and the light coming on. The hearing causes the heeding.

So here's what I suggest. Do not go one inch deeper in knowing the Word of God until you've taken one step farther in obeying the Word of God. What do you already know that you're not doing? Knowing isn't the sticking point. More knowing isn't going to catapult you into action. It's not the solvent that loosens your bonds, the shove that breaks your inertia. More knowing will only make matters worse.

You already know enough.

If you're not careful, claiming you need more knowledge will actually become your alibi for inaction. "Always learning," Paul says, "and never able to come to the knowledge of the truth."[8] Sometimes gaining knowledge is merely a strategy of evading truth.

Just do it.

Take something you already know. Maybe it's something as banal as tithing. You may be ignorant of the Greek and Hebrew words involved or of the history of interpretation concerning this, or unable to line up all the biblical texts that speak to it, or confused about whether you should tithe from your gross or from your net.

But you know enough just to do it.

Or take the manifold calls to unity and humility in Scripture. You've read them a hundred times, heard them preached a thousand. You know how unity and humility are rooted in the very example and nature of Christ himself. You know they are the most convincing testimony the church can give to a broken and wary world. You know they are marks of the church's foundation in God and announcements of the gospel's universal truth.

And more besides.

And you're not the exception. Your little tiff, your hurt feelings, your misgiving about the way the elders handled the land purchase — these do not entitle you to an exemption, warrant your forming a faction and stirring up dissension among the brethren.

You already know enough.

"Anyone who listens to my teaching and follows it is wise, like a person who builds a house on solid rock."[9]

Where else would you want to build?

Hear the Word, and heed the Word, in season and out.

Prayer

The kingdom of God is essentially a prayer movement. That's the kingdom's skeleton key, the secret to opening all its doors. "How should we pray?" Jesus' disciples asked him. "Thy kingdom come," he answered. He was pointing to yet another *beer* for in season and out.

The kingdom comes on the wings of prayer. The kingdom is a bloodhound, and its sharpest tracking scent is the prayers of the saints. The first, best posture for kingdom-seeking is on our knees. The first, best place for laying hold of it is in our prayer closets.

All this my wife has had to teach me, and still I'm slow to learn. She, by a trick of genes or temperament or just greater spiritual maturity, has a hunger for prayer that makes me look anorexic. I have a hunger for prayer that is topped up with a few bites, a couple of sips, a little sniffing at the thing. But she could stay at the prayer banquet most of the day, and it would only increase her appetite.

Essentially, her example is shaming me into a deeper prayer life.

But the deeper I go, the more something different from shame takes over. I am starting to understand what Cheryl has always known: prayer, even the sweaty bone-breaking kind known as intercession, is not an act of exertion but a source of replenishment. It is not fuel burned but fuel tapped. It is not the duty of the disciple but the privilege. It's a perk of friendship, like having the key to someone's boat or car and the freedom to use it whenever you like.

When I pray—not in the token, rote, rushed way I sometimes do, but in the lingering, savoring, soul-baring way my wife's taught me—I find ready access to the presence of God. And I find that I walk in greater spiritual power.

Hebrews tells us that we can come to the throne of grace whenever we want. This is astonishing. In the Old Testament, no one ventured near to God without due preparation. You had to be invited, chastened, chosen, cleansed. Even then, your chances of surviving the encounter were slim. People who were ambushed by God—Jacob at the river Jabbok especially comes to mind—walked away amazed by one thing: they saw God and didn't die.

But Jesus solved that problem. His death rent the curtain—top to bottom—that divided the manifest presence of God from all but a few. This was God's idea. It was God himself who removed the barrier that kept most of humanity from coming near to him. The last and greatest high priest, Jesus, changed the rules. He used his divine authority to rewrite the playbook. Now any of us who walks with Jesus can walk into the throne room of God, anytime, from anywhere, and not to bring God anything but to get from God whatever we need.[10]

This is called prayer. Even as I write this, it strikes me as sheer madness that I don't do more of it.

My season of winter was when I was least inclined to pray and most in need of it. I often in that season practiced a simple and ancient discipline called breath prayer. I breathed in a phrase from the Bible—"The Lord is my shepherd" was my favorite—and breathed out the corresponding phrase—"I shall not want." I'd do this until the cadence of it slowed my mind and my breathing, stilled my anxiousness. I'd do it until all I wanted was God's shepherding presence. I'd do it until I experienced God's shepherding presence.

This is not some Buddhist meditation technique, as cult hounds sometimes label it. It was a practice that grew up in the Eastern church's monastic life as a way to be faithful to the Bible's exhortation to "pray without ceasing." It was a way, simple and deep, to practice the presence of God in season and out, to pray when you're also grinding, laundering, haying, baking.

In my winter, it was my way of clinging. It was how I held on to God, and found he was holding on to me, even when it felt otherwise.

But there are times for me when prayer is not only a cry for the kingdom; it's a tangible experience of it. I've attended, so have you, prayer meetings so dull and depressing that even the devil must feel no need to stay awake. The prayers rise no higher than the ceiling, reach no farther than Aunt Mildred's bad knees, little Billy's meeting with the principal in the morning, dear Betty's interview for a new job on Wednesday. The tone is bemoaning, the tenor disbelieving, the subject matter banal. It's not that God doesn't care about the little things—sparrows, lilies, all that. He does. It's just that our prayers get stuck here, as though the main business of heaven is sorting out our bus schedules, smoothing out our little wrinkles, and getting our cars to run forever without maintenance.

I love those prayer meetings when we storm the gates of hell. When we wrestle God and refuse to let go until he blesses us. When we command mountains to throw themselves into the sea, and they do. I love those times when we cry for the kingdom and it comes, when we ask God to bring to us people far from him, and two days later seven show up, or we ask God to heal a marriage that looks shattered beyond mending, and he not only restores it but makes it the source of many other such healings.

Which leads me to what else I pray for besides God's presence. I also pray for God's power.

There's a story about prayer in Mark's gospel[11] that troubles and intrigues me. Jesus takes three of his disciples—Peter, John, and James—to witness his transfiguration. When they return the next day, they come down the mountain and straight into a skirmish. The rest of the disciples are in heated argument with the teachers of the law. A desperate father with a demon-afflicted son had come to the disciples for help. They're helpless. So, it seems, are the teachers of the law. Both sides are powerless in the face of radical evil and heartbroken suffering. So they do what God's people typically do to compensate for impotence: they fight.

Argue.

Name-call.

Faultfind.

Split theological hairs.

Jesus is disgusted with all of them. "O unbelieving generation.... How long shall I stay with you? How long shall I put up with you?"

And then: "Bring the boy to me."

"Bring the boy to me." No more lollygagging. No more he-saids and she-saids. No more my-theology's-better-than-your-theology, my-church-is-bigger-than-your-church, my-seminary-has-more-tenured-faculty-than-your-seminary. No more standing around quibbling over fine points of doctrine while the whole world is hurtling to hell, and fast.

"Bring the boy to me."

This irritates Jesus, having to ask this. It irritates him to the point of almost quitting. "How long will I stay with you?" It irritates him, because the father actually came to Jesus' disciples with the innocent hope that to bring a problem to them was the same thing as bringing the problem to Jesus. The father says to Jesus, "I *brought you* my son, who is possessed by an evil spirit.... I *asked your disciples* to drive out the spirit."

He actually thinks to bring a problem to Jesus' disciples is the same thing as bringing the problem to Jesus.

And that's what Jesus intends. Jesus nurses the hope that he can go away—up a mountain, up to heaven—and his followers will carry on his work.

How naive is that? Jesus actually expects that we will do greater things than he. He actually expects that as the Father sent him, he can send us. He actually expects that those who follow him will do the works of God on this earth. He actually expects that a desperate father with a tormented son can bring his problem to our church, and the problem will be dealt with.

"Bring the boy to me." It breaks Jesus' heart to say it. But the boy is brought. And with a word, Jesus does what needs doing: deals decisively with evil, heroically with the afflicted, tenderly with the brokenhearted. The demon doesn't walk again. The boy walks away free. The father walks away rejoicing.

The teachers of the law just walk away.

And the disciples—they follow Jesus. They walk where he's walking. Jesus goes inside, and they come shuffling after him. A question vexes them, and they need an answer: "Why couldn't we drive it out?"

Their question answers a question that's vexed me a long time. My question is, What's the difference between a disciple and a teacher of the law? Or ask it this way: what distinguishes a Christ-follower from those who are merely religious?

What's the difference between a disciple and a teacher of the law?

So far, in this story, nothing. Except one thing. The only difference I can see between a true Christ-follower and someone merely religious is that a Christ-follower is dissatisfied with his or her level of spiritual power.

"Why couldn't we cast it out?" They really want to know. They really want to live into the expectation Jesus has for them. They really want to live lives that fill the God-hungry with wonder, evil spirits with terror, desperate fathers with joy, tormented sons with peace.

Spiritual impotency, especially in the face of desperate need, actually bothers a Christ-follower.

Those teachers of the law, they've already moved on to the next theological squabble. They witnessed Christ's power. They must have had a fleeting moment of wondering what was amiss in their own

---

TIME-IN 28

THE KINGDOM INSIDE YOU

Jesus said the kingdom of God does not come about by careful observation (*paratereseos* is the Greek here, meaning "scrupulous vigilance, standing watch," literally, "to stand beside"). The kingdom, he said, is not a "Here it is!" or "There it is!" kind of thing.

It is within you (*entos humon*, literally, "inside you").

Then the debates start. What does Jesus mean, "inside you"?

At the very least, this: that there's no use looking for the kingdom *out there*—crack dens shut down, gay marriages banned, your city "taken for God"—until you submit to the kingdom *in here*—the voice of God in the inmost places, every thought taken captive and made to obey Jesus, a life of glad surrender to the King of Kings' bidding.

I was meeting with someone recently who was telling me about their attempts to change someone. "It's frustrating," they said. "They just don't get it."

"Can I ask you something?" I said.

"Sure."

"What does 'get it' mean?"

They got so tongue-tied trying to answer, I asked for a time-out to ask a second question. "Do you know the difference between a conviction and a crusade?"

"I don't know what you mean."

"Well, okay. A conviction is a belief inside you so large, so deep, so passionate, that it holds you more than you hold it. It

---

lives. But it never ruffled them enough to inquire further. They're off to the races, off to afternoon debate about prelapsarianism, off to hear Professor Itoldyouso lecture on three views of the millennial reign, off to whatever. No time for worrying about demon-wracked children and heart-stricken fathers, no time to live lives of wonder

defines you. It's anchored in your soul. You can't imagine yourself apart from that belief. It's truth you'd take a bullet for.

"A crusade, on the other hand, is an attempt to get those around you to agree with you, or else. It's an attempt to conform the world to your ideas.

"The problem is this: a crusade is usually an end-run around a conviction. A crusade is not an attempt to change the world on the basis of your deep convictions but to compensate for the lack of them. A crusade is trying to establish the kingdom *out there* before we've established it *in here*."

Try this. List all the ways you want things around you changed. Start small—things in your family, your work, your relationships. Then span out—things in the neighborhood, your church, the churches, your community, your district or region, your state or province, your country, the world.

The list might include better communication; a deeper honoring of one another; more passionate worship; less gossip; less domestic violence; better leadership; more prayer; better education; a fairer distribution of global wealth; better world diplomacy.

Then highlight the ones you feel especially strongly about.

Narrow it down to two or three. Now, write down beside those two or three the ways you will allow God to establish his kingdom inside you. How can you be a sign and symbol of God's kingdom in these matters?

That might be all the crusading you need.

or to give evil a reason to wish it hadn't come 'round—no time for the business of heaven when there's always the business of counting angels on pinheads.

"Why couldn't we cast it out?" The minute we stop asking that, as long as our power is insufficient to deal with the pain of a world God so loved, is the minute we've traded following Jesus for just attending meetings.

"Why couldn't we cast it out?" Jesus, in reply, says the most subversive thing: "This kind can come out only by prayer."

Only by prayer. Two things, neither in the story as it stands, immediately jump out.

The first: Jesus doesn't pray. Not here. Not now. He just says the word, power goes out from him, and one very noxious spirit gets clobbered.

The second: the disciples are not prayerless. They must have prayed. They're Jews, for crying out loud. They're Christ-followers, for heaven's sake. It's not possible that they've not prayed—and not just recently but right here, right now.

The real question is, What does Jesus mean by prayer?

And the best answer I can come up with is that he wants us to say, "Now I lay me down to sleep, I pray the Lord my soul to keep."

I'm kidding.

My best answer is that what Jesus means by prayer is for our lives to look more like his life. He sees prayer as Christ formed in us. He sees prayer as being transformed, from glory to glory, into his likeness. He sees prayer as abiding in him until his grace, his truth, his peace, his presence, his power so fill us and form us that we, just like him, can just say the word, and the word is done.

If certain evil spirits come out only with prayer, then it's true that certain manifestations of the Holy Spirit in us come about only with prayer. And the prayer Jesus wants us to pray most is for his kingdom—his rule and reign—to take up residence in us.

It's a prayer for all seasons.

Community

Community is a well I had to dig for myself. It's a *beer* I had to brew, so to speak. It's served me in season and out.

I woke up, age forty, to a hard reality: I had not one "three o'clock in the morning" friend, that person I could call any time, night or day, from any place, who would consider it their deepest honor to be roused from sleep or pulled from a board meeting or interrupted in the middle of a family dinner to help me. Not one. If life unraveled—my marriage crashed, one of my children was brought home by police, I was in a faraway city late at night and some trouble, inward or outward, beset me—I hadn't, besides my wife, a single friend in whom I could find refuge, seek counsel, ask to get up in the middle of the night and come sit with me.

At forty, I knew more people than I could name. I enjoyed the company of dozens. I had multiple social circles I moved within, and was even sought out.

I just had no three o'clock in the morning friend. The realization startled me.

I've always loved David. There's always been a part of me, half vanity, half valor, that's identified with him. David was only a boy when he faced down Goliath. All that giant's menacing girth, hair-raising taunts, soldierly skill provoked in everyone else paralyzing fear; in David, they raised faith. David defeated him with nothing but a slingshot and holy pluck. That story stirs my blood and tests my own mettle. David is a man of undaunted courage and unflinching trust.

But he's also a man of fierce independence. David needs no one but God. That is a good thing. But not always. Later, David will lose his heart's bearings, looking for anything but God to satisfy him. Among other reasons this happens, I think this reason ranks high: he was friendless. After the death of Jonathan, David never, by all appearances, got close to anyone or let anyone get close to him. He had henchmen, servants, colleagues, acquaintances. He had a virtual harem of wives. He had children by the score.

David had success: power, prestige, wealth, clout. Servants fawning, women doting, men appeasing. He had all this, but what he lacked was a friend: someone to watch his back, hear his heart, share his grief. He had no three-in-the-morning friend. And that, I'm guessing, made his soul thin.

Goliath wasn't the only giant David fought. There was another. His name was Ishbi-Benob. But unlike David's battle with Goliath, his one with Ishbi-Benob is virtually unknown. Here's the story: "Once again there was a battle between the Philistines and Israel. David went down with his men to fight against the Philistines, *and he became exhausted*. And Ishbi-Benob, one of the descendants of Rapha [that is, a giant], whose bronze spearhead weighed three-hundred shekels and who was armed with a new sword, said he would kill David. But Abishai son of Zeruiah *came to David's rescue*; he struck the Philistine down and killed him."[12]

Ishbi-Benob's bronze spearhead was precisely half as heavy as Goliath's.[13] The implication is that Ishbi was only half Goliath's size: a diminutive giant. David, a hero in his youth, has become weak and slow in middle age. He exhausts quickly. He succumbs easily. Fully armed, he still needs rescuing from a runty giant.

It's disappointing, though not surprising, that we don't herald this giant story. We've made an icon of David's battle with Goliath. We've largely ignored his battle with Ishbi-Benob. And is it any wonder? We don't celebrate weakness. We don't honor dependency. We don't value needing others.

We love the tale of the lone hero.

The tale of the struggling companion embarrasses us. Indeed, every indication is it embarrassed David, and likely was the trigger for his sin with Bathsheba. His contest with Ishbi-Benob was his last time on the battlefield. The closing line of that story: "Then David's men swore to him, saying, 'Never again will you go out with us to battle.'"[14] The opening line of the Bathsheba story: "In the spring, at the time when kings go off to war, David sent Joab. . . . But David remained in Jerusalem."[15] The humiliation of being too old for war, I think, set him up for some other means of conquest, some other way to feel young again.

David was a man after God's own heart, which is what I want to be. I wonder if he'd have been more of a man after God's own *char-*

acter if he'd had a friend or two close enough to rescue him in other battles. And would he have needed Nathan to confront him in anger if he'd always had Jonathan to do that in love?

At forty, I had people around who could rescue me from small giants, and many other predicaments I got myself into, the liabilities of warfare: unjamming the photocopier, dealing with a chronic complainer, covering a Wednesday night class I had to miss. I even had people willing to help me with my golf game, though that was beyond rescuing. But I had no one who could rescue me from myself. There was none who, if middle-aged ennui and some skewed sense of entitlement conspired to wreck my life, would step in on my behalf. There was no one to watch my soul. And though I was doing that—watching souls—for many people in a general sense, I was doing it for no one in particular.

So at forty, I decided to change that. I dug a well. I approached two men whom I liked—men who would have helped me in a battle with giants—and asked if they would be my lifelong three-in-the-morning friends. Well, it wasn't quite that abrupt. It unfolded slowly, over many walks, coffees, campouts, dinners, prayer sessions. We'd each take a risk—disclose some innermost thought, some lifelong secret, some personal struggle—and watch to see what the others did with it. We kept testing the watertightness of the friendship, whether things we poured in afterward leaked out.

They didn't.

That was nearly ten years ago. I renew my friendship with these men weekly. We've laughed together, cried together, argued with each other, rebuked one another. We've solved problems, built things, given courage. We've applauded and exhorted each other. We've been iron to sharpen the other's iron, and salve on one another's wounds. We were there for each other when Carol died. We are there for each other when one of our children isn't doing well. We're there when one of us is discouraged, or tempted, or frustrated, or under attack. We anticipate being there when our health starts to fail, and our minds start to wander, and our hands get shaky, and our eyes get runny.

We'll be there for each other when winter comes. And then as we each go away, one by one, we'll be there to say goodbye until there's no one left to say it. And then we'll meet again, and really know each other, and start all over, and go forever this time.

Friendship has been a good *beer*. It's helped me know where I've come from. It's helping me to know where I'm going. And many times, it's given me the courage I need to go back to the situation I thought unbearable. But, mostly, my friends have helped me recover God's presence, and I've found strength not just to return but to do it whistling and skipping.

TIME-IN 29

A THREE-STRAND CORD

Two are better than one,
>because they have a good return for their labor:
If they fall down,
>they can help each other up.
>But pity those who fall
>and have no one to help them up!
Also, if two lie down together, they will keep warm.
>But how can one keep warm alone?
Though one may be overpowered,
>two can defend themselves.
>A cord of three strands is not quickly broken.[16]

"Two are better than one." G. K. Chesterton writes this in *The Man Who Was Thursday,* when the protagonist finds a friend among those he thinks are enemies: "Through all his ordeal his root horror had been isolation, and there were no words to express the abyss between isolation and having one ally. It may be conceded to the mathematicians that four is twice two. But two is not twice one: two is two thousand times one."[17]

"Two are better than one." The writer of Ecclesiastes gives a host of reasons why. A friend makes our lives more profitable (a better return), more comfortable (warmth in the cold), less lonely (a helping hand in an accident or a failure), less vulnerable (defense against an attacker), less frail (not easily broken). A friend decreases life's harm—an economic downturn, a false step, a chilly night, an armed assailant, a quick unraveling—and increases life's goodness—more abundance, more warmth, more safety, more strength.

I've found that friends do all this.

But mostly, I've found such a friend in Jesus, who no longer calls me a servant, but his friend.[18] As my friend, he yokes up with me to do work, to give a better return. He reaches out a hand to me when I fall, from clumsiness or willfulness, and helps me back to my feet. He covers me when the night is very long and very cold. He fights with me and for me when my enemy attacks. He weaves a strand of holy companionship into the cord of my life. It's not quickly broken.

This book began with a close look at Psalm 88, which ends "darkness is my closest friend."

Yes, it sometimes feels that way.

But the Man for All Seasons has joined himself to us. He's called us his friends.

Spend time now thanking your Friend that, no matter how cold the night gets, or hell-bent your enemy, or hard your work, or grievous your fall, he's right here with you, in season and out.

AFTERWORD

I wrote parts of this book in two of my favorite places. One's called Fireweed, a retreat house not far from where I live, named after the plant that, when it blooms, flames the hillside with bright red flowers. It's thirty minutes up the Trans-Canada Highway, and ten minutes in. But it's hidden far enough in the backcountry, in the folds of woody hills and marshy dales, down twists and turns of narrow country road, that it may as well be hours away. The house is large and has big picture windows looking out on a field stretching down to a reedy lake, and beyond that a dense stand of forest. When I arrived, the place was chilled. I built and stoked a hot wood fire downstairs, and turned up the gas fireplace upstairs, and put on a pot of coffee, and by midmorning the house was so warm I had to shed my sweater. I wrote without interruption from early morning till bedtime, and stopped only to eat a quick lunch. Just before dinner, I walked down to the lake.

It was a grey day, damp and chill. The grass around the lake was matted from a heavy snowfall a month before. Thin crusts of snow still lay in patches in the swales, and covered the makeshift boardwalk that provides a footpath through the marshy bog to the edge of the lake. The boardwalk leads to a rickety dock, where two dinghies, one yellow, one green, lay bottoms up. I walked as close as I could get to those two little boats, and pondered going farther. The dock was half submerged and clad in ice, and I pictured myself tiptoeing out on it, edging toward the boats, and then its giving way beneath my weight, or tilting up like a seesaw and pitching me backward in the half-frozen water. I pictured dragging my drenched, besmirched, hypothermic self up the hill to the house, tromping mud down the hall to the bathroom, teeth chattering, skin turned porcelain white. So I stayed where I was. But I stayed there a while, as shadows sifted down through the trees. I listened to birds with trilling melodic voices sing in the grasses, and others with throaty urgent cries answer from the woods and, deeper still, an owl emit a low and haunting call, like a solemn warning. And I watched the light keep shifting downward, and darkness gather in the fir boughs and pool in the grasslands. Up the hill, lights blazed from the house. I started back toward it, and stopped at the woodshed—an old horse stable—to gather and carry an armload of firewood for the stove.

I had dinner at the Crow and Gate, a charming country English pub a few minutes' drive away. I got the beef dip, and a dark chocolate porter, and sat close, but not too close, to the fire, under an old photo of Winston Churchill, half smirking, half scowling, looking over my shoulder. I read from a book of poems as I waited for my meal, and jotted a few notes in my journal, and called Cheryl on the way back.

The date: February 2.

Dead of winter.

The other place is called Galilee. It's a tiny cottage perched high above Ganges Harbour on Saltspring Island. Getting to Galilee involves a twenty-minute drive from where I live, a twenty-minute ferry ride to Saltspring, and a twenty-minute drive across the island. The place I stay is at the end of a narrow twisting driveway that dips and climbs through thick coastal forest and comes out at a clearing. There the cottage stands. It looks like a place a writer or an artist, or a gnome, might hide in and ply their craft, undisturbed by anything but birds and dragonflies. It has a large window, floor to ceiling, I look out as I write. The window frames a stunning view of ocean and forest and islands, and beyond that, mountains. I have to discipline myself not to daydream.

When I arrived, the place was cooking. I opened both doors at either end of the cottage, and got a cool breeze flowing through. Midmorning, I took a break from the writing to cut the lawn, trying to steer, as I'd been instructed, around the wild daisies, trying to avoid, as I knew I should, all the rocks and tree roots hidden in the tall grass. At midday, I took another break and drove to the village of Saltspring. At one of the village bakeries I got a bowl of smoked salmon chowder, with a sourdough roll, and a cup of strong coffee. I checked my email, sent text messages to my wife and children, then poked around a few stores. I came back and wrote a poem with fridge magnets:

> through the raw
> ache of worship
> he sits
> as some delicate
> finger of eternity
> parts the waters
> in two
> and shows a road
> beneath

Not a great poem, but all I could muster with the limited vocabulary the fridge magnets provide. But I did write, and edit, and came away with this book more or less finished.

The date: May 28.

Late spring.

My second day at Fireweed, I drove to a provincial park called Hemer, ninety-three hectares of coastal forest and frog-ridden lakes that John and Violet Hemer donated to the province for the enjoyment of all. Hemer has a broad walking trail, strewn thick with fir needles, that loops around its perimeter, and other trails that crisscross between the loop. I walked briskly and chose a route that zigzagged. The forest was cool, and the two lakes I passed were still sheeted in ice.

As I walked, I prayed. But it was more a conversation, a heartfelt talk with a good friend, which I suppose is what prayer is. I told Jesus what I was afraid of, what I hoped for, what I regretted, what I cherished. I told him about this book, where it felt thin, or bloated, or forced, and I asked him, when we got back to Fireweed, if he could help me with that. I told him how thankful I was for my wife and children. I told him how astonished I was at what he'd done with my life so far, given the raw materials I handed him. And I asked him if he had anything to tell me, and he did, which I'll keep to myself.

I prayed prayers like that at Galilee, too, as I sat on a weathered wood bench in the hot sunshine and looked out on the wide expanse of blue-grey harbor. I thanked God, and sought him, and laid my heart before him.

I pray like that in the dead of winter, and through late spring, and into summer, and during fall, and then back 'round again. I'll pray like that, God willing, when my next book is written, should there be such a thing. I'll pray like that when all these books are long forgotten. I'll pray like that when I'm too old to drive, or walk, or eat beef dip or clam chowder, or write poems, even with the aid of fridge magnets.

I'll pray like that until the day words fail me, and I have no breath left for speaking. And even then, he will not forsake me. Especially then, in that season, he'll walk with me, and lead me home.

Whom shall I fear?

But I want to end by telling you my prayers for you. I pray that this book has met you in whatever season you're in, and prepared you for whatever seasons await. I pray that it has helped you find your voice, your stride, your rhythm, in season or out. Mostly, I pray that you have, with or without my help, found Christ wherever you are. And that, even more, you've discovered that, wherever you are, he's found you.

He will never leave or forsake you.

NOTES

INTRODUCTION:
FOR EVERYTHING, A SEASON

1. Eccl. 3:1, 9–11 TNIV.

CHAPTER 1:
WINTER

1. Eccl. 3:1–8 TNIV.
2. Eccl. 12:1–8 TNIV.
3. TNIV.
4. Walter Brueggemann, *The Message of the Psalms* (Minneapolis: Augsburg Fortress, 1984), 78, 80.
5. Ps. 88:8, 18 TNIV.
6. Luke 7:21–23 TNIV.
7. Luke 7:24–28.
8. The book ends with a section on friendship, and you may want to read that now (pp. 309–13).
9. See, for example, 2 Cor. 1:8–9; 12:1–10.

CHAPTER 2:
WINTER ACTIVITIES

1. John 15:1–2.
2. 2 Cor. 1:8–10 TNIV.
3. 2 Cor. 4:16–18 TNIV.
4. As of this writing, Thomas' condition, against all medical predictions, has vastly improved. He's in residence in a Victoria hospital for physical therapy — and this after, earlier in the year, he'd been consigned to palliative care. We're hoping for a miracle. Please pray.
5. This story was related to me by a friend of mine who attended St. John's for a time.

CHAPTER 3:
SPRING

1. Isa. 35:6−7.
2. C. S. Lewis, *The Lion, the Witch and the Wardrobe* (1950; Hamandsworth, Middlesex: Puffin Books, 1978), 110−11.
3. Rom. 8:18−21 TNIV.
4. Isa. 55:10−12.
5. Isa. 35:3−4.
6. Matt. 11:5.
7. As I was finishing the edits for this book, I received news that Jim had died— nearly ninety, in his sleep, and smiling.
8. Isa. 35:8−9.
9. I've been a pastor long enough to see close up that the highway to hell may start fun, fast, and easy, but it doesn't continue that way. It becomes arduous, tortuous, painstaking. You can get off it any time, but the longer you stay on, the more you pick up the rules of the road. Those take some undoing.

CHAPTER 4:
SPRING ACTIVITIES

1. As I did my final edit on this, I was preparing in one week to perform Susan's marriage to Bill, a wonderful man she met at our church.

CHAPTER 5:
SUMMER

1. Rev. 22:2.
2. Luke 21:29−31.
3. Zech. 8:2−3, 4, 20−21 MSG.
4. Eccl. 3:10−11 TNIV.
5. Ezra 3:10−11.
6. Heb. 11:10.

CHAPTER 6:
SUMMER ACTIVITIES

1. 1 Tim. 6:17.
2. A. W. Tozer, *Knowledge of the Holy* (San Francisco: Harper and Row, 1961), 47.
3. Eccl. 12:1.
4. Phil. 3:1; 4:4
5. 2 Cor. 8:9.
6. Perhaps the last pure act of Edenic living, of completing the joy of having something by sharing it, was when Eve, after taking and eating the forbidden fruit, "also gave some to her husband." It's our last glimpse of humanity acting in pure holy impulse. From then on, all motives of sharing have a slight taint at best.
7. Mark 4:6.

8. Ps. 19:4–6, emphasis mine.

9. The accolades for the Word paid by Ps. 19:7–10.

10. Prov. 10:5 NLT, emphasis mine.

11. For example, Exod. 23:19.

12. Rom. 8:23; 1 Cor. 15:20, 23.

13. James 1:18; Rev. 14:4.

14. This past summer I did my most ruthless pruning yet. Even as I type this, I feast on the sweetest grapes I've ever eaten.

15. Luke 21:20–31 TNIV, emphasis mine.

16. Luke 21:7–12 TNIV.

17. Luke 21:14–15, 18, 28 TNIV.

CHAPTER 7:
FALL

1. Heb. 6:7–8.

2. Heb. 12:11, emphasis mine.

3. Heb. 12:15, emphasis mine.

4. Gal. 6:7–10 TNIV.

5. 2 Cor. 9:6–11 TNIV.

6. Prov. 24:30–34 TNIV.

7. John 4:35, emphasis mine.

8. John 4:36–38 TNIV.

9. 2 Cor. 9:6, 8, 10–11 TNIV.

10. 2 Cor. 9:9–14.

11. 1 Cor. 9:11.

12. Billy Graham, *Just As I Am* (San Francisco: HarperOne, 2007), 705.

13. Heb. 12:7–11 TNIV.

14. James 3:18.

15. Dialogue of a group of pastors with Bishop André Mfitmukiwa in Toronto, Canada, 14 May 2009.

16. Eph. 2:14.

17. Col. 1:24.

18. Phil Callaway, "The Shark Chaser," *Leadership Weekly*, 18 December 2006, 54.

CHAPTER 8:
FALL ACTIVITIES

1. Mark 2:19.

2. Luke 15:32, emphasis mine.

3. C. S. Lewis, *Reflections on the Psalms* (New York: Harcourt, Brace, and Co., 1958), 97.

4. Ezra 7:10 NRSV.

5. TNIV, emphasis mine.

CHAPTER 9:
FALL ACTIVITIES

1. Judg. 6:3–5 TNIV.
2. Judg. 6:27.
3. Of course, Rishabh's parents are Hindus in a land overridden with statues of Hindu gods. It's hard not to make the connection between Baal and, say, Vishnu, and wonder—politically incorrect as this is—whether the endemic poverty and hunger and corruption of countries such as India are not linked, in both sociological and spiritual ways, to their religious systems.
4. Greg Hawkins and Cally Parkinson, *Follow Me: What's Next for You?* (Barrington, IL: Willow Creek Resources, 2008), 112.
5. Mal. 3:8–12 TNIV.
6. Gen. 3:17.
7. Rom. 1:23–24 TNIV.
8. Judg. 6:25–26.
9. 1 Cor. 1:26–29.
10. Judg. 6:27 TNIV. This scene is almost a mirror image in miniature of Judges 7:10 and 19, where Gideon is afraid to attack the Midianites and so, to gain confidence that God is with him, takes along a servant, and then launches the attack with a hundred men by his side, two hundred still in waiting. The one servant is a distillate of the ten, and the hundred men a multiplying of that number. I like these details in the story, because they speak to my own fear, my own need for a company—whether one hundred, or ten, or just one—of fellow Baal wreckers and Midianite destroyers by my side.
11. Judg. 6:28–32 TNIV.

CHAPTER 10:
BALANCING (OR NOT)

1. Isa. 43:24.
2. Heb. 11:21.
3. 1 Cor. 9:24.

CHAPTER 11:
ABIDING

1. Phil. 4:13.
2. Col. 3:17, emphasis mine.
3. Luke 13:6–8.
4. See Luke 13:1–5.
5. Interview with Gene Heyman, by Charlie Gillis, *MacLean's*, 1 June 2009, 19–21.

CHAPTER 12:
SEEKING

1. Ellie Lee, "A Kind of Wisdom," *The Moth* (podcast), 15 June 2009.

CHAPTER 13:
WALKING (IN THE LIGHT)

1. Col. 1:29.
2. Gal. 5:25.
3. Much scholarly debate has been generated by this detail, Nicodemus coming at night: was he skulking in shadows, or simply busy during the day, or is this part of John's grand motif, worked throughout his gospel, of darkness and light? No definitive answer exists, though it's worth noting that Jesus ends his conversation with Nicodemus by contrasting those who love darkness and those who choose light. But what strikes me most about the detail—Nicodemus coming at night—is what it says about Jesus: he's available to all and sundry, highborn and lowlife, anywhere, anytime. He's available in the middle of the night.
4. John 3:8–9.
5. John 3:14–15.
6. See John 12:32, where Jesus repeats the idea of his being lifted up, and John comments that Jesus was referring to "the manner of his death." But note also how Jesus broadens the scope of the impact of his being lifted up: in John 3, it affects "everyone *who believes*"; in John 12 it draws "all men." I'm not a universalist (the belief, in its extreme form, that everyone is saved), but those who are have some good authority for their position.
7. John 3:16–23.
8. John 8:31–32.
9. Actually, the word *grace* is rare in all the Gospels: neither Matthew nor Mark uses it at all, Luke only once, and John six times, three in the span of four verses in chapter 1 of his gospel (14, 16, 17), once in his second letter, and twice in Revelation. The latter uses are mostly in his salutations. It's Paul who uses the term on every page, with an almost obsessive force, though both the letter to the Hebrews and the letters of Peter, especially his first, make heavy use of it.
10. John 16:8–11.
11. 1 John 1:5–7 NASB.
12. Luke 19:1–10.
13. Phil. 1:27–28.
14. Phil. 4:6.
15. Acts 16:25.
16. Matt. 10:28.
17. Rev. 2:11; 20:6, 14; 21:8.
18. C. S. Lewis, *The Voyage of the Dawntreader* (1952; Hamandsworth, Middlesex: Puffin Books, 1977), 194–95.
19. Rev. 11:15.
20. Rev. 21:23–25.

CHAPTER 14:
BEING (A TREE)

1. Colin Tudge, *The Tree* (New York: Three Rivers Press, 2005), 3.
2. See Jared Diamond, *Collapse: How Societies Choose to Fail or Succeed* (New York: Penguin, 2006), 136–56, esp. 138–39.

CHAPTER 15:
SUSTAINING

1. Eph. 4:14.
2. Let me shamelessly promote my book *The Rest of God: Restoring Your Soul by Restoring Sabbath*.
3. "Make every effort" is a refrain in the New Testament. See especially 2 Peter 1:1–9, which—to shamelessly promote another of my books—I deal with extensively in *Hidden in Plain Sight: The Secret of More*.
4. Phil. 3:19.
5. Phil. 3:12.
6. Heb. 12:11.
7. Acts 20:27 NKJV.

CHAPTER 16:
KNOCKING (ON HEAVEN'S DOOR)

1. Eccl. 3:11 TNIV.
2. Jared Diamond, *Collapse: How Societies Choose to Fail or Succeed* (New York: Penguin, 2006), 107.
3. The reason Adam and Eve were banished from the garden was not because they ate from the tree they were commanded not to eat from (Gen. 3:11). For that, the ground was cursed. They were banished from the garden *so that they might not eat* from the "tree of life" and so "live forever" (Gen. 3:22–23). That's the tree at the center of the New Jerusalem—the garden becomes a city—which bears crop twelve months of the year, and whose leaves heal the nations (Rev. 22:2). Our *miru* is that tree.
4. Eccl. 3:11 TNIV.
5. Col. 3:1.
6. 2 Cor. 4:18.
7. 2 Cor. 4:16.

CHAPTER 17:
PERSEVERING

1. Phil. 3:10.
2. Isa. 9:2.
3. Phil. 3:10–14 TNIV.
4. Rom. 5:1–5.

5. James 1:2–8.
6. My book *Hidden in Plain Sight* is largely an exploration and application of Peter's seven virtues.
7. Heb. 10:22.

CHAPTER 18:
IN SEASON AND OUT

1. Gen. 16:1–6.
2. Gen. 16:7–14.
3. John 4:1–26.
4. Timothy Keller, *The Reason for God: Belief in an Age of Skepticism* (New York: Dutton, 2008), 161.
5. John 4:23–24, emphasis mine.
6. See 2 Samuel 6.
7. Matt. 15:27.
8. 2 Tim. 3:7 NASB.
9. Matt. 7:24 NLT.
10. Heb. 4:14–16.
11. Mark 9:14–32.
12. 2 Sam. 21:15–17, emphases mine.
13. See 1 Sam. 17:7.
14. 2 Sam. 21:17.
15. 2 Sam. 11:1.
16. Eccl. 4:9–12 TNIV.
17. G. K. Chesterton, *The Man Who Was Thursday: A Nightmare* (1908; Hamandsworth, Middlesex: Penguin, 1987), 88.
18. John 15:15.